Contents

SECOND

Starting
Your Career
as a
Freelance
Writer

BY MOIRA ANDERSON ALLEN

CARVER
COUNTY
LIBRARY

Supported by the
City Council and Economic
Development Commission of
Norwood Young America

Allworth Press books may be purchased in bulk at special discounts for sales promotion, corporate gifts, fund-raising, or educational purposes. Special editions can also be created to specifications. For details, contact the Special Sales Department, Allworth Press, 307 West 36th Street, 11th Floor, New York, NY 10018 or info@skyhorsepublishing.com.

15 14 13 12 11   5 4 3 2

Published by Allworth Press, an imprint of Skyhorse Publishing, Inc.
307 West 36th Street, 11th Floor, New York, NY 10018.

Allworth Press® is a registered trademark of Skyhorse Publishing, Inc.®, a Delaware corporation.

www.allworth.com

Cover and interior design by Mary Belibasakis
Page composition/typography by Integra Software Services, Pvt., Ltd., Pondicherry, India

ISBN: 978-1-58115-760-4

Library of Congress Cataloging-in-Publication Data

Allen, Moira Anderson, 1959-
   Starting your career as a freelance writer/by Moira Anderson Allen. – 2nd ed.
      p. cm.
Includes bibliographical references and index.
ISBN 978-1-58115-760-4
1. Authorship–Vocational guidance. 2. Authorship–Marketing. I. Title.
   PN151.A49 2011
   808'.02023—dc22
                                                      2010041776

Printed in the United States of America

Introduction

This is the book I always wanted to write. As a writer and writing instructor, I searched in vain for a book that, to me, really answers the questions writers ask about launching a freelance career. A book that explains, in clear detail, what to do first, what to do next, what to do after that.

It's not that there aren't any books on freelance writing on the market. Indeed, there are dozens. So what makes me think I can write one that covers the topic better than the rest?

The answer is: Because while I'm a writer, I'm not *just* a writer. I'm also an editor. I've sat on both sides of the desk. I know what it's like to send out queries and submissions and wait, seemingly forever, for a response—but I also know what it's like to *receive* those queries and submissions, and what makes the good ones stand out from the rest. I know how to *get* an acceptance, and I also know what inspires me to *give* one.

In addition, having spent the past ten years as the editor and publisher of Writing-World.com, one of the world's largest Web sites for writers, I've answered literally hundreds of questions from writers about nearly every aspect of the writing business. Consequently, I know what questions writers *ask* about launching a successful career.

This book will guide you through the steps needed to start freelancing, and the steps needed to make your career successful. Whether you want to freelance as a sideline to your day job or while taking care of a home and family, or whether you're interested in going "full-time" and supporting yourself as a writer, this book will give you the tools for success.

You may want to read this book more than once as you progress in your career. But whether you read it once or a dozen times, there is one even more important thing you must do to become a successful writer. And that is: Put the book down and *start writing!*

Moira Allen
editors@writing-world.com
www.writing-world.com

PART I

Getting Started

❧ 1 ☙

So You Want to Be a Freelance Writer

Writing for publication is one of the most rewarding careers I can think of. It offers the opportunity for independence, creativity, and the occasional moment of fame. It allows you to speak to others—to entertain, to educate, to inspire, to motivate. It gives you a chance to earn an income by doing something you love. It may even give you a chance to change the world, or at least to improve one small corner of it, by giving your readers the tools they need to make their lives better. And there's nothing quite like the thrill of seeing your name in print—not just the first time, but every time!

It's also one of the easier careers to break into. You don't need any special qualifications to become a freelance writer: No special degrees or educational background, no certification, no business license, no "permission." All you really need to do to get started is to sit down and *write*. Plus, thanks to the magic of the Internet, you can launch a successful writing career from just about anywhere in the world; you're no longer limited by problems of international language differences, postage, and currencies.

As a *creative* career, freelance writing can be far more lucrative than many other creative or artistic outlets. I enjoy crafts, for example, but when I have a choice between spending an hour making an item that might sell for $25, or spending two hours writing a how-to crafts article that might sell for $500, the decision is a no-brainer!

At the same time, freelance writing can be arduous and frustrating. It takes time to get a writing career launched, and even longer to become "successful." The publishing marketplace has become an increasingly hostile environment for writers, as many publications are run by corporations that are interested only in the bottom line. Rejection is an inevitable part of this business—a part every writer must learn to accept gracefully.

And make no mistake: freelance writing *is* a business. Writing for publication isn't simply an exercise in creativity; it is a process of developing a *product*. The business side of freelancing includes determining what types of markets are available to you, and the types of materials you can sell to those markets. As a business, freelance writing also has its mundane side—handling correspondence, keeping records and financial accounts, and so forth.

The good news is that a writing career is remarkably flexible. It adjusts to your hours, enabling you to invest as few or as many hours as you wish. Most freelancers begin as moonlighters, writing in their "spare" time while handling a day job or taking care of a family. Moonlighting gives you a chance to develop your skills, build a portfolio or client base, and build a nest egg against the day that you decide to go full-time. It also gives you a chance to determine, *before* you make that jump, whether this is the career for you. Indeed, many writers never do go full-time, but freelance as a way to supplement their regular income.

WHAT IS A FREELANCER?

A freelance writer is, by definition, a writer who is self-employed. As a freelancer, you do not draw a paycheck, but work independently, writing what you want and when you want, and offering your work to any market that will buy it. If you enter into a more formal relationship with a publisher (e.g., by becoming a columnist for a magazine), you may become an "independent contractor" for that publication, but you will not be an employee. This independence is what many freelancers cherish most about the business.

Beyond that, the term "freelancer" can be applied to a variety of writing activities and markets. This book covers the following types of freelance writing:

• **Writing for magazines.** Nonfiction magazines represent the largest, most accessible, and highest-paying market for freelancers. There are literally thousands of print magazines that accept freelance material in the United States alone, and hundreds of other potential markets internationally. Though many predicted that the Internet would cause the "death" of print periodicals, readers still prefer them—and advertisers still find them the best way to reach customers. Hence, they remain a strong market for writers. The downside of magazines is that they work months in advance; when you sell a piece to a magazine, you often won't see it in print for six months to a year.

• **Writing for online periodicals.** Webzines, e-mail newsletters, and sites associated with offline entities (such as stores, catalogs, and media) offer an attractive market for freelancers. Most online markets do not pay as well as print markets, however, as they generally attract less advertising and subscriber revenues. The online marketplace has been shrinking steadily in the past decade; many would-be publishers rushed to establish e-zines, thinking that there was easy money to be made on the Internet, only to find that readers were less inclined to pay subscription fees to online periodicals when so much information could be found on the Web for free. But paying online markets do still exist. Online markets typically work on a faster schedule; your material may get published within weeks (or even days) of submission. Despite what many experts predicted, writing for online markets is little different from writing for print; publications still want solid, information-packed pieces with a beginning, middle and end.

• **Writing for newspapers.** There are at least as many newspapers in the United States as magazines, if not more, and many are open to freelance contributions. As Sue Fagalde Lick explains in chapter 15, however, newspapers generally look for both a local angle and a "news" angle (i.e., what makes an article timely?). Most local and regional papers pay less than magazines, but it's often possible to sell the same piece to several noncompeting papers. Newspapers also work on a much shorter schedule than magazines, usually publishing material within weeks of acceptance.

• **Writing nonfiction books.** Few freelancers *start* their careers by writing nonfiction books, but many find this a logical "next step," particularly when they've written a number of articles or columns in a particular topic area, or when they have a particular area of expertise. An agent is generally not needed to sell a nonfiction book, and you can usually obtain an advance before you begin writing.

• **Writing and editing for businesses.** Writing business and corporate materials can provide more steady work and income than writing for periodicals. The key difference, however, is that when writing for business customers, you will not be producing your own material, but creating and editing materials (such as brochures, reports, sales literature, documentation, etc.) as dictated by your customer. This type of freelancing requires good editing skills and (sometimes) some business or technical expertise. Fortunately, thanks to the Internet, it's now possible to write for businesses outside your local area. Dawn Copeman discusses business writing in Part VIII.

Other freelance activities include editing (such as developmental editing, technical editing, copy-editing and proofreading); speechwriting; teaching and speaking; writing educational and curriculum materials; writing humor, essays, and poetry; writing fiction (both short stories and novels); and even illustrating and cartooning. For most freelance writers, nonfiction and/or business writing tends to be the primary source of income.

HOW MUCH CAN YOU EARN?

One of the first questions would-be freelancers ask is "how much can I earn?" The answer, of course, is "it depends." Your income potential depends upon your skill, areas of expertise, business acumen, the amount of time you can devote to writing, and more.

The first thing to understand is that freelancers often don't set their own rates. If you write for periodicals, you must generally accept the pay range offered by those markets. Some markets offer flat "per-piece" rates (ranging from $25 to $1,000 or more), while others pay by the word (anywhere from 1¢ to $1 or more). Many publications also offer a range of rates, depending on the author's experience and the complexity of the article; needless to say, newer writers are generally paid at the lower end of the scale.

New writers tend to make one of two mistakes when looking at these figures. The first is to say, "Wow! I can sell an article for $1,000! I'll be rich!" If the first potential market that pops into your head is *Redbook* or *Cosmopolitan,* think again. The top-paying markets can afford top-of-the-line writers—writers with years of experience and a hefty sheaf of clips. While new writers *can* occasionally break into these markets, the odds are against you. Writing for *Redbook* isn't the way to launch your career—and it's a good way to get frustrated if that's where you're trying to start.

A second and equally damaging mistake, however, is to assume that, as a new writer, you can only write for low-paying markets. While lower-paying markets *are* more open to new (and inexperienced) writers, that doesn't mean you have to start out writing for a penny a word. In reality, the markets most open to new writers are those that pay anywhere from $25 to $500. This includes the majority of special-interest publications (see chapter 14). The key to cracking this type of market may lie more in your non-writing credentials than in your actual writing skills.

To determine how much you can hope to earn, therefore, you'll need to look at the following questions:

1) **What markets can you write for?** Begin by locating markets that match your interests and experience. For example, if you're an animal lover, look for pet publications. If you travel, look at travel publications. Don't waste time on publications that aren't within your area of expertise, no matter how much they pay. For example, if you know nothing about computers, don't expect to sell your first article to *PC World!* (You can get to those markets later.)

2) **How much do they pay?** Check the pay range of your target markets. If you find that you've chosen a field with only a handful of publications, brainstorm topics to expand your range (see chapter 11). This will give you an idea of the payment range you can expect. (I also recommend submitting your material to the *highest*-paying market on your list first, and working your way down to the lower-paying markets if and only if your submission is rejected by your first choice. Otherwise, if you submit to—and are accepted by—a lower-paying market *first,* you've lost any chance of selling that piece to a better market.)

3) **How much time must you spend per article?** If it takes you ten hours to complete an article, you'll obviously be able to write (and sell) fewer articles per week or month than if it only takes five hours. This also tells you how much an article is really "worth." For example, it's obviously better to sell a ten-hour article for $100 than for $50. On the other hand, a ten-hour article

that you sell for $100 is actually worth *less* than a two-hour article that you can sell for $50 (the first pays $10 an hour, the second pays $25).

4) **How much time do you have?** If you can invest five hours a week in writing, and you estimate that it will take five hours to write a feature article, that translates into one article per week. However, you'll also need to allocate time to market research, queries, correspondence, and other administrative tasks, so in reality, you may be able to produce only one article every other week. Keep in mind, too, that *writing* an article a week isn't the same thing as actually *selling* an article per week.

It's also important to remember that freelance income doesn't start arriving immediately. Launching a freelance career involves a start-up period, during which you're conducting market research and sending out your first queries and submissions. If you write primarily for print magazines, you'll find that it takes six to eight weeks to get your first responses, and another month or so before you see your first check—while it can take six months or more to get your first published "clip." Newspapers and online publications tend to work more quickly; newspapers tend to publish material within a few weeks of submission (at most), while some online publications may publish a piece within days, giving you virtually "instant" clips. Typically, however, you'll start to see a steady inflow of assignments (and payments) within about six months.

With so many variables involved, there are no hard-and-fast figures on how much a freelancer can expect to earn at a particular career stage. It's not unrealistic, however, to hope for revenues of between $5,000 and $10,000 in one's first year of part-time freelancing, and a steady increase thereafter.

WHAT DOES IT TAKE TO BECOME A FREELANCER?

As I said earlier, one of the great things about this career is its lack of "prerequisites." You don't need a particular degree or educational background. You needn't have majored in English or journalism (in fact, this can hinder rather than help, as academic writing is very different from "consumer" writing). You don't need to be young (or old); you can launch a career as a freelancer at 20 or 50 or 70.

What you do need is the following:

1) **Writing ability.** Most people embark on a freelance career because they know they have good writing skills, and would like to turn those skills into a source of income. Others, however, wonder if they "have what it takes."[1]

If you fall into the latter category, the best way to find out whether you're a "good" writer is to start submitting your work for publication. Keep in mind that you *will* be rejected—and that this will often have nothing

---

[1]Note that some sources of feedback are less reliable indicators of actual writing ability than others. Positive comments from friends and family are nice, but not necessarily a guarantee that your work is ready for the market. Similarly, don't rely on "good grades" in an English course (or even a writing course), as the academic world has different criteria from the publishing world.

to do with your ability. What you're looking for is a pattern. If your first 20 to 30 submissions are rejected with nothing more than a form letter, there's a good chance your writing needs work (or that you're targeting the wrong markets or querying with inappropriate ideas). If, however, you're getting rejections with feedback, that's an indication that you're on the right track. Editors don't waste time commenting on "hopeless" writers. And, of course, acceptance is the best news of all!

If you *are* getting a stream of rejections, you may want to seek additional feedback. One approach is to join an online or real-world writing or critique group. Another is to take a writing course, again either online or through an adult education program. Again, look for patterns in the feedback you receive: Do you consistently hear that you have problems with organization, spelling, or grammatical errors?

The key to being a "good" writer is to accept the fact that you can always become a "better" writer. One has to be almost schizophrenic in this business: one has to silence that little voice that says, "I'm not good enough," and at the same time, be honest enough to say, "I may need to improve."

2) **Business sense.** While *writing* is often considered a creative process, *freelance writing* is a business. Your goal as a freelancer is not simply self-expression; it is the development of materials that you can sell to publications. This means being able to make business decisions about what (and how) to write. Instead of just saying, "I'd like to write about dogs," for example, one must ask, "What can I write about dogs that would interest an audience of experienced dog owners?"

The business side of freelancing includes regular market research. It also means handling a fair amount of "administrivium"—negotiating contracts, billing clients, keeping accurate income and expense records, maintaining reasonably coherent files, and so forth. This book will also give you tips on how to manage those essential tasks.

3) **Professionalism.** If you can *appear* professional, editors will assume that you *are* a professional—no matter how little experience you have. This means learning how to send a query, format a manuscript, handle e-mail correspondence, meet deadlines, negotiate contracts, etc. It also means being able to manage one's emotions and to behave courteously and professionally at all times—even when dealing with editors who *don't*. Nothing will ruin a freelance career faster than a reputation for responding unprofessionally to rejection—e.g., by complaining, begging an editor to reconsider, or sending flaming e-mails.

4) **Motivation.** Thousands of people *desire* to write, but never actually do. To become a freelancer, your desire to write must be stronger than your desire to do any number of other things. Becoming a freelancer means taking steps

to change your life, and these steps aren't always comfortable. It can mean changing your habits to squeeze in a few extra hours to write. It can mean giving up things that you enjoy, such as time spent reading or watching television, or even (to a certain extent) time spent with your family and friends.

Freelancing also requires the courage to sit down and face the keyboard and start translating your dream of writing into reality. I don't know of any successful writer who considers writing an *easy* job. Freelance writing means tackling challenges—projects that take you out of your comfort zone and cause you to push your abilities to their limits. There are days when you won't even consider writing to be *fun*—when you'd rather do just about anything, including dig ditches, than face the keyboard. (Don't worry; we all have those days, no matter how many years we've been writing.)

Motivation may also mean sticking to your decision even when no one around you supports it. While many freelancers are blessed with supportive families, others aren't so lucky. If, for example, your decision to freelance means leaving a paying job, you may find that family members resent that loss of income. Your family may also resent having to take on extra chores so that you'll have more time for writing (though it won't kill anyone to have to do their own laundry). Perhaps hardest of all, however, is when family and friends simply can't seem to understand *why* you want to write. When your mother keeps asking you when you're going to get a "real job," or your friends insist on calling you at home during the day because they know you're not actually "working," just smile and keep typing.

5) **Perseverance.** At times, freelancing can seem like a long, uphill struggle. Your file of rejection letters will *always* be larger than your file of acceptances. You will experience setbacks and discouragements. You will experience moments when you wonder if you'll ever sell anything (or ever sell anything again), or whether you were dreaming when you thought you could become "a writer." A successful freelancer isn't one who never has those problems or those doubts; a successful freelancer is one who perseveres in spite of them.

6) **Discipline.** One of the drawbacks of freelancing is that you don't have anyone "forcing" you to be productive. You don't have a boss standing over your shoulder, nagging you to get back to work, or telling you what to write and when. Often, the only deadlines you have are those you set for yourself. To be a successful freelancer, you need to be a self-starter—and you need to be able to finish what you start.

Many articles recommend that you write for a certain number of hours every day. Often, however, this isn't practical. I recommend that you strive for a *weekly* minimum, and get in that writing time whenever you can. Also, don't stress over *when* you write—e.g., "two hours before breakfast." Discipline doesn't lie in formulas; it lies in forcing oneself to ignore all the excuses we have for *not* writing.

And now for the standard caveat: If you're dreaming of instant fame and fortune as a writer, then I'd advise you to seek another career. Freelance writing is not a quick path to riches or glory. Those who embark on this path with visions of overnight success rarely last long, and their names are quickly forgotten.

That doesn't mean that you *can't* become famous, and even wealthy, as a writer. Those who have achieved this kind of success, however, didn't do so because they were looking for it. Instead, they set out to follow the dream of doing what they loved for its own sake. If you love to write, there are few things more satisfying than being able to do what you love for a living—and as one writer once said, if you do what you love, the money will follow.

❧ 2 ❧

Getting Started

A career in freelance writing requires very little "startup investment." It does, however, require a few basic tools—equipment, resources, supplies. Here are some of the things you'll need to set up your "writing office"—even if that office is just a corner of the kitchen.

These tools and resources fall into two categories: The absolute necessities, and the optional extras. The necessities are items that you'll need to acquire before you can go very far in your writing work—even if this means laying out some expenses before you earn any income. The "extras" are important—but can usually wait until you see a profit.

THE NECESSITIES

A workspace of your own
The very first thing you need to establish is a *place* to write. While some writers have launched their careers from a corner of the kitchen table, it helps immensely to have a space—even a very small space—that you can call your own. Many writers feel that this space also requires a door that can be closed against interruptions, distractions, and family members. Another advantage of an enclosed workspace is that it's more likely to qualify for the home-office deduction.

At the very least, you'll need the following:

- A desktop (even if it's a table) for your computer
- Good lighting for your computer and reading areas
- A flat surface to spread out notes, books, and other materials
- A place to file research notes, articles, correspondence, etc.
- A place to store your writing supplies
- A handy shelf for your most useful reference books
- A chair that provides good back support

You don't have to go to the office supply store and buy a mahogany desk (though I recommend shelling out for a good chair that will give you adequate back support). Plenty of folks make do with a couple of boards laid across two filing cabinets and a bookcase made of boards and bricks. The key is to make that space *yours*—and to make sure that your family respects that space.

A computer of your own

Not only will the majority of your potential markets expect you to be able to submit material electronically (usually via e-mail), but they will also expect to be able to communicate with you by e-mail, and expect you to be able to review their guidelines on the Web. If you're serious about freelancing as a business, having your own computer is essential.

Notice that I said "your *own* computer." Many households have a "home computer"—but often, all family members share that computer. If that's the case in your home, you'll find that your "writing time" generally takes second place to homework, games, checking stocks, downloading MP3 files, and general surfing. It's difficult enough to find time to write without having to compete for computer time as well.

If you don't have your own computer, this should be your first, and most important, business investment. It doesn't have to be expensive; for as little as $600 you can usually get a system that includes a screen, keyboard, and even a printer. You can also get good deals on used computers; many computer outlets sell "reconditioned" computers, and you can also find used hardware and software on Amazon.com and other sites.

Make sure that your computer is equipped with Microsoft Word, as this is the program most commonly used by publishers. Word documents can be produced both by PCs (Windows) and the Macintosh, so you can use whichever "platform" you're most comfortable with.

If you don't have space for a full-size computer, consider buying a laptop. Laptops now have just as much power and memory as a desktop model, with the added advantage of portability. If you do choose a laptop, however, I recommend getting a separate keyboard and mouse; for long writing sessions, you'll find a full-sized keyboard much more comfortable (and far more ergonomic) than a laptop keyboard. I also recommend getting a full-sized flat screen if you can afford it; it takes up very little desk space and is much easier to read.

Today, happily, any computer you buy will now come fully equipped with a host of peripherals that once had to be purchased and set up separately. Your system should have at least one read/write CD/DVD drive that will enable you to make back-up disks of your information. It will undoubtedly have a built-in modem and Ethernet connection, enabling you to access the Internet. It will have several USB ports that will enable you to use additional peripherals (and if it doesn't have enough, you can always purchase an extra USB hub).

Some computer systems come complete with a keyboard and mouse, but others require you to purchase these items separately. There is a wide range of keyboard types on the market, ranging from standard to high-end ergonomic.

You may also want to consider a wireless keyboard and/or mouse, which can help reduce the number of cables running across your workspace. (Some people are concerned about the cost of batteries; my wireless mouse tends to need new batteries every four to five months, which I consider sufficiently economical.)

Even though many publishers will expect you to submit material electronically, you'll still need a printer. Today, the options in that department are virtually endless. I recommend getting one of the many excellent "all in one" printer systems that combine an inkjet printer system, a copier, a scanner, and a fax machine. This type of system is particularly useful if your office space is limited.

Don't grab the cheapest printer you can find. Instead, make sure you know how much print *cartridges* will cost. I once purchased a very nice little printer for less than $20—and spent several hundred dollars on cartridges before I retired it. If you don't need color printing, consider an inexpensive black and white laser printer, such as a Brother. These workhorses will churn out hundreds of pages at a fraction of the cost of inkjet cartridges.

An Internet account

If you already have a computer, or even a "family" computer, you probably already have an Internet service. Quite probably, your service is provided either by your television cable company or your phone company. If you're adding your own personal "writing" computer to the household, you may need to talk to your Internet service provider about networking this new computer to the existing system. Sometimes you can do this yourself by obtaining a router. You should already have a modem, often provided by your service provider; to network an additional computer, you'll connect the modem to the router, and then run cables from the router to each computer on the system. If that's not practical (i.e., the computers are in different rooms and you'd have to drill holes through the walls to get there), consider investing in a wireless router. Again, you can usually obtain this service from your network provider, or you can set it up yourself.

You'll also need an e-mail account. The service that provides your Internet access will undoubtedly provide you with one or more e-mail accounts as part of the service (some give as many as ten different e-mail account names, so every member of the family can have separate accounts). You can also opt for a free online Web-based service such as Gmail (from Google), Yahoo, or Hotmail. There are advantages to a Web-based service; you have the option of checking your mail online and leaving it on the host server, which reduces the risk of downloading viruses and other malicious e-mails to your own system. Another advantage of such a system is that you can access your e-mail online from anywhere—which is particularly useful if you need to be able to check and send e-mail while on the road.

A phone

Just as you need a computer of your own, you also need a phone of your own. This should be part of your basic workspace. It's usually easiest to conduct telephone interviews at your computer, so that you can jot down notes or look up information while you're talking. Your business phone needn't be fancy; you can pick up a cheap one for $10 or less.

You may also want to install a second phone *line* for business use, particularly if it's going to be difficult to ensure uninterrupted phone-time when you're working. The cost of a second line, including installation, is deductible as a business expense (you can't deduct the cost of your first, "personal" line, though you can deduct the cost of all business calls). A less expensive alternative is to subscribe to a second *number* on your primary line, with a "distinctive ring" that enables you to distinguish between personal and business calls. A fax machine can also be set up to respond to a "distinctive ring," so that you can have your phone and fax on the same line.

Having a second line, or second number, enables you to ensure that your business calls are always answered professionally—or by a separate answering machine when you're not available.

The Writer's Market

There is still no substitute for this comprehensive annual guide to markets. Published every fall, *Writer's Market* lists approximately 3,000 magazine markets, plus book publishers, writing contests, and markets for other products such as greeting cards, screenplays, and more. Listings include contact information, payment rates, rights, and what each publication wants to receive from writers.

Writer's Market comes in a basic edition (book only) and an "online edition" (book plus access to an online market database, which is located at *www.writersmarket.com*). One can also subscribe to the online database *without* buying the print book (which can be useful if you live outside the United States and can't easily order the book itself). I recommend getting the print book if you can, however, regardless of whether you intend to use the online database; when researching new markets, there's nothing quite like being able to page through the book itself, marking interesting-looking publications.

Basic writing supplies

You'll need the following:

- Several reams of good-quality, 20-lb. white bond paper[1]
- A box of 9x12 mailing envelopes
- A box of #10 (business size) envelopes
- Blank CDs (both for back-up and for submissions)
- Postage in various denominations. (Invest in an inexpensive postage scale that lists current postal rates up to one pound, and buy postage that corresponds to those rates. And here's a tip: When the postage rates change, which they do with depressing frequency these days, don't bother buying a new scale. Just locate the new rate table at *www.usps.com*, print out the new rates, and put them somewhere near your scale.)
- Your own supply of pens, pencils, felt pens/markers, erasers, paper clips, rubber bands, rulers, Post-it notes, etc.

---

[1]U.S. and Canadian writers will use 8.5x11 paper; writers in most other countries will generally use A4 paper.

- File folders (and labels); also hanging folders if your file cabinet uses them. (For the economy-minded, there's nothing wrong with scavenging used file folders from your office!)
- Note-pads, both large and small. Large note-pads are great for jotting down interviews or research notes; small ones are good to keep by your computer (and everywhere else) to jot down ideas, reminders, etc.

A professional letterhead

You can design a letterhead at no cost on your computer, and save it as a file to use whenever writing a letter, or have it printed at a local print shop. Include your name, address, phone, fax, and e-mail. Avoid cute logos like pens or parchments, and don't use a "title" (like "author" or "freelance writer")— these are signs of an amateur. I recommend using a linen or parchment stock in a neutral color such as ivory or gray for letters (but not for manuscripts); this helps set them apart from the sea of white paper that clutters the average editor's desk.

Here's an example of a simple letterhead design:

Moira Allen
_____

1234 Mystreet • Mytown, VA 20151
(XXX) 555-1234 • (XXX) 555-1235 (fax)
editors@writing-world.com

I use Zapf Chancery for the name and Palatino for the address. This example is reduced to fit the page size of this book; for an 8.5x11 sheet of paper, I use a 24-point font for the name and a 12-point font for the address.

OPTIONAL EXTRAS

A fax machine

It's helpful to be able to receive contracts from editors by fax, and some editors may also wish to fax galley proofs of your manuscript. Today, you can usually get an inexpensive all-in-one printer that includes a fax machine. This will also be a plain-paper fax, which means that you don't have to worry about the ink fading over time. However, this is also the day of "junk faxes," so unless you are expecting a fax from an editor, it's a good idea to keep the fax unplugged when you're not using it.

A copier

You'll find that you're constantly running to the local print shop to copy contracts, clips, correspondence, and a host of other materials. Having your own copy machine saves valuable time and will eventually pay for itself. Again, getting a printer that doubles as a copier is a good solution—and many now copy in color as well as black-and-white.

Computer peripherals

In addition to the essentials of a computer and printer, I recommend the following equipment:

• **A flash drive.** These handy little USB "sticks" come with many names and in many sizes. They provide a great way to transfer information from one computer to another, or to carry information with you. I use mine primarily to back up the day's work, so that I know that my most recent information is always stored in a second location at the end of the day. This frees me from the necessity of having to make constant CD backups.

• **An external hard drive.** For keeping backups of your writing, finances, and other files, nothing beats a portable, external hard drive. You may not wish to acquire one of these right away, but when your back-up CDs start piling up, it can be an excellent investment.

• **A label-maker.** Even though it's technically possible to print envelopes on your printer using Word templates, it's a pain—particularly if (like me) you have a printer that has a fit if you try to feed it anything thicker than a sheet of paper. It also won't help if you need a label for a large envelope (i.e., with a thick manuscript) or a package. The solution: a LabelWriter. This handy tool lets you print mailing labels with the touch of a button—just paste the address from a letter into the label-maker window. (It's also useful for printing labels for other purposes, such as file labels and even CD labels.)

• **A scanner.** If you have non-digital photos that you'd like to market, this is an easy way to convert them to electronic files. If your photos are prints, a flatbed scanner will do the job. If they are transparencies or negatives, you'll need either a flatbed scanner that has a transparency converter, or you'll need a film scanner. If you have large-format slides or transparencies, this will require a greater investment—or, you can opt to have your slides professionally scanned.

A "writer's bookshelf"

In addition to *Writer's Market,* you'll want a good dictionary that defines *obscure* words as well as everyday words. (A dictionary should define the words you *don't* know!) You'll also want a thesaurus (Roget's is good, as is Webster's). If you plan to write technical, medical, or scientific articles, it's wise to invest in the appropriate dictionaries for those, too. Over time, you'll also probably collect some basic references on writing, as well as books that relate to your particular areas of interest or expertise. Here are some worthwhile books for writers:

- *The Writer's Guide to Queries, Pitches and Proposals,* by Moira Allen
- *The Writer's Digest Guide to Manuscript Formats*
- *Every Writer's Guide to Copyright & Publishing Law,* by Ellen Kozak
- *How to Write a Book Proposal,* by Michael Larsen
- *The Complete Guide to Self-Publishing,* by Tom and Marilyn Ross
- *The Self-Publishing Manual,* by Dan Poynter

A separate bank account

It's a good idea to keep your business income and expenses separate by setting up a separate bank account. Banks charge whopping fees for "business" accounts—but as long as you're receiving checks in your own name, you don't need one. If you write under a pseudonym or business name and will receive checks under that name, you may need to set up a "doing business as" or get a business license; check with your bank for details. (You can, however, write under a pseudonym and still get paid under your real name.)

Spend a few days setting up your writing space. Take the time to get it just right. Make sure it is comfortable: You're not going to become enthusiastic about writing if each session puts you in desperate need of a chiropractor.[2] Make it esthetically as well as ergonomically pleasing: Put an attractive picture on the wall, a potted plant on the desk. If you can afford to go beyond the merely functional, pick out a desk that appeals to you visually—a desk that says, "This is the desk of a writer!" Take time to determine the best arrangement for your equipment; make sure everything is within easy reach—that you don't have to climb over the printer to reach your files, for example.

Then, leave it alone. Rearranging one's workspace and reorganizing one's files are two of the most common forms of procrastination. It *feels* like you're working, but you're not. Resist the temptation to keep tinkering with your space, and sit down and start *writing*. After all, the best tools in the world aren't going to help you if you don't use them!

---

[2] I do recommend using a chiropractor, however. Because of the amount of time spent at the keyboard, writers are prone to neck and back troubles.

❧3❧

Making Time to Write

A re you wondering when you'll find enough time to start writing? If so, I have good news and bad news. The good news is you'll never have more time than you do right now. The bad news is... well, that *is* the bad news.

Time is never "found." Time can only be "made." If you decide to wait until your kids are in school, or in college, or you have enough money to quit your day job, or retirement, you could wait forever. The only way to make those writing dreams come true is to start looking at the time you have *now*—and find ways to make that time work for you instead of against you.

TREAT TIME AS AN INVESTMENT

Some say, "time is money." A more accurate statement might be that "time is *like* money." We have only so much, and must make decisions about how and where to spend it.

Writing, like any new career, requires a start-up investment of time. Many new writers, however, feel uncomfortable with that initial investment. Those long, unpaid hours at the computer or keyboard often feel "wasted" or "self-indulgent." Worse, many writers have family members who share this view.

This start-up time is essential, however. It takes time to build your skills, sell that first article, and develop a client base. If you sit down today and send out your first set of queries, it still may be two to four months before you receive a response, six months before you make a sale, and eight months before you actually see your first check. But if you don't invest time in that initial "launch" period, you'll never see that check at all.

EXAMINE YOUR "TIME BUDGET"

"Making time to write" doesn't mean finding "free" time; it means reallocating time from other projects and activities. Before you can do that, you must discover exactly where you're "spending" your time.

A good method is to purchase an appointment book that breaks the day into 15-minute segments. For two weeks, record where every block of your time goes—including eating, sleeping, brushing your teeth, etc. Be honest: If you lingered for an hour over breakfast reading articles about the latest movie star divorce, write it down. (At least record it as "celebrity research.") If you're not sure how much time you actually spend on an activity, buy a timer that works as a stopwatch—i.e., it "counts up"—and use it to track those activities.

The results of your log may surprise you. Do you ever have those days when you feel as if you never sit down from dawn to dusk—yet can't say what you accomplished? This log will help you discover where that time went. You may be surprised by how long certain tasks take, and how many "unnoticed" tasks nibble away at your day. You may also find that you're spending a great deal of time on tasks that you don't care about nearly as much as you care about writing.

EXAMINE YOUR PRIORITIES

No matter what you're doing now—working, raising a family, going to school—you already have a "full" schedule. Your first reaction to the thought of scheduling writing time into that schedule is probably "How? Where?"

Making time to write means making tradeoffs. You may have to give up some activities in order to reallocate that time. A good exercise at this point is to look at your log and categorize the various activities you pursue. Possible categories include:

• **Unavoidable tasks.** Your day job would be included here!

• **Necessary tasks.** Obviously you're not going to give up cooking dinner, washing clothes, getting dressed, eating lunch, etc. However, some of these tasks can be reassessed, rescheduled, or combined with other tasks (for example, instead of going out for lunch, consider spending that hour at your desk reviewing sample magazines or *Writer's Market*).

• **Tasks you enjoy.** Don't give up everything you enjoy; that's a sure way to burn out. If you feel that you would truly lose something of value by giving up a particular activity, put it in this category.

• **Tasks you perform because you think you "should."** Volunteer activities often fall into this category: You may not enjoy them, but you feel obligated to continue with them. Certain types of housework also fall into this category: Is it absolutely necessary to press the sheets?

• **Tasks someone else could perform.** We often handle tasks for others (such as hanging up a spouse's shirts) that they could just as easily handle themselves. Sometimes, delegating such tasks not only frees time for you, but also helps others become more responsible and independent.

• **Tasks that take an inordinate amount of time.** Did it really take three hours to do laundry, or buy groceries, or wash the car? Why? In many cases, we lose time through distractions or "make work" without realizing what we are doing.

• **Tasks that are purely recreational.** Reading, television, and computer games all fall into this category. So, in some cases, does "surfing the Internet" and handling e-mail. Don't imagine that you have to give up all recreational activities to become a writer; however, if these are occupying a large number of hours, you may wish to reexamine your priorities.

ELIMINATE TIME-WASTERS

We all have them. Some are conscious; some, however, creep into our lives in the guise of habits, procrastination devices, and assumptions about what we "should" and "shouldn't" do. Here are some of the most common:

• **Television.** Record shows during the weekend (when you could be writing) and watch them during the week (when you may be too tired to write). Ask yourself if you're watching certain shows because you enjoy them, or simply out of habit. Let the rest of the family watch their favorites without you. If you eliminate two one-hour shows per week, that's two hours you've gained for writing. (Also, try combining TV with other tasks, like ironing or exercise.) The same applies to movies. Some folks rent three a night—one for him, one for her, one for the kids. Try alternating the "his and hers" movies instead, and let the kids watch theirs without you.

• **Junk mail.** No law says that you have to *open* junk mail. Develop the habit of tossing anything you don't want—ads, catalogs, etc.—straight into a trash bag or recycling bin. Spend time only on mail that matters.

• **Magazines.** Do you have a stack of magazines you never read? Publications you only skim? Consider canceling them (and save some money in the bargain). Similarly, do you need a daily paper, or could you live with the weekend edition? (If it takes you a week to read the Sunday paper, consider canceling that too!)

• **Errands.** Errands take more time than you think, because they include travel time and "home" time (e.g., putting away groceries). They also drain your energy. Try to combine as many errands as possible on a single trip; run errands that must take you to different parts of town on different days. Keep lists, so that you don't forget something and have to run out again. If you do forget something and can live without it, save it until your next trip (or send someone else!). Try to schedule a specific day of the week for errands, so that you can plan around it.

• **Telemarketers.** Your mother taught you that it was rude to hang up on people—but she wasn't raised in the age of telemarketing. The best solution is to let your answering machine pick up; if you're in the midst of a project, turn off the ringer. Invest in caller ID to help screen calls. If you feel that you *must* pick up, tell the caller firmly that you're not interested and ask to be placed on their "do not call" list. (Some telemarketing recordings will provide an option, at the end of the recording, to be removed from the list. Usually this option is #2 on your dial, so try pressing that to see if it takes you to the removal option.)

• **Household chores.** Sometimes, vacuuming can look more appealing than a looming deadline. When it comes to chores, I've learned to ask, "Will this still get done if I don't do it now?" I know that sooner or later, I *will* empty the dryer or the dishwasher—but if I leave my desk to empty it *now,* I may not recapture that 15 or 20 minutes I could have spent writing. Another option (really!) is to hire household help to handle things like washing floors and vacuuming. Finally, make sure your family members are doing their fair share of the work; do you really want to explain to an editor that your article is late because you had to pick up your kid's socks?

TEACH OTHERS TO RESPECT YOUR TIME

Many of us have learned to drop everything when someone requests our attention. It could be a spouse, a child, a coworker, or that friend who calls every day to talk about her problems.

If you don't guard your time, no one else will. It is not enough to simply ask others to respect your "writing time." You must reinforce that request by refusing to drop what you're doing whenever someone interrupts you. Otherwise, people *will* interrupt—not out of malice or lack of consideration, but because you have given them no reason not to.

Many "writer moms" (and dads) enforce the "if it's not on fire or bleeding, don't bother me" rule. This is sometimes easier to do if you have a door that you can close, but that's not always essential. What is essential is convincing others that you mean what you say: When you say, "I am writing and cannot be disturbed," don't stop writing unless the house is on fire.

Protecting your time means cultivating the art of saying "no," "later," and "I have to go now." At first, this may seem the most difficult task of all, but eventually you will realize that your new attitude hasn't caused the rest of the world to view you as an ogre—and you're actually getting some quality writing done!

If you're looking for time to write, don't wait until tomorrow or next week or until the kids have grown up and moved out of the house. Start today. You really have all the time you need.

ᴧ4ᴦ

Setting Goals

One of the greatest challenges writers face is the lack of "structure" in our job. There's no one to tell us what to do, when to do it, how to do it—or even whether we've done it well. One way to overcome that challenge is to learn how to set goals.

While you may yearn to become a six-figure novelist who appears regularly on Oprah, that's not a goal. It's a dream—and the only way you'll achieve that dream is by setting well-defined goals.

DEFINING EFFECTIVE WRITING GOALS

To be effective, goals should meet three criteria: They should be *measurable, attainable,* and *meaningful.*

Measurable
Many writers start with "qualitative" goals: We want to be a "good" writer, or a "better" writer, or a "successful" writer, or a writer who produces "worthwhile" material. But how do you define good, or successful, or worthwhile? Because these terms are so difficult to measure, such goals seem to continually slip from our grasp.

Goals are useless if you can't determine whether they've been met. (After all, it's always possible to become a "better" writer.) Thus, quantifiable goals—goals that can be measured by some form of output or results—are more effective. For example, you might set a goal of writing a certain number of pages per day, or sending out a certain number of queries per week. If you dream of becoming "rich" (or at least "self-supporting"), define a specific income goal—and a time in which you hope to reach it.

Attainable
The gulf between where we are and where we'd like to be often seems too great to span. Goals can help by breaking the journey into short, attainable steps.

If your dream is to become a best-selling novelist, but you've never set pen to paper, consider setting an attainable goal such as attending a writing course, taking a class online, or simply studying a book on novel-writing. A second goal might be to write your first story, the outline of your novel, or your first chapter. A third might be to seek feedback, perhaps by joining a critique group or by sending your story to an editor. Each goal marks a step toward your long-term dream, and each is attainable in its own right.

To set attainable goals, you must be honest with yourself about what you are able to achieve at this stage in your writing career. If you have never earned a penny from writing, for example, it would be unrealistic to set the goal of becoming "self-supporting" in a year. Similarly, if you've never written anything longer than a holiday newsletter, it would be unrealistic to expect yourself to complete a 600-page novel in six months.

Attainability also means recognizing what is physically possible in the world of writing. I once spoke with someone who was frustrated at having "failed" to become self-supporting by writing science fiction short stories—despite the fact that markets for such work average around 5¢ per word or less. To earn even $25,000 per year (exclusive of taxes), one would have to write and *sell* 500,000 words per year (an average of two 5,000-word stories per week).

Meaningful

In writing, it's easy to be sidetracked by goals that appear worthwhile, but that don't lead in the direction you want to go. This can often be the result of competing goals. For example, you may dream of becoming a novelist, but face the very real need to put food on the table. Consequently, it's easy to postpone that novel (which won't earn you a dime until it's finished) for more immediately lucrative projects. In a situation like this, remember that competing goals don't have to be an either/or proposition: You could resolve this problem by devoting 25 percent of your writing time to your novel, and the other 75 percent to articles.

Another source of sidetracking is the pursuit of someone else's goals or recommendations for "success." Writing magazines are full of sure-fire secrets and formulas, but often fail to mention that these strategies don't work for everyone. For example, if you've set the goal of "getting up every morning to write before work," that may be fine—unless you happen to be a night person, in which case you'll either hate those hours of writing, or hate yourself for being unable to achieve the goal you've set. Similarly, if you've been told that a good writer always keeps a journal, but yours bores you to tears, you may come to the mistaken conclusion that you aren't a "real" writer—or waste a lot of time in a pursuit that has no meaning for you. At the same time, be careful about passing up opportunities just because they don't seem immediately fulfilling. Taking a writing class, for example, may not seem exciting, but it could help you toward your long-term goals.

SHORT-TERM VS. LONG-TERM GOALS

A wise writing strategy includes a mix of short-term goals ("Today I'll locate five craft markets") and long-term goals ("This year I'll begin writing that novel").

A good way to determine your long-term goals is to ask yourself where you want to be in six months, one year, five years, or ten years. By answering those questions, you define your vision and chart your course—and you'll be better able to determine whether a writing project will contribute to your goal or distract from it.

Long-term goals often build upon one another. For example, your goal for your first year of freelance writing might be to build as many clips as possible. Once you've established a portfolio, you might devote your second year to targeting more prestigious, better-paying markets. You might decide to move from being a "generalist" to a "specialist"—establishing yourself as an expert in a certain field. Conversely, you might decide to broaden your writing horizons by moving from tightly focused subjects to more diverse topics.

While long-term goals help you determine where you're going, short-term goals help you decide how to get there. If your one-year goal is to "sell ten magazine articles," your short-term goals might include conducting market research, writing queries, or submitting a certain number of articles per month.

Short-term goals are usually measured by "output." Output goals are those in which you have complete control over the results: Mail ten queries per week, or write three articles or stories per month. Typical output goals include:

- Number of hours spent writing per day (or week)
- Number of pages produced per day (or week)
- Number of queries submitted per week or month
- Number of projects (articles, stories, or chapters) written per month or year

Note that these output goals have short time frames. A short-term goal doesn't become a long-term goal simply by expanding the quota (e.g., moving from "10 queries a week" to "520 queries a year"). Instead, long-term goals are best measured by results. While you can control your output, you cannot always control the results. Even though you meet your weekly quota of queries, you can't control the editorial decisions and market factors that determine whether those queries will be accepted.

REVIEW YOUR PROGRESS

To determine whether you're on schedule, ahead of schedule, or falling behind, it's important to review your progress regularly. Have you met your output goals, have you exceeded them, or did you set them unrealistically high? If you've met those goals, are you any closer to your long-term "result" goal—or does it seem as distant as ever?

Such assessments can help you determine whether you need to change your long-term goals, or the short-term strategies you're using to meet them. If, for example, your one-year goal was to "get something, anything, published," and you've accomplished that goal in the first month, it's time to set a new long-term goal. If, on the other hand, you've sent out ten queries per week for six months without a single positive response, it may be time to reevaluate your short-term goals: Perhaps you need to target different markets, reexamine the ideas you're pitching, or learn how to write a more effective query. In other words, if six months of "output" haven't brought you closer to your long-term "results" goal, don't waste another six doing the same thing!

Goals are not chains, meant to lock you into some sort of writer's bondage. As your interests, dreams, and skills change, your goals can (and should) change as well. A goal that had meaning a year ago may not seem so important now, while another goal you might not have dared aspire to suddenly seems attainable. Remember that goals are not your destiny. They are simply effective tools you can use to *reach* that destiny.

❧5❧

Coping with Rejection

Rejection slips are the writer's gremlin, the nagging suggestion that we don't measure up. What can we do about them? How can we live with them? How do we make them stop?

Unfortunately, rejection is part of being a writer. Not just a beginning writer, either; experienced writers get them as well. One of the most important steps you can take as a writer is to learn how to cope with rejection, how to understand what it means to your career, and how to move on.

The first step in handling rejection is to learn how to separate yourself from your work. You may pour your heart and soul into your writing, but you must also establish "boundaries" between yourself and your creation. Your writing may be like a child to you, but like any child, it must go out into the world to succeed or fail on its own merits. If you can't develop such boundaries, you'll go nuts—and stop. Success will become impossible if you cannot bear the pain of failure.

BUT *WHY*?

You've probably heard that editors who reject your work aren't rejecting *you*—and that's true. However, they may also not even be rejecting your work. Lack of quality is only one reason for rejection. There are many others. Pieces are often rejected for one of the following reasons:

• **A similar piece is already on file.** "Similar" can mean simply relating to the same topic—for example, if you submit an article on Antigua to a travel magazine, and they have another article on Antigua on hand (even if it's vastly different from yours), they won't accept another.

• **A similar piece has been assigned.** Great minds *do* think alike—and you'd be amazed how often two or more writers will query on a similar topic.

• **A similar piece was published within the last two or three years.** Many publications won't repeat a topic for at least that long. Internet publications may not repeat a topic that they've *ever* published, if their entire archives are still available online.

It's also possible to write an excellent article that still doesn't quite mesh with an editor's tastes in terms of style, tone, approach, angle, viewpoint, or even length. Again, this doesn't mean that your article was poor; it means that it came close but not quite close enough.

Another reason for rejection is sheer volume. If an editor can accept five articles per month out of a pile of 500, it isn't only the "bad" articles that are going to be rejected. Perfectly good articles will be rejected as well. Your article may be perfect in every way, yet be sent back simply because it was number six in the stack from which the editor could only accept five.

"GOOD" REJECTION SLIPS

Is there such a thing as a "good" rejection slip? Absolutely. Any rejection slip that offers information is good—because it helps you understand the reason for the rejection. Some magazines offer a "checklist" letter, listing common reasons for rejection and "checking" the one that applies to you. Finding out that someone else had already been assigned to the topic is a lot better than assuming the editor thought your article stank.

Even better than checklists, however, are rejections that include a personal note. Even a scribble (or, these days, a short e-mail note) shows that the editor thought enough of your piece to respond personally. Treasure those scribbles; they mean you're making a positive impression.

Still higher on the list of "positive" rejections is the "please try again" note. When an editor asks you to come back with another submission, believe it: No editor will say this unless s/he means it. This is often the result of a submission that "just misses" acceptance for one of the reasons listed above. Quite often, the editor truly wishes s/he could purchase your piece, but can't—and doesn't want to lose the opportunity to grab you as a contributor. Whenever you're asked to try again, *try again!*

SELF-HONESTY

While there may be dozens of reasons why an editor rejected your piece that have nothing to do with quality, a writer must also be willing to ask honestly whether, in fact, quality *was* the issue. When we write, we often become so involved in a piece that an accurate assessment of quality becomes difficult. Often, our work isn't as good as we thought it was—or wasn't what our target market required.

Good writing is a skill, not a gift—and skills are refined over time. Sure, there are occasional "prodigies" who craft the perfect bestseller the first time they pick up a pen—just as there are "prodigy" musicians who play perfectly the first time they pick up the violin. For the rest of us, perfection is achieved by plodding—and by endless practice that may, for a time, make everyone around us cover their ears and wince.

The reality of writing is that when you start, you think you're pretty good. After a year, if you've been writing steadily, you're likely to look back on those first efforts and wonder what on earth you saw in them. After you've been writing for five years, you may look at those first-year masterpieces and wonder why you didn't burn them on the spot. This process never ends: As you continue to improve, you'll feel this way twenty years from now. To some, this scenario sounds depressing—but what would be even more depressing is the idea that you *can't* get better!

Writing is a somewhat schizophrenic process. We must be able to look at each piece we produce and say, honestly, "This is the best I can do." At the same time, we must also be able to say—equally honestly—"I can do better." Both statements are true. What you write today is the best you can do—today. Tomorrow, quite probably, you'll do better. But only if you don't stop writing today.

IT SANK. GET OVER IT.

Someone created a T-shirt with a picture of the Titanic on the front and, on the back, the words: "It sank. Get over it." The same can be said of rejection.

"Getting used to" rejection doesn't mean that rejection loses its sting. It doesn't. Nor is that a bad thing: I suspect that the day rejection ceases to hurt is the day one has lost one's passion for writing. Pain isn't a bad thing. Pain simply means we care.

At the same time, there are things you can do to ease the sting. The next time your material comes back with one of those awful slips, try one of these:

• **Have a rejection party.** "Celebrate" your rejection with a pizza, a dish of ice cream, a trip to the movies. You have a right to celebrate: You have to be a writer to be rejected.

• **Start a rejection slip file.** Besides being useful for taxes (it proves to the IRS that you're conducting a business), it can come in handy down the line, when you're famous. Then you'll be able to say, with a smug flourish, "Well, I was rejected forty-eight times before my story/novel/article was accepted by Megabucks Publishing..."

• **Send your material to the next publisher on your list.**

• **Write something else.** Better yet, start writing something else the minute your last piece is finished and out the door. Rejection stings less when your mind is occupied with a newer, and therefore more interesting, project.

Remember, there is something worse than rejection, and that's never writing (or submitting) anything to be rejected in the first place.

PART II

Starting Your Article

❧ 6 ☙

Finding Ideas

One of the most common complaints of new writers is "I don't have anything to write about." This isn't true. Everyone has *lots* of things to write about; the trick is to figure out how to convert one's experiences into marketable article topics.

But first, you need to know what *makes* a marketable article topic! And that means knowing what editors want.

WHAT DO EDITORS WANT?

To answer this question, take a look at the contents of any magazine. You will find that *most* of the articles involve some type of "how-to" information. A health magazine, for example, will offer information on how to eat right, lose weight, overcome fatigue, stay fit, recognize the symptoms of a serious illness, and so forth. A pet magazine will discuss how to take better care of your pet. A crafts magazine will give you project tips and designs, or suggest equipment.

The next category is "pure information" that doesn't necessarily help a reader accomplish anything. Profiles and historical features usually fall into this category. Some magazines (such as *Discover* and *Smithsonian)* focus entirely on information. While a few "information-only" publications (like *National Geographic)* have a large audience, most such publications (such as *Military History* or *Discovering Archaeology)* have a much narrower market.

You'll also discover that most publications run very few "personal experience" articles—often no more than one per issue. Some don't run any. Those that do tend to focus on *exceptional* experiences—a family's battle to save a sick child, for example. Magazines that publish personal essays or opinion pieces (such as *Reader's Digest* or *Guideposts)* are even more rare and considerably harder to crack. While some publications include a "reader essay page" in the front or back, these receive hundreds of submissions each month, which means high odds against breaking in.

The answer to "what editors want," therefore, is simple. First, editors want articles that will help readers improve some aspect of their lives. Second, editors want articles with interesting information. Unless a publication focuses on information, however, you'll find that the ratio of "how-to" pieces to "information" pieces is often as high as ten to one.

To break into the periodical market, you need to become reader-focused, rather than "author-focused." As you begin to mine your experiences and expertise for article topics, you'll find that you have many opportunities to share information and help readers improve their lives.

DIGGING FOR IDEAS

The first step in coming up with article topics is determining where to look for ideas. Here are some places to start:

- Your personal life—home, family, personal history, life experiences
- Your interests and hobbies
- Your workplace, expertise, or professional background
- Your education
- Your memories—whether nostalgic or traumatic
- Your activities—vacations, family events, community activities, etc.
- Your observations—the people, places, and things around you
- Your interests—things that intrigue you, even if you don't know much about them (yet)

Ideas also come from the *process* of developing ideas:

- From brainstorming a topic
- From reviewing magazines and looking at articles
- From researching market sources
- From researching a topic (your research for one article can lead to "spin-off" articles for other markets)

Here's the million-dollar question: *Do I have to write about what I know?* Writing about what you know has several advantages:

- It saves work.
- It gives you an "instant credential" (your experience).
- It's easier to research.
- It's more comfortable.

It also has disadvantages, however:

- It's easy to overlook what you know, because it's so familiar.
- Too-familiar subjects may seem boring, and not excite you as a writer.

- It's easy to get stuck, and fail to expand your knowledge base or market potential.

One way to move beyond "what you know" is to write about what interests you. You know what you'd like to learn more about, what you find absolutely fascinating. An alternative to writing about what you know, therefore, is to write about what you *don't* know—but wish you did!

No matter what you write, you're going to end up doing research. So why not research subjects that are of interest to you? You don't have to know a lot about them to start with. You simply need to believe that, because this fascinates you, there's a good chance that it might fascinate someone else.

BRAINSTORMING IDEAS

As you begin to develop ideas, imagine that your mind is working like a camera lens. Sometimes you want to "zoom out" to get the "big picture"—to see the perspective, the surroundings. At other times you need to "zoom in" to sharpen your focus, to concentrate on the details. This process goes back and forth as you work your way from "idea" to "article topic."

A good way to start is with a wide-angle focus. Take another look at the list of idea sources I provided earlier. Jot down the areas you would like to explore for article ideas. For example, let's try "personal life."

If I were "brainstorming," I'd write this topic at the top of a piece of paper or computer file. (By the way, sometimes ideas flow better when you use old-fashioned approaches. If you find you're not getting anywhere by staring at the computer screen, take a pad of paper and a pencil to another room and work there. Sometimes the computer brings out our "inner editor" and we need to shut that off by taking a more physical approach to writing.)

Anyway—you've put "personal life" at the top of your "idea" page. Now, shut down that inner voice that is whispering, "No one wants to know about my personal life!" This is true, actually—but that's not what we're here for. We're here to find out what aspects of your personal life might lead to articles that people *will* want to read. So—let's jot down a few things about "personal life."

- **Family.** Do you have a spouse? Children? In-laws? Parents? Grandparents? Siblings? Extended family? Family members that don't speak to each other? Family members in other countries, or of other cultures? Are you adopted? Is anyone in your family adopted? What about topics like marriage, divorce, childbirth, or death?

- **Holidays.** Jot down a list of the holidays you celebrate. Does your family have special ways of celebrating particular holidays? Does it avoid certain holidays? Does your family celebrate holidays that are less familiar to the general public? Are holidays joyful or stressful? What are some of the activities you share with your children during a particular holiday? This category might include birthdays as well.

- **Pets.** Do you have a family pet? How about past pets? Pets of your childhood? How do you take care of it? What problems do you experience with your pets? What activities do you pursue with your pets? What challenges have you faced and overcome? What tragedies have you endured? How do your pets interact with your children?

- **And so on...**

This is part of the "zooming out" process. Notice that we started with a single idea—"personal life"—and expanded that idea into at least three subtopics (family, holidays, pets). We then expanded each of *those* topics into several more specific areas. If you try this exercise with all eight of the subject areas proposed at the beginning, you could find yourself with dozens of potential topics.

This is also a good exercise to do with a partner—a spouse, significant other, or writing buddy—who can help you come up with ideas you might otherwise miss. Someone who knows you is likely to think of things that you might overlook simply because they're too "familiar."

FOCUS AND EXPAND

So far, none of the subjects listed above is sufficiently focused to serve as an article topic. The next step, therefore, is to zoom in even more closely—and then to expand once again.

On another sheet of paper or file, select *one* of the topics that you generated. For example, you might select "holiday activities" as an area to explore further. However, this is still too general. Zoom in further: What holiday? What activities?

The immediate temptation is to tackle "Christmas," because it offers so many topics. On the other hand, it's also the holiday that gets the most "ink"—which means you're competing against a lot of other writers. So let's focus on a holiday that gets a little less press: Easter. It's time to brainstorm again, jotting down everything you associate with Easter. Here's my list:

- Eggs
- Bunnies
- Easter baskets
- Easter egg hunts
- Onion-skin Easter eggs
- Rabbits—good for pets?
- Chicks—same question
- Easter history/folklore
- Easter in other countries—Greek Easter candles
- Easter trees...

Now we're getting somewhere. Some of these topics are still a bit vague (what about Easter eggs, exactly?), but others are ripe for the plucking. Let's see what articles we might be able to generate from this list.

- **Easter baskets.** Is there someone in your town who makes fancy Easter baskets? (Check the classifieds for a "gift basket" store.) That might make a profile for a local paper.

- **Onion-skin Easter eggs.** Sooner or later, I'll get around to writing *my* holiday article on this family tradition.

- **Rabbits/chicks: Good for pets?** Your local paper might be interested in an article on why one shouldn't give bunnies or chicks to the kids. Interview a representative of your local humane society, and check online to find statistics on how many bunnies are sold in pet shops at this time of year.

- **Easter history/folklore** This is a perennial favorite. I know, because it was one of the very first articles I ever sold to a newspaper—and I am still selling that exact same article nearly 30 years after I first wrote it. No reason why you can't do a bit of research and sell something on this topic too!

- **Easter in other countries.** We visited Greece on our honeymoon, and I was struck by the sight of families returning to the islands after shopping on the mainland, all carrying elaborately decorated Easter candles. This might be an interesting feature for a travel magazine or travel section of a newspaper.

- **Easter trees.** These are very popular in Germany, and have a made a limited appearance in the United States, but haven't really caught on yet. This could be a nice, crafty "how-to" article on how to make your own—something you could sell to a local paper, or to a crafts or home-decorating magazine. Or you could slant this as a children's activity—how kids can make an Easter tree—and aim for a family publication such as *Family Fun*.

I've just identified five articles that I might be able to write, with very little effort, from this one subject. Easter, however, was itself a subtopic of a larger category—holiday activities. Imagine how many more article ideas you could generate if you looked at other holidays! You can follow other branches—holiday foods, holiday safety, holiday reminiscences, nontraditional holidays—and develop dozens of possibilities.

Keep in mind, too, that you're likely to find areas in which your categories overlap. If you have children, it's going to be easy to put together topics that combine "holidays" and "children"—crafts, safety tips, inspirational stories, etc. Or you might combine "holidays" and "grandparents" for a nostalgic look back at holidays in your past. And so on...

DON'T ELIMINATE THE NEGATIVE

Chances are that the topics that first strike you as good article ideas are positive. Maybe some of the more negative things that came out on your list made you shudder and move on quickly. But don't overlook the value of "negative experiences" in this exercise. Let's say, for example, that you hate Christmas because that's when the entire "clan" gets together—and everyone picks up the old fights where they left off the previous year. By the time the holiday is over, you're so stressed that you wish Christmas could be banned forever.

Not a very happy picture, right? Besides, who wants to hear about your troubles? No one, perhaps—but stop and think for a moment. Do you suppose you're the only family with this problem? Might there not be hundreds of families who go through something similar every year, and hate it just as much as you do? Can you write something that speaks to those families?

Here's where "writing what you know" meets "writing what you don't know." What you *know* is that you hate Christmas because it involves a huge, stressful family gathering. What you *don't* know is how to change that. If you could find out, you could share that information with other families—and write an article that might make a profound difference in many lives!

One approach might be to write a story that portrays your family in such a way that others see *their* families in your experience—and find, at least, a way to laugh about it even if they can't change it. Or, you could look for someone who *does* know how to change this family dynamic—a professional counselor, for example. Try running a search on "holiday stress" and "family gathering" and see what comes up. (Find out more about conducting research online in chapter 9.) Chances are, you'll find not only online information but also names of experts you can interview for more tips.

Once you begin brainstorming ideas and mixing and matching idea categories, you stop worrying about "what to write." Instead, you'll start wondering whether you'll ever have time to write up all the great article ideas you've developed!

❦ 7 ❧

Categories, Subjects, Topics, and Slants

If you went through the exercises in the previous chapter, you should have a selection of ideas for articles. Some of those ideas are nearly ready to go. Some of them aren't. The goal of this chapter is to help you bring at least one of those ideas to the starting gate by choosing the right market, the right audience, and the right slant for that audience.

I talked about "zooming in" and "zooming out" as one way to help you develop ideas. Another way to look at article development is to view it as a process of refinement. You start with the raw ore—a lump of material, such as knowledge or a loose collection of ideas ("my family")—and refine that ore through a succession of stages until you have "pure metal" that you can work into an article.

To begin this process, you need to be able to recognize the difference between a *category* of ideas, a *subject,* a *topic,* and a *slant.* Each of these is a stage in the refinement process, bringing you closer and closer to an article.

CATEGORY

This is where most writers start. A category is not an idea for an article; it may not even be a subject. Often, it's a catchall bin full of ideas, subjects, etc., that interest a writer. For example, if I were to say, "I want to write historical articles," I'm speaking of a category. I haven't defined a subject—I haven't even defined a period or type of history. However, I *have* defined the area in which I'd like to proceed, both in developing article topics and in locating markets. The same applies if I said I wanted to write about "health" or "pets" or "families" or "cooking."

Choosing a category is an important step. It tells you where to start your refinement process. It tells you, for example, that you should start researching markets that fit into this category. If your category was "pets," how many pet magazines or related markets (such as online pet stores) are there? What do they want? Do they accept freelance material? Gathering the answers can help you move on to the next step.

SUBJECT

This is the next level. Once you have a category of interest, pick a subject out of that category. If your category is "holidays," your subject might be "Christmas." From my category of "history," I might choose a subject such as "Mary, Queen of Scots." However, these are still not article topics. You can't simply write an article about "Christmas"— because the obvious question an editor is going to ask is, "Well, what about it?" Similarly, many lengthy books have been written about Mary, Queen of Scots; if I want to write an article about her, I must choose something more specific.

TOPIC

This is where the process starts to get interesting, because this is where you begin to develop the seed of your actual article. Let's suppose that I know lots and lots about Mary, and I've decided to focus on her years of imprisonment under Queen Elizabeth. That's the beginning of my topic. But what am I going to say? I could still spin this off into four or five (or more) articles. That's where it's helpful to have done some market research, to find out what type of article might actually *sell*.

So…Off I go to Barnes and Noble, to see what kind of magazines might accept an article on Mary. Obviously, *Redbook* is out. However, I pick up copies of *BBC History Magazine, Renaissance, Realm, British Heritage,* and *Scottish Life.* I flip through my treasures, and discover that *BBC History Magazine* is written primarily by experts, and generally focuses on topics being covered by BBC. *Renaissance* (which is produced by the Society for Creative Anachronisms) is nice, and might be a place for a general historical piece. *Realm* focuses more on travel, and I can't figure out how to contact them. *Scottish Life* focuses more on modern life than on history. *British Heritage,* however, focuses on visiting places with an interesting historical background. I decide to focus on that market.

By studying the publication, I know that it focuses as much on *location* as it does on *history,* so a general article about Mary's imprisonment probably wouldn't sell here. But a guide to the various *castles* in which Mary was imprisoned sounds ideal. It also would provide great photo opportunities. So now I've refined my topic to something specific and workable: "The castles in which Mary was imprisoned."

SLANT

I have a topic, but what am I going to say about it? I can't just say, "Mary, Queen of Scots, was imprisoned in X castle, which is located *here,* and looks like *this."* I need to look at that magazine again, and determine what slant is going to attract the editor. Since *British Heritage* focuses on places people might like to visit, my slant is going to be: "How you can visit the castles that imprisoned a Queen." In my article, I'm going to take the reader on a guided tour of the castles where Mary was imprisoned. Where are they? What are they like? Can you still visit Mary's accommodations? I'll provide a bit of history of each castle, details about

Mary's stay, and what you'll find if you visit today. The article will have a nice sidebar on how to get there, any pertinent tour details, hours... If I've read my market correctly, this is exactly the sort of thing (a mixture of travel and history) that should get this editor's attention.

The point is, you can't sell an article on the basis of a category ("history") or a subject. You *may* be able to sell an article on the basis of a topic, but it's difficult. Your best chance of selling an article is to research markets as part of your "refinement" process, choose one that you like, and *slant* your article directly toward that market.

Here are some tips on how to develop a workable slant.

- **Step out of your shoes and into the reader's shoes.** When you begin generating ideas, you're looking at areas of your life and experience and interests that might provide good material. To translate that information into potential articles, however, you have to step out of your "writer" shoes and into "reader" shoes. Start asking, "*Why* would a reader want to know about this? *What* would a reader want to know about this? *How* can this material be useful or helpful to the reader?"

- **Think "how-to" whenever possible.** The vast majority of what is published in magazines and other periodicals (not counting "news") focuses on a "how-to" component. The number of magazines that focus exclusively on "information" (history, news, etc.) is actually small. Most publications are looking for articles with "take-away" value —something the reader can apply in his or her life.

- **Think in terms of a *phrase* when developing your slant.** Try to avoid "slants" that are simply "subjects" ("haunted castles" or "Christmas decorations"). Express your slant in an active phrase: "Tour the haunted castles of Scotland," or "Decorate your home Victorian-style." Your slant may even become the title for your article: "How you can decorate your home ..." "Best places to visit in ..." etc.

- **Forget about "I" (the writer) and focus on "you" (the reader).** To be an effective writer, it's vital to move past your own experiences and perceptions and focus on the reader: How this can help *you*, why *you* should visit this location, how *you* can get the most out of a trip to..., ten ways that *you* can overcome this problem, why *you'll* love this product, etc. Putting "you-the-reader" into your slant is the most important step you can take toward winning editors.

Once you have a slant, you have something else that is vital to the next step: Your *core concept*. You have the central idea, theme, point, or whatever you choose to call it, that your article is "about." You should be able to sum up your slant and core concept in a single sentence—"My article is about how you can ..." Everything else must relate to this core concept, and that's what we're going to look at in the next chapter.

❧ 8 ☙

The Outline Demystified

I don't know any writer who likes the prospect of creating an outline. That's probably because we all remember being taught that horrible "1,2,3 - A,B,C" format in high school. (Hands up, everyone who used to get around those exercises by writing a paper first, and then creating the outline after the paper was done!) Relax—I'm not going to talk about that kind of outline.

An outline is simply a way to construct a road map of where you want to go with your article. Another way to look at an outline is to think of it as a filing cabinet. When you research your article, you're going to gather a lot of information. How will you know what to put in and what to leave out? By creating an "outline" that, in a sense, places "headers" on the files in your cabinet, you'll know whether the information you've gathered fits into the "files" that you have—or whether it doesn't. If you don't have a "file" for that information, chances are that the information doesn't belong in your article.

For example, when I decided to go full-time as a freelancer in 1996, one of the first articles I pitched was a piece on "cancer in cats." I chose to write the article because my own cat had recently died of cancer. When I got the assignment, I roughed out the areas I planned to cover:

- Types of cancer
- Breed-specific cancers
- How to detect cancer
- My experience with a cat with cancer
- Preventing cancer
- Treatments
- Hope for the future
- Hi-tech treatments
- Diagnostic techniques

A quick look at this list showed me that some ideas were actually sub-categories of others. "Breed-specific cancers" fit under "types of cancer," while "diagnostic techniques" fit under "how to detect." "Hope for the future" fit under "treatments." One category also stood out as *not* fitting with the rest: "My own experience." I ended up with four "file folders" to work with:

- Types of Cancer
- Detecting Cancer
- Treating Cancer
- Preventing Cancer

This, by the way, is an outline. It can be as simple as that. Besides serving as a framework for my article, it provided a framework for my research: I knew what types of questions I had to ask, based on the information I wanted to include. I researched the article on the Web and by interviewing experts, asking questions based on my four topic areas—and "filing" that information in the appropriate place. If information came in that didn't fit into one of these four areas, I knew that it probably didn't belong in my article.

I also had a slant or "core concept"—"What you need to know about cancer in cats." (Note, again, how a slant can make a great title: "Is your cat at risk of cancer?" or "How you can reduce your cat's risk of cancer.")

Having that core concept or slant is vital. It tells you what is vital to your article—what is at the center of your idea—and what isn't. If you have information or thoughts that don't relate directly to the core concept, then that information probably doesn't belong in the article.

FIVE WAYS TO APPROACH THE OUTLINE

As I said above, I'm no fan of the "1,2,3 - A,B,C" approach to outlines. This approach tends to get one bogged down in the mechanics—Is this a subset of #2? Should I move this section *here*? There are easier ways to put your ideas and information in order.

1) **Ask yourself what questions a reader would ask.** What would a reader want to know about this subject? Make a list of those questions. For example, a reader interested in cancer in cats might want to know:

   - How common is cancer in cats?
   - What kinds of cancer affect cats?
   - What cats are at greatest risk?
   - How can I tell if my cat has cancer?
   - What can I do if my cat has cancer?
   - What kinds of treatments are available to me?
   - What are their success rates?

- What are their risks to my cat?
- How long will my cat live if it has cancer?
- Can I prevent my cat from getting cancer?
- Where do I go to get more help?

Sometimes, simply jotting down a list of questions is all you need to define the basic areas your article will cover, and even the order in which you might wish to cover them.

2) **Think in "subheads."** Most published articles are divided into sections with subheads. This is a good way to organize your information (and putting in your own subheads always pleases an editor). The four "file folders" that I developed for my feline cancer piece would also serve very nicely as subheads:

- Is your cat at risk?
- Protecting your cat from cancer
- Detecting the signs of cancer
- Choosing a treatment plan

Subheads help you organize your information logically. You'll also be able to determine whether your article is "in balance." If you have 250 words under one subhead and 1,000 under another, chances are you need to reorganize the article.

3) **List events or concepts chronologically.** What happened first? What happened next? What happened after that? What happened last? This approach works well for an article that focuses on events that occurred over time—e.g., a historical piece, a personal profile, etc. For example, women's magazines often publish stories of how a family coped with a child's illness. A chronological outline of such an article might look like this:

- Family notices something isn't right with the child
- Family goes to traditional doctor
- Family gets reassurances, goes home
- Child gets worse
- Family seeks more help; gets more reassurances
- Child gets worse
- Family gets desperate; seeks more information
- Family finds special doctor/support group/information online
- Family locates specialist/special treatment/new cure
- Family is warned of risks of treatment

- Family goes ahead with treatment
- Child gets better

4) List points in logical order. Many how-to articles have an obvious logical order: Do this first, do this next, do this next, and do this last. Your outline here may consist simply of a list of things to do, and the order in which the reader should do them. This works well for a how-to article, for example.

A travel article might also have a logical order, based on the order in which one would see or visit a location. If, for example, you'd start at Point A and travel to Point X, a logical way to present your information is in the order in which the traveler following your route would encounter it. This works even for a single location: Trace the route a traveler would take if walking through a site, such as a castle or museum.

5) Make a list. List all the pieces of information that you'd like to include in the article. Then, go over that list and assign numbers to each item based on its importance or priority. For example, if you're writing a piece on ways to improve communication between spouses, jot down a list of all the suggestions you want to cover. Which tips are most important? Which are less important? Which could be omitted without any real harm to your article? You may find, when you're done, that you have a selection of *key* points, and perhaps a few "leftovers" that aren't as useful. In some cases, your list may become the actual structure of your finished article ("Five ways to improve communication with your spouse"); in others, it may become the "hidden" structure that underlies your piece, even though you aren't numbering the points in the final article.

WORKING WITHIN A WORD BUDGET

A final consideration to keep in mind as you outline an article is your word budget. Every magazine has length requirements for feature articles. Such articles typically range from 1,000 to 3,000 words, with the most common length being 2,000.

One of the most common amateur mistakes is to propose an article that seeks to address more topics than can be covered effectively within the required word count. Editors are quick to spot this error—and equally quick to reject such queries.

For example, I recently reviewed a query letter from a woman who wanted to write about a controversial treatment for breast cancer. So far, so good. However, in 2,000 words or less, the writer wanted to cover traditional cancer treatments, alternative treatments, a profile and history of a woman who chose such a treatment, interviews with her doctor and other patients, and a discussion of why women aren't told about alternative treatments.

As an editor, I'd reject this query as being unfocused and impossible to cover in 2,000 words. In addition, since the woman had only begun treatment, the writer would have been unable to offer a conclusion—i.e., did it work?

Resist the temptation to throw everything you have, including the kitchen sink, into your article! Remember, *if it doesn't relate to your core concept, it doesn't belong in your article.*

This can be tough. You do all that research and have all that great information, and it's *hard* to throw some of it out. But don't despair. Chances are, you can use your extra information to write a completely different article for another publication. There is also the option of including sidebars to your main article.

Think about your word budget as you develop your outline. Keep in mind that the more subtopics you include in your article, the fewer words you'll be able to allocate to each topic. If you have four major subtopics, you can devote approximately 500 words to each of them. If you have ten, you can give each no more than 200 words. (Keep in mind that you'll also need an introduction, a conclusion, and some allowance for "transitions.")

This brings up the difference between an "in-depth" article and an "overview." If you have only a few subtopics (three to five), you can write an "in-depth" article. If you have a lengthy list of subtopics, then you'll probably end up writing an overview. An article titled "Ten Tips on Beating Holiday Stress" is almost certainly going to be an overview—it will give you ten ideas, but not a lot of in-depth information on any one of them. An article titled "Put an End to Holiday Stress," which involves an interview with a therapist and four or five basic suggestions, is likely to be more in-depth.

Should you focus on an in-depth piece or an overview? This gets back to your market research. What type of piece does the market you're targeting prefer? Choose the type of article that seems most likely to appeal to the editor, and audience, of your chosen market. (*Family Circle,* for example, loves lists: 100 ways to clean your house with basic products, 50 inexpensive "dates" to share with your spouse, 30 things to do on a rainy day.) Just be aware that the more subtopics you have, the less information you can provide about any of them.

ᛝ*9*ᛢ
Conducting Research on the Web

Now that you've selected an idea, developed it into a topic, and perhaps even outlined your article, the next step is to fill in the gaps. While you may have chosen a topic that draws upon your own experience and expertise, chances are that you're also going to have to do some research before you can actually write your article.

Once, this was a writer's most time-consuming task. Thanks to the Internet, however, research that once took days (or weeks) to complete can often be handled in a few hours or less. No longer do you have to drive to the library, comb through catalogs to find a likely reference, search for the reference only to find that it's been checked out (or missing since 1992), ask for another book through interlibrary loan that will take weeks to arrive, and so forth. While libraries are still rich sources of information, a lot of the searching we once did in the stacks can now be accomplished with the touch of a button.

DEFINING EFFECTIVE SEARCH TERMS

Internet search engines enable you to research general subject areas—e.g., everything you wanted to know about 17th-century costumes—or look up the answers to specific questions ("What is the planetary mass of Jupiter?").

The key is defining an effective search term (or set of terms). Your goal is to choose terms that will bring up the most relevant sites, while excluding those that are irrelevant.

To accomplish this, your terms should be as specific as possible. Often, a good way to accomplish this is to specify two, three, or more precise words that you want to find within the same document. For example, if you wanted to research "cat care," simply searching on "cats" would bring up a host of inappropriate sites. However, by entering terms such as "cats" and "care," you'll get more focused results. An even better approach is to ask yourself what type of phrase an article on "caring for cats" would be most likely to contain—e.g., "how to care for your cat" or "how to take care of your cat."

Another approach is to determine what terminology an expert would use. If you're researching "cancer in cats," for example, using a combination of terms like "cats" and "cancer" will certainly produce good results. However, searching on "feline oncology" may be even more productive, as this is the terminology that would be used by veterinarians.

To search for more than one word in the same document (e.g., "cats" and "cancer," simply type both words into the search engine. If you wish to search for a specific phrase (for example, a person's name, a book title, or a quotation), enter it in quotes. If you wish to *exclude* irrelevant results from a search, try putting a minus sign in front of the word you'd like to exclude. For example, if you want to search for information on limericks, but wish to exclude search results relating to Limerick, Ireland, try entering the word "limerick," followed by "-Ireland."

Keep in mind that search engines are specific. They can't "guess" or provide information that is "close." They can only find *exactly* what you enter. (Needless to say, spelling is important—though Google now does a fairly decent job of trying to come up with alternate spellings if your search term does not provide any results.) Most engines rank the results based on how many times your search term appears in a document, or how close to the beginning of the document it appears (along with a number of other variables). That doesn't mean, however, that you should look only at the first few results provided. You may find that the perfect site is number 30 on the list, or even number 50. (If you scan three pages of results without finding a likely site, however, you probably need to refine your search.)

Another thing to keep in mind is that different countries use different spellings. If you're using American spellings, your search results may exclude non-U.S. sites that could offer valuable information. If a word has both an American and a British spelling, try both (e.g., "catalog" vs. "catalogue"). Similarly, if you're searching for information about a specific date, remember that while the U.S. format would be "May 4, 2001," the European format would be "4 May 2001."

IS IT ACCURATE?

There's a flip side to the joys of searching out data—the question of whether what you find is accurate!

Unfortunately, the Internet offers just as much misinformation as information. One classic example is an article that appeared in *The Boston Globe* in July 2000, touching on the grim fates of the 56 men who signed the Declaration of Independence. This article was based on an e-mail that has been making the rounds since about 1995—an e-mail that was also passed along as "fact" by Ann Landers. As *American Journalism Review* columnist Carl Cannon pointed out, this e-mail (and the *Globe* article) was, in fact, almost entirely false.

According to the oft-quoted account, five signers of the Declaration were captured by the British and tortured to death as traitors, while nine fought and died in the Revolutionary War. In reality, no signers of the Declaration were tortured by the British, while two were merely injured in the War (none died). One signer who supposedly "died in poverty" actually became governor of Pennsylvania.

The Internet is also a hotbed of urban legends, hoaxes, and scares. You've probably gotten an inbox-full of "virus threats" characterized by the tell-tale phrase, "Please pass this on to everyone you know." Perhaps you've heard that the government is about to start charging everyone for using e-mail, to help subsidize the Post Office (it isn't). Even accurate information (such as the news that certain cold medicines were to be withdrawn from the market) gets circulated long after its "time," until it becomes misinformation simply because it is out of date.

How can you determine whether the information you find is accurate? It's impossible to be 100 percent sure—but by asking the following questions about everything you read, you'll improve your chances of getting "the right stuff."

• **Does the author, site, or information appear to exist primarily to support a particular point of view?** Why is this information online in the first place? Does the material contain an obvious bias toward a particular point of view, agenda, or belief? If so, chances are that the material will at least be slanted toward that bias—even if it is, itself, factual—and there's also a very good chance that information that does *not* support the author's views will be omitted.

• **Does the site seem "overly emotional"?** It's often easy to spot "emotional" sites—they're full of boldface phrases and LOTS OF CAPS. They often look as if the author is "shouting" at you. If a site uses phrases like "Don't believe what those Commie bastards in government are trying to pull off!!!" I'm inclined to believe that the author has an axe to grind—and that accuracy may not be the highest priority.

• **Is the author trying to sell something?** I'm always wary of sites that purport to offer "valuable medical information" that "doctors won't tell you"—but just happens to be available in the author's book, or that supports a line of products such as supplements or exercise equipment. That doesn't mean that an author who is trying to sell a book is necessarily providing misinformation—but if the information seems primarily offered as a sales pitch, beware!

• **Who is the author?** Does the author have any credentials? The Internet is a place where absolutely anyone can post anything. Keep in mind, however, that a *lack* of credentials does not necessarily mean that the information will be inaccurate; the Internet is also a place where thousands of ordinary folks post highly accurate information, based on their personal research. If the author doesn't have credentials, look for references (e.g., a bibliography) that can help confirm the information provided.

• **Is the site up to date?** Many sites post a copyright notice, usually at the bottom of the page. If the copyright notice has not been updated in the last five years, that's a good indication that the site hasn't been either. Some sites also post a "last updated" notice. Another way to determine if a site is current is to test a few of its links. If you find that most of the links are "dead," you can assume that the author has not updated the information recently.

• **Does the information agree with other sites on the same topic?** When I see ten sites that list Shackleton's death on January 5, and only one that lists it on January 4, I'm inclined to believe in the voice of the majority. By reviewing several sites on a topic, you'll get an idea for what the "accepted facts" are—and be able to spot a site that seems out of line.

Here are some other ways to protect yourself—and your writing—from inaccuracies:

• **Never assume that information in an unsolicited e-mail is factual** unless you have checked it thoroughly or are familiar with the original source. E-mail has been the most prolific source of legends, myths (like the "signers of the Declaration" story), virus hoaxes, urban legends, and outdated information. E-mail gets forwarded forever—and it seems to appeal to the gullible who pass on stories like "I passed out in a hotel room and woke up without a kidney." Hoaxes also include warm-fuzzy stories, such as tales of sick children needing prayers or greeting cards. *Never* cite information that comes from an unsolicited e-mail without verifying its accuracy.

• **Check the hoax pages for stories that are too good (or too bad) to be true.** (For example, Osama bin Laden does *not* own Snapple!) You'll find information on common hoaxes and urban legends at the Urban Legends Reference Pages (*www.snopes.com/snopes.asp*), and information on computer virus hoaxes at the Computer Virus Hoax Page (*http://vmyths.com/*).

• **Don't rely on a domain suffix to "validate" information.** Don't assume that a ".com" suffix indicates a "commercial" site; anyone can use this suffix and some of the best information on the Web is available through .com addresses. Conversely, don't assume that a ".edu" site must be accurate; this does not necessarily indicate that the site is *sponsored* by a university, only that it is hosted on a university server.

• **Use common sense!** Often, your own instincts will be the best guide. If something looks fishy, don't trust it just because it's online—or even because it seems to be backed by some impressive credentials.

USING PUBLISHED SOURCES

While it's appropriate (and often necessary) to conduct research online and in other published sources when writing an article, how you *use* that research in your article is another issue. Editors aren't fond of articles that are filled with quotes drawn from other published materials (such articles tend to look too much like college research papers). Editors much prefer "live quotes" that you've gathered from interviews.

If you use quotes from published sources, it's important to be sure that you aren't crossing the subtle line between "research" and "plagiarism." It isn't always easy to determine where this line is; a certain amount of quoting, for example, is usually considered "fair use" under copyright law. Here are some dos and don'ts to consider when quoting published sources.

• **Use the information to *support* your article, not to actually *write* that article.** I once reviewed a piece on pet training that was based entirely on quotes drawn from various authors' published books. If the quotes had been removed, there would have been no article—which indicated that the writer really didn't have an original article of her own.

• **Use quotes sparingly.** The question of whether something is "fair use" often depends on the amount of material being quoted. You aren't likely to get in trouble if you quote a few lines or even a paragraph from a published work, but be cautious of using anything more extensive.

• **Ask yourself whether the author of the material you're quoting would have a problem** with the amount of his or her work that you're including in your own. (Another way to approach this is to ask yourself whether *you* would have a problem with someone quoting similar amounts of material from *your* work.)

• **Make sure that your quotes don't contain the "essence" of the previously published work.** If you quote an author to the extent that reading your article is like reading a condensed version of the author's own work, you have a problem.

• **If possible, go to the authors you're quoting and get "live" quotes** instead of using material from their published works.

• **Attribute the information.** You don't need to footnote your information; simply provide a reference within the text, such as "Dr. Gordon Chalmers of the American Institute for Research notes in his book, *Good Stuff by Chalmers*, that..." Make sure that the reader will not draw the mistaken conclusion that a piece of information originates with *you* rather than with your *source*.

• **Provide a list of references for the editor.** Some publications insist that all facts be supported with references and documentation, so be sure you can show where your material came from.

The good news is that copyright infringement lawsuits are actually extremely rare; it's not likely that an author is going to take you to court for having used too many quotes from his or her published work. However, the question of "can I be sued" should be of far less concern than the question of "will this damage my reputation as a writer?" Editors who see an article chock-full of quotes from published sources aren't going to take you to court; they're simply going to send you a rejection slip.

❧10☙

Conducting Interviews

While you can get loads of wonderful information from the Internet (or from books or magazines), it's important to remember that an article is not a research paper. Forget about finding lots of information in previously published resources and spitting it back out in ten pages. While some publications accept material that is "pure research" (such as historical topics), most editors don't want articles that draw heavily on published sources. What they want is "live quotes."

Interviews frequently scare new writers. We feel that we don't have the credentials to ask for an interview—that we may even insult an expert by approaching them. I'll share a little secret: If you're not the outgoing, go-get-em type, you may *never* enjoy doing interviews. (I've been doing this for more than 30 years, and I still don't like making that call!) But this can be your little secret (and mine). You can hate interviews—and still present a professional "face" to your interviewee.

MAKING CONTACT

Your first step is to find appropriate experts to interview. If you're doing a profile, obviously your main interviewee is the subject of that profile—but you may also want to interview people who know that person (a boss, a spouse, a friend). If you're covering a particular topic, you'll want to interview people who are experts on that topic. For an article on "cancer in cats," for example, you need to interview someone who specializes in animal cancer treatments. The easiest way to find experts is often to search on your topic online.

Many writers wonder whether to contact prospective interviewees before or after you have an assignment. Having a list of interviewees can certainly help you *get* an assignment; conversely, actually having an assignment is more likely to encourage interviewees to talk to you. I generally contact interviewees only after I have an assignment in hand. However, if I believe that my query will be strengthened by the promise of an interview by an important expert, I will contact that person in advance and ask if he or she would be willing to talk to me *if* I obtain the assignment. (So far, no one has ever said no!)

I don't recommend actually conducting interviews before you have an assignment. This could prove a waste of your time and theirs. (There are exceptions to this rule as well, of course; for example, if you're traveling and come across someone perfect for an interview, don't miss the opportunity!)

The next question is whether to interview by phone, e-mail, or in person. If you're profiling someone local, an in-person interview is usually best, as you'll be able to pick up more visual details—the person's appearance, environment, mannerisms, etc. Telephone interviews are the next most personal way to talk to someone, and are particularly useful if you expect to need to ask lots of questions and get clarification on the answers. They're also useful if you want to let the interviewee take more control of the interview and more or less "follow their lead," rather than keeping the discussion to a predefined list of questions. (When setting up a telephone interview, be sure you know what time zone your interviewee is in—and that you know exactly what time the interview is supposed to occur in *both* time zones. There's nothing so embarrassing as discovering that the call you thought you were supposed to make at 9 a.m. your time is actually being received at 6 a.m. by your interviewee.)

E-mail interviews can also be very effective. They are less intrusive than telephone interviews, and can be more comfortable for you if you're nervous about actually talking to someone. Just be sure that they are equally comfortable for the interviewee. Some people like the option of writing down their responses; an e-mail interview gives them more time to consider the questions, come back to them, and so forth. Others, however, don't like writing, and may give much less useful responses "on paper" than they would by phone or in person. (I'll discuss e-mail interviews in more detail below.)

Once you find a potential interviewee and decide how you'd like to conduct the interview, the next step is asking for the interview. Remember, *they don't need to know you're nervous.* You may be shaking in your boots; they'll never know. If you're going to interview someone by phone or in person, the first contact should usually be made by telephone. Simply call the person and explain who you are and what you are writing about. For example:

"Hi, my name is Moira Allen, and I'm working on an article for Cats *Magazine about cancer in cats. Would you be willing to talk to me about some of the treatments your clinic provides for feline cancer patients?"*

If you don't have an assignment yet, just say, "I'm working on an article about..." Nine times out of ten, they'll never ask what publication it's for. If they do, just say "I'll be pitching this to..." and fill in the magazine name.

If the person says "yes" to the idea of doing an interview, ask when would be a good time. Frequently, the person is likely to say, "This would be a good time," so *be prepared to do the interview on the spot.* Have your interview questions ready and make sure you've called when *you* have time to do the interview. It's embarrassing to have to tell your interviewee, "Oh, gee, sorry, I don't have time to talk to you right now; can we schedule an appointment?" If the person *does* want to do the interview at another time, he or she may want to know how long the interview will take, so you should have a time estimate (e.g., half an hour). Generally, you should call the person for the interview (it should be on your nickel). The exception is when a person can't guarantee being available at a certain time, and so would prefer to control the timing of the interview by calling you. (Businesses, for example, will often prefer to call you, and will often arrange the call through a secretary.)

If you aren't comfortable simply cold-calling a person, or can't find a phone number, try to make contact by e-mail. The same approach works just fine (leaving out the "Hi" part). Close your e-mail with something like "Could I call you next week to discuss this?" Include your phone number; some people will be happy to call you back.

BEFORE THE INTERVIEW

By taking the right steps to set up your interview, you can ensure that you make a good impression, get the information you want, and (perhaps) gain a contact you can use for future articles.

• **Prepare your questions in advance.** By having a list of questions handy, you'll be able to answer an interviewee who asks, "What do you want to talk about?" Create "open-ended" questions rather than questions that can be answered "yes" or "no." For example, if you're interviewing a children's author, don't ask, "Do you enjoy writing children's books?" (If the author just says "yes," you have to come up with another question, like "why?") Instead, ask something like "What do you enjoy most about writing children's books?" or "What is the most fulfilling part of writing children's books?" These questions will elicit a more in-depth answer.

• **Ask for a specific amount of time.** Do you want half an hour? An hour? This will help your interviewee schedule the appointment (and is especially important if you're scheduling through a secretary).

• **Be honest about your purpose.** If you don't have a firm assignment, don't pretend that you do. (You can, however, explain that you're pitching the article to a specific market.) Don't claim credentials that you don't have. Unless you're trying to interview a celebrity, you'll find that most people are willing to talk to "ordinary" writers.

• **Don't confuse time zones.** Always refer to the interviewee's time zone when making appointments—e.g., "I'll call you at 2:00 p.m your time." Don't even mention your own time zone; if you say something like "I'll call you at 4:00 p.m., which is 2:00 p.m. my time," you may confuse the interviewee as to which time you're actually calling.

• **Let the interviewee schedule the interview.** Often, you'll be asked what time is convenient. Instead of setting a time yourself, suggest a range of times, such as "any afternoon next week," or "any time on Wednesday or Thursday." This gives the interviewee flexibility to work you into the schedule. Try not to leave interviews to the last minute; while many interviewees try to be helpful with respect to deadlines, you never know when someone will be out of town, too busy, or otherwise unavailable.

• **Ask the interviewee how s/he would prefer to be interviewed.** Many people now prefer e-mail interviews, as this allows them to respond on their own time, and gives them the leisure to provide more in-depth answers. However, if you feel that you may need to follow up on questions, or have more control over the interview, you may prefer to push for a telephone interview. (Another option is to send your initial questions by e-mail, and then follow up on any additional questions or clarifications by phone.)

• **Be prepared to e-mail your questions to the interviewee in advance.** Business executives often prefer this, as it enables them to prepare for the specific types of information you're looking for. This won't always work if you're conducting a sensitive, personal, or controversial interview, but it does work if you're just gathering basic facts.

DURING THE INTERVIEW

Keep your interviewee happy with the interview process by remaining courteous and professional—no matter what! As long as you remain polite, your interviewee is unlikely to be offended, even if your questions are sensitive or controversial.

• **Be prepared.** Again, having a list of questions prepared in advance can help you guide the interview in the direction you want it to go. It can also help you double-check to make sure you've gotten all the information you need. Note that you may not actually ask every one of your questions; often, an interviewee's response to one question will give you the answers to other questions.

• **Remember that the interview is about the interviewee, *not* about you.** You're there to gather information, not to judge the person or the material. It doesn't matter how you feel about the person, whether you agree or disagree with his/her perspective, or whether you like what you hear. Keep in mind that if you remain calm and nonjudgmental, you're likely to get far more material than if you react negatively to the interviewee's responses.

• **Interact with the interviewee.** Don't just fire off questions and jot down the answers. Respond. Make "uh-huh" and "I see" and "Oh, really?" noises. Let the interviewee know you're listening and genuinely interested in the information. Volunteer an occasional comment that shows you understand what you are being told.

• **Let the interviewee set the tone.** Don't assume familiarity; let the interviewee determine whether the discussion proceeds formally or informally. Don't volunteer personal information or "chat" unless the interviewee has indicated this seems appropriate.

- **Pay attention to nonverbal parts of the interview.** If you're writing a profile and interview someone in person, jot down details about the person's surroundings, appearance, tone of voice, etc.—anything will give the reader a clearer picture. Did the person's clothing clash with the "personality" you expected? (For example, a rich CEO wearing torn cutoffs.) What did you notice about the person's environment? Was it filled with mementos, or barren and austere? Did it seem to reflect the interviewee's interests and personality, or clash with them? What did you notice about the person's body language and facial expressions—did the person seem comfortable or tense? Pay attention to questions that make your interviewee tense; they could lead to important information. (Don't be afraid to ask "tough" questions when appropriate.) Does the person's facial expression or body language match the words? For example, if someone says, "I have a wonderful marriage," but sits back with crossed arms and a frown, you might have doubts as to the truth of the statement.

- **Keep the interview "on track."** Interviewees will often go off on tangents. In some cases, a tangent can bring up more interesting information—but if you're being given only a short period of time for the interview, and the tangent isn't giving you the information you need, you'll need to bring the conversation back on track. One way to do this is to use the interviewee's earlier responses to redirect the interview, e.g., "Getting back to what you were saying earlier about..."

- **Don't be afraid of silences.** Silences are wonderful tools. They make people uncomfortable, and people thus tend to try to *fill* a silence. If you're not getting a response to a question, or if the response seemed too short or insufficient, just wait a moment without saying anything—often this will cause the person to say more. Don't rush to fill silences yourself!

- **Always thank the interviewee when the interview is over.** A common question is whether to tape interviews or transcribe them by hand. I prefer both. I hate transcribing taped notes, so I try to write everything down, but a recording provides a good backup if I can't read my handwriting, or if the interviewer talks so fast (or gives so much information) that I can't get it all down. It's also a good way to support your article later, in case an interviewee claims you've misquoted him. (Always save your tapes for a couple of years!)

When I interview by phone, I usually type responses directly into the computer. Some answering machines will enable you to make a recording of a conversation; if you do so, however, be sure to inform the interviewee that you're taping the call. Different states have different laws about the legality of taping a telephone call without the knowledge of the other party; for more information on taping interviews, see "Can We Tape?" at *www.rcfp.org/taping/*.

AFTER THE INTERVIEW

An interview isn't necessarily over just because you've hung up the phone. You may need to come back for more information or clarification. You may also want to call upon that person's expertise for other articles. The following courtesies can help keep you in the interviewee's good will.

- **Send a thank-you note by e-mail or snail-mail.** Let the interviewee know when and where the article will be published, or provide that information once you have it.

- **Ask your editor to send complimentary copies of the issue to each interviewee.** Be sure to include a list of interviewees (with their addresses) when you send in your article. If an editor balks, ask for extra copies to be sent to you, so you can send them yourself.

- **When the article is published, send a copy with another thank-you letter.** I like to contact interviewees once an article comes out to make sure they received a complimentary copy from the editor. If they didn't, send them a copy yourself; it will be appreciated. (In some cases, the editor may send you a PDF file of your article; this makes it very easy to forward a copy on to your interviewees.)

Many interviewees will try to pressure you into letting them "review" (and in some cases, "approve") an article before it goes to the editor. The consensus among authors and editors on this point is to say *no*. Never promise to let an interviewee see your article before it goes to press. Never give an interviewee any "approval power" over your article. If an interviewee puts any pressure on you to do this, simply say you're sorry, but your editor won't permit it.

One reason many interviewees want to see an interview before it is published is because they've had bad experiences with writers who want to put their own, biased spin or slant on an interview. In such a case, be understanding—but firm. (If you have done previous interviews that demonstrate your balanced and professional reporting style, share those with the interviewee; they may put his mind at ease about your approach.)

The only exception to this rule is when you're interviewing someone about a highly technical subject and want to be absolutely sure you've gotten all the information right. In such a case, the only interest the interviewee is likely to have in reviewing the article is the same as yours: accuracy. If I have any doubts about how I've transcribed and presented the interview information, I may pass it back to the interviewee for a check—but *not* for any form of pre-approval.

E-MAIL INTERVIEWS

E-mail can be an effective and convenient way to conduct an interview, and is often appreciated by busy experts who don't have time for a face-to-face or telephone interview. It enables you to compose questions carefully rather than "on the fly," and gives your interviewee time to respond carefully as well.

(Another plus is that the interviewee gets to do all the typing!) E-mail also offers a good way to follow up on a traditional interview, when seeking clarification or additional information.

E-mail interviews are less effective when you're trying to develop a profile that includes not only the individual's words but also your observations of the person's appearance, actions, skills, emotions, tone of voice, etc. They are also less effective if you don't know enough about a subject to develop useful questions, or when you're more likely to get information from the natural flow of questions and answers than from a predefined script. In an e-mail interview, you can't change direction if a more promising tangent emerges from the conversation; you can't nudge the interviewee back on track if the conversation strays or ask follow-on questions if your first questions don't elicit enough information; and you can't ask for immediate explanations or clarification.

The following strategies can help you develop and refine an e-mail interview:

- **Determine your goals before writing your questions.** Decide exactly what you need to know; then develop questions that will best elicit that information.

- **Ask open-ended questions rather than questions that can be answered "yes" or "no."**

- **Explain why you're asking a particular question,** so the interviewee knows what type of response you're looking for.

- **Let the interviewee know what audience you're writing for,** so the interviewee will know how detailed or technical the information should be.

- **Keep your questions as clear, uncomplicated, and short as possible.**

- **Keep your list of questions short.** Ten is good; twenty is likely to tax an interviewee's patience.

- **List your questions numerically,** and leave space between each question for the interviewee to insert the answer.

- **Include a final "open" question**—e.g., "Is there anything else you'd like to say on this subject that hasn't been covered above?"

- **Let the interviewee know when you need the answers.** Remember that the interviewee is doing you a favor, and is under no obligation to meet your deadline.

- **Don't be afraid to ask for clarification,** or to follow up on questions or answers that beg for additional information. And always thank your interviewee!

E-MAIL SURVEYS

Another way to gather information via e-mail is to conduct a survey. E-mail enables you to send a list of questions to hundreds of potential respondents, at no cost.

At the same time, caution is in order. Some respondents may regard a survey as a form of spam. Your e-mail should state the nature and purpose of the survey as quickly, succinctly, and courteously as possible. Assure respondents of privacy, and guarantee that you won't cite anyone by name or organization without permission. If you're soliciting comments as well as statistics, ask respondents to indicate whether or not they may be quoted, and how they should be cited.

Like interview questions, survey questions should be short, clear, and well organized. Unlike interview questions, however, survey questions should encourage "yes/no" answers, or answers to a multiple-choice selection. Respondents are more likely to answer a short questionnaire than a long one.

An easy format is to follow each question with the answer options (e.g., "Yes" or "No") on separate lines. Place a set of parentheses in front of each option, with space for a response. Here's an example from an e-mail survey I sent to a number of magazine editors:

1) Do you accept e-mail queries?
( ) Yes
( ) No

2) How do you prefer to receive manuscripts?
( ) Hardcopy (printed)
( ) On disk
( ) By e-mail, in the body of the message
( ) As an e-mail attachment

This enables the respondent to simply insert an "x" in the appropriate space and mail the form back as a reply. If you're offering a multiple-choice question that could have more than one answer, indicate whether you want the respondent to "check only one" or "check all that apply."

To ensure your respondents' privacy, place all your survey addresses in the "BCC" (blind copy) field of your header. Leave the "TO" field blank. If you have a large number of addressees, send the survey in several batches rather than all at once.

When you mail your survey, several may bounce back immediately as undeliverable. Keep track of these bounces so you know exactly how many surveys actually reached their destination. This will enable you to calculate the correct percentage of responses. For example, if you send out 100 surveys, get ten back as undeliverable, and receive fifty responses, you have a 55 percent response rate.

The bulk of your responses will typically arrive in a flood within the first two or three days of your mailing. After that, the flood will taper to a trickle. At some point, you'll have to decide when it's time to cut off the survey and tally the results, even if you're still getting an occasional response. If possible, set up a filter in your e-mail program to route responses to a separate mailbox until you're ready to tally them.

Once you've completed the survey, make a list of the respondents and send them a thank-you note for participating. If respondents are interested in the results of your survey, let them know when and where the article will appear.

USING INTERVIEW MATERIAL

Once the interview is finished, write up your notes as soon as possible, while it is still fresh in your mind. Try to be as clear and accurate as possible.

You'll often find you have too much information to actually fit in your article, but that's fine. Some of what you've gathered might spin off into another article, or you might find that a personal experience makes a great sidebar. Interview material is like raw ore; your task now is to refine it, and find the "precious metal" hidden inside. (By the way, by granting an interview, the interviewee is considered to have granted you the "right" to use those responses, not only in the original article but also in other articles you might choose to write.)

The one absolute rule of using interviews is this: *never twist a person's words to imply something other than what the person meant.* Do not use quotes out of context, or partial quotes, as a way to make it seem someone said something they did not.

Other issues are less clear. For example, there are two schools of thought on "cleaning up" quotes. Let's say you have interviewed someone who does not express himself clearly or in an educated way. Maybe his quote sounds something like "Well, uh, y'know, really, that's tough, but I'd have to say, I think, probably, I'd want to see the guy fry, y'know?" Some writers and editors suggest using the entire quote. Others who would use only the last eight words (or even cut the final "y'know"). The "use it like it is no matter what" school says that if a quote is grammatically incorrect, you still use it just "as is"; other writers feel this can cause unnecessary embarrassment for the interviewee, and that minor corrections to grammar are acceptable as long as they don't change the meaning (and tone) of the quote.

This can get a bit sticky when you're doing e-mail interviews. When you interview someone on the phone, you don't know whether the person knows how to spell, and you don't care, because you're writing it down yourself and are therefore responsible for the spelling. But what if a person has sent you an e-mail interview full of misspellings? Should you use it verbatim (or riddle it with "sics" to indicate that he, and not you, was the source of the misspellings)? My view is that, unless you have a *profound* reason to keep those errors, it's better to clean it up. Not everyone has a perfect grasp of spelling, and I believe an interviewee should not be made to look stupid—especially when that person has done me the favor of giving me the information I asked for.

I compared interview material to ore, and that's exactly what it is. You don't want to dump everything the person said into your article. Instead, you want to mine it for quotes that add *spice* to the article (assuming it is not a straight Q&A piece). That doesn't mean you can't use more of the person's material; however, you'll find your article usually works best if you paraphrase most of the interview and add direct quotes that bring home the point you're trying to make.

Here's the text of an e-mail interview I conducted with author Kate Elliott:

The American Heritage Dictionary defines culture as "the totality of socially transmitted behavior patterns, arts, beliefs, institutions, and all other products of human work and thought characteristic of a community or population." According to the OED, the word "culture' is related to 'cultivate" in the sense of tending crops.

Words grow from specific roots for a reason. Definitions of "cultivate" include "To improve or prepare (land), as by plowing or fertilizing, for raising crops... To grow or tend... To promote the growth of... To nurture... To form and refine." (American Heritage Dictionary)

I think that these definitions and that relationship between culture and cultivation can give writers clues as to how to approach writing, and creating, a "believable" culture in fantasy or science fiction novel.

For that purpose, one can draw out the metaphor of tillage, however labored it might become in time: When the writer creates a culture in the sf/f field, she starts with untilled ground, a kind of blank slate. That ground has to be prepared, tended, formed, and refined. A culture, likewise, must show arts, beliefs, institutions (to whatever extent), technologies, and roles. In the role of "cultivator," the writer can, in addition, not merely impose her own notions onto that developing culture but see what comes of giving it a little room to evolve naturally in the course of planning and writing the novel.

Here's what I wrote in the final article:

Elliott likes to draw an analogy between "culture" and "cultivate," two words that spring from the same root. "When a writer creates a culture, she starts with untilled ground, a kind of blank slate. The ground has to be prepared, tended, formed, refined. Likewise, a culture must show arts, beliefs, institutions, technologies, and roles. In the role of 'cultivator,' a writer doesn't simply impose her own notions onto that developing culture, but gives it a little room to evolve naturally in the course of planning and writing the novel."

Finally, remember that an interview is *not* about the *interviewer*. I've read too many interviews in which the writer keeps intruding upon the interview—with thoughts, reactions, interpretations, personal observations, etc. For example, I've seen interviewers write things like "I really felt a connection with what Mary was saying about her marriage, because of my own bad experiences...." If the article is about *Mary,* what is the interviewer doing in this picture?

This can be not only intrusive (the reader sees more of the *interviewer* than the *interviewee),* but also unethical if the interviewer attempts to "interpret" the interviewee's comments for the audience—especially if the interviewer is trying to cast the interviewee in a bad light. If you feel that an interviewee is a horrible person, let that person's words *speak for themselves*—and let readers draw their own conclusions.

❦ 11 ❧

Starting Your First Draft

Few things are more intimidating than the blank page (or screen) when you have a deadline. You may have known exactly what you wanted to say when you wrote your query, but now, perhaps, you have a stack of research notes and no idea how to get started. Or, perhaps you're stuck on the first sentence. This doesn't just happen to new writers; it happens to us all. Here are some ways to get that article going.

STEP ONE: IDENTIFY YOUR SUBJECT

The first step is to ask yourself whether you know exactly what your article is supposed to be about. Now that you've done your research, your brain may be stuffed with all sorts of information, and you're having trouble "sorting it out." It's time to go back to the basics.

Make sure you can state the central concept (or "thesis") of your article in a *single sentence*. Make sure, as well, that this sentence has no more than one "and" in it. For example:

TITLE: "Your child's first hike"
Market: Family-oriented travel or hiking publication
Good Topic Sentence: "How to introduce your child to hiking safely and enjoyably."
Bad Topic Sentence: "How to introduce your child to hiking, and what to pack, and where to go, and a look at my own experiences taking the kids on hikes, plus a look back at my first hike when I was a child..."

TITLE: Discover the new Olympic sport of skeleton!
Market: Winter sports publications
Good Topic Sentence: "What 'skeleton' is and how to get involved."

Bad Topic Sentence: "What 'skeleton' is, how to get involved, profiles of some notable 'skeleton' athletes, a history of skeleton and the Olympics, and places where you can learn how to do it, plus some of the risks…"

The purpose of a topic sentence is not only to help you focus on the central point of your article, but also to *limit* you. Everything in your article should relate to that topic sentence. If it doesn't, then it doesn't belong in this article, no matter how interesting it may be. A tightly focused topic sentence will keep you on track; a rambling topic sentence will get you lost.

Another way to define your topic sentence is to turn it into the question that would be asked by the reader. For example:

- How can I introduce my child to the sport of hiking?
- What is "skeleton" and how can I get started in this sport?

By turning your thesis into a question, you know exactly what your article has to "answer." Here are some other sample questions that would make good "core concepts" for articles:

- Should I refinance my home?
- How can I learn to crochet?
- How do you cook chestnuts?
- How can I communicate more effectively with my spouse?
- What do I need to know about "natural" vitamins?
- Where can I stay in New York for less than $200 a night?
- What are some romantic things I can do for less than $20?
- How can I keep the kids entertained on a rainy day?
- What would be an ideal gift for my mother-in-law?

Not every article idea can be expressed as a question, but you might be surprised by how easy it is to turn *most* ideas into questions. From there, the process becomes much simpler: Your goal is to *answer* the question.

STEP TWO: IDENTIFY YOUR SUBTOPICS

Once you've defined your topic statement, identify subtopics that support the original thesis. For example, your article on a child's first hike might cover:

- How to make a trip enjoyable
- How to make a trip safe

An article on whether to refinance one's home might include:

- Circumstances in which refinancing is a good idea
- Circumstances in which refinancing is a bad idea
- How to get more information

Each of these subtopics may lead to more logical subtopics.

- **Child's hiking trip → Safety → Risks:** Common trail hazards, including sunburn, dehydration, toxic plants, insect bites, animals/snakes, injuries such as cuts, bruises, sprains.

- **Child's hiking trip → Safety → Precautions:** Warning your child about hazards, things to pack in case of hazards, how to protect against sunburn, etc.

- **Child's hiking trip → Safety → Remedies:** What to do if any of the hazards are encountered (e.g., how to treat poison ivy, snake bite, etc.)

If you have too many subtopics, remember that you can always pull one out and use it as a sidebar. The key is to make sure that everything you're trying to cover in the article *directly* relates to your core topic. If it doesn't, save it for another piece.

STEP THREE: IDENTIFY YOUR AUDIENCE

Besides establishing the question your article will be answering, you also need to know who will be *asking* that question. If, for example, your article is covering "How to plan for retirement," you need to know who will be reading the piece. The questions asked by a 20-year-old single woman would be very different from those asked by a 40-year-old man with children about to enter college, or a recently divorced woman, or someone who is self-employed.

Going back to our "child hiking" article, you would want to know whether you're writing for experienced hikers, or a more general magazine whose readers may *not* be that experienced. You'll have to explain many more basic concepts to the latter audience, while the more experienced audience might be more interested in high-tech equipment suitable for kids, or the best hiking trails for kids in a particular region.

STEP FOUR: IDENTIFY YOUR LIMITS

Be sure you know how long your article is supposed to be. I discussed "word budgets" in chapter 8: You have only so many words to allocate to each point in your article. The more points you want to make, the fewer words you can budget to each point. The fewer points you need to cover, the more in-depth your coverage can be on every point.

While there is no hard-and-fast rule about how many words you should devote to a single subtopic, I feel that for an in-depth article, you need a budget of at least 300 to 500 words. A 2,000-word article would give you room for four major subtopics.

If you need to cover a larger number of subtopics, your article will become more of an "overview." Overviews often work well as "list" articles. For example, you might write an in-depth piece on "how to keep your children entertained on a rainy day"—*or,* a list titled "Ten ways to keep your kids entertained..."

STEP FIVE: IDENTIFY YOUR STRUCTURE

Next, determine the best order in which to present your information. Often, once you know the question, a logical order for the answer may be intuitively obvious. You may also have defined this order in your outline. Here are some typical ways to structure your article:

- **Logical Order.** What comes first, what comes next, what comes after that? What is the first question a reader would ask, the second, the third, and so on?

- **Chronological Order.** What happened first? What happened next? What happened after that?

- **Instructional Order.** What should the reader do first? What does he do next? What is step one, step two, step three?

- **List Order.** Lists work well for articles like "Ten ways to entertain your children on a road trip" or "Twenty ways to clean up stains and spills." Shorter lists work fine without numbers; longer lists often benefit from numbering. Your number can also become your title.

If all else fails, try what I call "sculpting." Just write down paragraphs, at random, based on your research information. Don't worry about putting them together in a logical sequence, or polishing them; the goal is to get something on the page. I call this "sculpting" because it reminds me of the process of throwing wads of clay into a pile that will eventually become a sculpture. The first step is to simply get all the clay in the right place. *Then* you can worry about shaping and smoothing.

STYLE AND PRESENTATION

Once you know what your article will include, you need to address *how* you want to write it. This section looks at some of the "tools" you can include in your basic article-writing toolkit.

Style and Voice

Most of us evolve our own distinctive style over time. However, style is also dependent on the market you're writing for. Your articles may have a great deal of stylistic variation, while still retaining your unique "voice." Some issues to consider here are:

- **The level of the audience.** Knowing your audience's reading level, and its level of knowledge/expertise on your subject, will have considerable influence on how you approach your article. Does your audience expect technical terminology, or simple writing with lots of explanations? Does it expect the author to be a friendly, handholding guide or a more authoritative "expert"?

- **The appropriate "narrative voice."** Should you write your article in first-person ("I/we"), second person ("you"), or third person ("he/she/they/one")? Again, this depends on the publication. Some publications use *no* first-person narratives; some prefer it. Some types of articles (such as how-tos) rely on the second person ("Do this, then do this."). Some prefer third: "One can achieve this effect by..."

• **Personal vs. impersonal.** Some publications prefer more personal, conversational articles; some prefer articles to be very impersonal, presenting information without a sense of the author being "present" in the article. I prefer a balance: I like articles to be accessible and "user-friendly," but I don't care for "chatty Kathy" pieces that ramble on about what the writer thinks about everything s/he is discussing.

Presentation Elements

You don't have to write every piece as a straight narrative from beginning to end. There are lots of ways to add variety to your writing, including:

• **Anecdotes.** Used sparingly, anecdotes can spice up a piece, providing personal examples to illustrate your information. Your entire article can be based around an anecdotal example, or, you could open with an anecdote that introduces your subject, and then close with a concluding anecdote that shows how your introductory story "turned out."

• **Interviews/quotes.** These should also be used sparingly. Instead of quoting everything a person says, paraphrase the bulk of the information you obtain through interviews and use direct quotes that highlight the content of your article.

• **Statistics.** Some people love numbers; some people don't. Statistics can be a useful way to back up your point, but they can also cause some readers to nod off. Watch out for sentences like "In 2009, 50 percent of the 1,750 hotels in the 55-mile radius of Metropolis experienced a 92 percent increase in their revenue, for a total of $72 million..."

• **"Made up" anecdotes.** Some publications like to illustrate a point with "artificial" anecdotes: "Because John backed up his computer data, his business didn't fail when his computer crashed. Unfortunately, Mary didn't..." I've never been a fan of this approach, but some editors like it!

• **Personal experiences.** Even in a more factual "how-to" piece, you can use personal experiences to illustrate your topic. For example, if you were writing about caring for a pet with diabetes, you might use your own experience to help put the reader at ease (if you can do it, he can do it!), and provide a logical way to "walk through" the information. Keep in mind that in such article, the experience is the "vehicle" for your information, not the *point* of your article.

BEGINNINGS, MIDDLES, AND ENDS

Every article needs a beginning—an introduction that "hooks" the reader and draws her into the article. Generally, your introduction should be no longer than one paragraph. Use it to establish what the article is about and why it will be relevant, or interesting, to the reader. (You will often find that your query hook works well as an article hook, or vice versa!)

The "middle" of your article—or rather, everything that falls between your introduction and conclusion—should fulfill the promise made by that introduction. Don't promise anything you can't deliver! Also, make sure the tone of your article matches the tone of the rest of the article; don't open with a joke and move on into an article that is morbid and depressing.

Your conclusion should provide a sense of closure to the article. The reader should feel that everything that needed to be said has been said. Try to *mirror* your introduction in your conclusion. For example, if you open with an anecdote, close with an anecdote. If you open with a quote, close the quote. Bring the reader "full circle" with the conclusion of your piece.

One common approach to "beginning/middle/end" is to set up your article as "problem/solution/call to action." Here, the introduction establishes a problem to be solved or question to be answered. It may explain *why* this issue is a problem, *why* the reader needs to know more, *why* the reader needs to take action. For example, a common type of health article is "symptoms you can't afford to ignore." The introduction explains that these symptoms can be signs of serious illness—establishing the *problem* that needs to be solved. The middle goes over the symptoms and what they could mean. The end is a "call to action"—if *you* see these symptoms, go to a doctor!

Articles that cover a personal experience should conclude with "the end of the story." There's an obvious corollary: *Don't try to write an experiential article until you know the end of the story!* For example, if you've just gotten divorced, don't try to write an article about "surviving divorce" until you've actually gone through the process and are in a position to look *back* on it. (See chapter 12 for more information on writing personal experiences.)

SIDEBARS

Once you've finished your article, chances are that you'll have information left over that is perfect for a sidebar. Editors love sidebars. Some publications require them; for example, travel magazines generally require sidebars that explain basic "how to get there, where to stay" information. In other cases, sidebars add extra information or interest to a feature. (Note that you don't need to format a sidebar when submitting it; just add it to the end of your article with its own heading and word-count.) Here are some basic types of sidebars:

- **Lists.** If you have a list of short pieces of information, consider pulling this out into a sidebar. For example, on that article about hiking and children, consider making a list of trail hazards, or first aid supplies to take along, or equipment to take. If it's for a regional publication, consider listing local trails that are good for children.

- **Personal experiences.** Sometimes a short personal account makes a good sidebar to a longer, more factual piece. When I edited *Dog Fancy,* I always liked to balance a technical medical article with a personal article about the same topic.

- **Factual information.** The reverse is also effective: Try balancing a personal article with a brief overview of factual information on the topic.

- **Quizzes.** Editors love quizzes. For example, I sold *The Writer* the quiz in chapter 39 as a sidebar to an article on how to survive as a full-time freelance writer.

- **Where to find it.** A sidebar on where to find more information, where to buy products mentioned in the article, where to find organizations related to the topic, etc., are always useful. Consider listing online resources as well.

Sidebars are (a) a great way to use extra information you can't fit into your article, (b) a sneaky way to get past a word limit, and (c) a good way to get extra money, because editors often pay extra for sidebars.

FIVE FLAWS THAT CAN LEAD TO REJECTION

Articles with excellent ideas and information can still be "marginalized" by structural flaws. The good news is that these flaws are usually easy to correct. Following are five flaws I often see in otherwise well-written manuscripts:

Rambling Introductions

If your introduction wanders on for three, four, or even five paragraphs, you have a problem. Such introductions often fall into one of these categories:

- **The personal introduction,** in which the writer introduces herself, her background, her credentials, or a personal experience that "sets the stage" for the article itself.

- **The analogy,** in which the writer compares what she is about to discuss to something else. For example, I've received many articles that compare writing to gardening ("learn to prune") or cooking ("choose the right ingredients").

- **The "setting-the-stage" introduction,** in which the writer takes several paragraphs to explain background information.

If 500 words of your 1,500-word article is "introduction," you're cheating the reader—and yourself. The reader loses because he gets only 1,000 words of information—and you lose, because if the editor cuts the introduction, you'll only get paid for 1,000 words instead of the 1,500 you actually wrote.

The solution: Limit your introduction to a single paragraph, or two at most. You don't need to spend a lot of time describing how you found out about a problem, or how you talked to five people to get your information, etc. Cut to the chase, and pack the body of your article with information too useful to cut!

Explaining "Why" but not "How"

Another common flaw is the tendency to write about the importance of doing something—without explaining *how* to do it. For example, a writer may explain why one needs to develop believable characters in fiction, but not how to actually do it.

The solution: Limit the "why" part of your article to the introduction—e.g., a paragraph on why believable characters are important. Use the rest of your article to show the reader exactly how to solve the problem you've established.

Instead of giving the reader "ten reasons why characterization is important," offer "ten steps toward building stronger characters."

Asking the Wrong Questions

Even experienced writers can fail to ask (and answer) the questions a reader is most likely to ask about a subject. It's not enough to write about what you know; you also have to figure out what the reader *doesn't* know.

The solution: Put yourself in the reader's shoes. If necessary, find someone who knows less about the subject than you do, and ask that person what he or she would want to learn from your article. Common "reader" questions include:

- What is it?
- Why should I be interested?
- How can I get involved?
- What do I need to know/learn/buy/obtain to get started?
- What are some of the perils and pitfalls, if any?
- Where do I get more information?

An article that answers all of these questions, on any subject, is likely to please readers *and* editors.

Lack of Organization

Some articles appear to have been jotted down as ideas came to the author, without any reordering. Even if an article contains good information, most editors don't have time to reorganize it paragraph by paragraph. If a piece has to be rewritten for it to make sense or to read well, it is likely to be rejected.

The solution: As I said above, identify the logical structure of your article, and (as I mentioned in the preceding chapter), "think in subheads." By establishing specific sections, you'll find it easier to determine where the information belongs.

No Conclusion

A surprising trend in articles crossing my desk is the lack of endings. All too often, when an author runs out of information, the article just stops.

Like that.

Endings are important: They bring closure, wrap up the loose ends, and help the reader make sense of what has gone before.

The solution: Always provide a conclusion to your material, even if it's just a couple of sentences. One way to conclude an article is to summarize what you've already said. Another is to refer back to the introduction: If you opened with an anecdote or analogy, consider closing with a related anecdote or analogy. If you asked a question in the introduction, recap the answer in the conclusion. Don't just leave the reader wondering whether the typesetter somehow lost the last paragraph of your article!

While these five flaws aren't the only reasons for rejection, they offer a useful checklist to keep in mind the next time your article comes back with a polite "no thank you." And by avoiding them in the first place, you'll greatly increase your chances of getting an acceptance letter the first time around!

❧ 12 ❧

Personal Experience Articles

When I was editor of a national pet magazine, my desk was swamped with "personal experience" articles—accounts of some funny, moving, or tragic event in the author's life. And every day, the majority of those articles went straight to the rejection pile.

It wasn't because they were poorly written. Many were quite good, and every bit as funny or moving as they claimed to be. We simply could not use them because they did not match our editorial focus.

Personal experience articles often make up 75 percent or more of a typical magazine's unsolicited submissions. Yet they are the least likely to be accepted. The reason is that personal experience pieces are typically about the *writer*. Editors are looking for articles about the *reader*.

That can create some tough odds. For example, if an editor could purchase ten articles per month out of 100 submissions, a personal experience piece might have a 1-in-75 chance of acceptance—while a service article's chances could be as high as 9-in-25. (Of course, in reality editors receive far more than 100 articles per month, and may purchase fewer than 10.)

You can beat those odds by offering an editor the best of both worlds: A personalized service piece. To do this, you must ask yourself how your experience relates to the reader. For example:

- Is this an experience the reader might wish to share or enjoy?
- Is this an experience from which the reader can learn or benefit?
- Is this an experience the reader might wish to avoid?
- Is this an experience that will help the reader cope with difficulty?

EXPERIENCES TO SHARE

Have you had an experience others might wish to share? Perhaps you've achieved a success or a goal, or simply had a good time. Would others want to do the same? If the answer is yes, you're in the ideal position to tell them how.

For example, perhaps you've just come back from a great vacation. Tell us about it! Most travel articles are personal experience pieces at heart. But they are written in such a way as to become the reader's experience as well—either vicariously, or by enabling the reader to duplicate the experience.

If your vacation involved a fascinating destination, tell us how to get there, what to see, where to find the best food and lodgings, or what to expect from the culture or environment. Tailor your account to your audience: Will your readers want to know about the most challenging hiking trails, the best restaurants, or how to get a bargain in the shops or bazaars? Should your article focus on little-known details of an exotic culture, or the nuts and bolts of travel and hotel arrangements?

Focusing on the service aspects of your article broadens the market dramatically. That story of your "best camping trip ever" can discuss equipment and supplies for one magazine, the "ten best campgrounds" in a particular region for another, and how to get the kids unplugged from their Gameboys and into the great outdoors for a third. In short, you should be asking not only how the reader can benefit from your experience, but also how many *different* types of readers might be able to benefit.

Keep in mind that your experience should be one a reader would like to share in the *future,* not one he or she has already shared. Readers aren't interested in articles about things they've already done. They are interested in new experiences, in things they might want to do—so show them how!

EXPERIENCES THAT ENRICH

If any single focus dominates the article market, it is "how to improve your life." Self-improvement themes fill magazines of every description: How to improve your health, well being, relationships, careers, skills, homes, hobbies. Nothing attracts a reader like the promise that an article will make life *better.*

To tap into this market, explore areas in your life that you have made better. Topics may range from the deeply personal (overcoming a fear, meeting a challenge) to the seemingly trivial (brightening your work area with potted plants). Any improvement that you've made in your own life could be an improvement someone else would like to emulate.

Suppose, for example, that you quit the corporate rat race to start your own business. Presumably, your goal was to improve your life (I've never read an article about someone joining the *corporate* world to improve their quality of life!). Your article could tell us not only why you did it, but how—including the advantages and disadvantages of the decision.

Has your decision led to more quality time with family members, more freedom to control one's life and destiny, more opportunities to enjoy the "little things" like gardens and sunsets and the freedom to linger over the morning's coffee and bagel? On the downside, can you help the reader cope with the difficulties of developing good work habits, handling the lack of social interaction, and coping with no steady paycheck or benefits?

Self-improvement articles don't necessarily have to be based on life-changing experiences. In many cases, an area of your life that *hasn't* changed can also be the basis of an excellent article. For example, is your relationship with your spouse running smoothly, with few hassles or arguments? Are your children well-behaved, getting good grades, and staying off drugs?

If your life is going well, keep in mind that thousands of readers would love to know your secrets for a successful relationship or how to raise happy and well-adjusted children!

EXPERIENCES TO AVOID

Sometimes the experiences from which we learn the most are the negative ones. Writers, of course, don't simply learn from their mistakes; they write about them. At least, they should!

Experiences that you wish you could have avoided often make wonderful service articles. What would you have done differently, if you had known then what you know now? What would you do differently today? It may be too late for you to avoid that problem, but it's never too late to help another.

Unpleasant experiences don't necessarily lead to unpleasant articles. Someone once said that comedy equals tragedy plus time. Sometimes, the best time to write about your experience is when you're finally able to look back on it and laugh. The resulting article will not only be useful, but entertaining as well.

For example, what about that disastrous family hiking trip you took in the MegaBugga Woods? The trip during which your dog broke its leash and tangled with a skunk, you got the worst sunburn of your life, and your child became a hands-on expert at identifying poison ivy? By the time your sunburn faded, you knew you had an article! Throw in a sidebar on how to identify toxic plants, or the type of protective clothing to wear, or first-aid supplies to carry along, and you'll have an article that could find any number of markets.

Of course, not every unpleasant experience lends itself to such lighthearted treatment. Some are more serious, and should be handled with sensitivity and care. Yet even potentially devastating experiences can often be avoided with the proper precautions. If you've suffered through such an event, you will be providing a valuable service to others by putting those precautions on paper.

EXPERIENCES TO ENDURE

Some painful or traumatic experiences cannot be avoided; they can only be endured. When someone faces a tragedy or loss, they often want to hear from someone else who has been through a similar experience: Someone who understands, who knows how it feels, whose advice and comfort comes from the heart.

That's the big difference between a "coping" article written by an expert, and one written by an ordinary person who has been there, endured, and somehow managed to pull his or her life together again. Experts have good advice (which you may be able to incorporate into your article), but your experience humanizes that advice and makes it meaningful to the reader.

Writers will never run out of markets for articles on how to cope with grief, trauma, or loss, because people will never cease to experience these things. And because traumatic events affect different people in different ways (even within a single family unit), an effective article can reach many different markets.

For example, suppose you're writing about losing a job. You might focus on how this experience affected you, and how you coped with feelings of anger, loss, helplessness, and frustration. You might write about how you found a new job. You might deal with issues of financial adjustments, or how to find support during your job hunt.

Your options don't end there, however. Unless you're single, with no one to support but your cat, the loss of your job will affect others as well. How did it affect your spouse? How did it affect your children? How could a reader help his or her own family members cope?

Any type of loss, large or small, raises issues and emotions that must be dealt with, either as an individual or as a family. By using your own experience as the basis for a service article, you send the message that resolution and recovery are possible.

FIRST EXPERIENCES

Remember the first time you _____ (fill in the blank)? Remember the novelty of the experience? The emotions it evoked? The insights revealed to you? These factors make "first experience" articles very tempting to writers, who want to share those feelings and insights with others.

Unfortunately, magazines are flooded with "first experience" pieces ("my first puppy," "my first baby") that are poorly conceived and even more poorly written. Many guidelines even flatly state "no first experiences." You can still beat the odds, however, by finding ways to match experience to market.

1) **Look for readers who haven't shared your experience.** If you want to write the story of your first dog, remember that every reader of a *dog* magazine has probably already had a similar experience. The discoveries that seemed new to you will most likely be old hat to these readers. Instead of thinking "dogs = dog magazine," look for an audience that *will* find your experience new and different. An article about the difference a new pet made in a single parent's relationship with her child, for example, might sell to a family or parenting magazine.

2) **Look for an uncommon element.** A "my first dog" story will sell to a pet magazine if there's something unique about the dog, its owner, or their relationship. For example, I once accepted an article about a canine escape artist who chewed through a chain link fence to get free. Readers appreciated the conflicts faced by this writer: Could she confine the dog without harming it, or would she have to give up this "problem pet"? Your resolution must be appropriate to the audience; had the author sent the dog to the pound, we wouldn't have bought the article.

3) **Look for an unusual perspective.** A story about "my first trip to the supermarket" would be as exciting as Valium—unless, perhaps, the supermarket is in a foreign country and you can't speak the language, read the labels, or guess the prices. The "outsider looking in" approach can often be a key to a sale. But there's a catch: You must know enough about the "inside" to understand what makes your perspective unique and different. I once sold an article to a dog show magazine on my reactions to what seemed, to me, the bizarre world of dog shows. To do so, however, I had to know enough about the sport to understand what would come across as humor, and what would come across as ignorance or even stupidity.

4) **Look for smaller "first experiences."** Instead of writing about your first dog, write about a specific event. How about the first time your dog became ill, or your first obedience class or dog show, or the first time you took your dog camping? Such stories can focus on areas where others may not have shared your experience—or where they may be able to learn from it.

EXPERIENCE AS EXPERTISE

While some publications seek writers with expert credentials, others seek writers who have the kind of expertise that only comes through personal experience. While an expert can provide useful technical information on a topic, it is the writer like you—the one who has "lived it"—who can bring that information to life for the reader. Your experience brings you special credentials, including:

• **Understanding.** You may have a better understanding of the needs and interests of a reader than an expert. You know what aspects of a topic need to be communicated to a reader like yourself—and how to get that information across. For example, while a veterinarian might write about the pathology of a particular pet disease, you can share what it means to be the owner of a pet who has that disease.

• **Communication.** Writers serve as translators between the technical experts and the audience. The veterinarian you interview might tell you about histolytes and platelets, but it's up to you to convert this information into terms the reader understands—and to frame it in a meaningful context.

• **Balance.** An article written by a leading authority on a particular subject may be brilliant, but one-sided. Writers, however, can examine controversies from all sides, following up leads and exploring various angles by interviewing experts with differing opinions or in different fields.

• **Tact.** Some experts simply aren't good at communicating with a "lay" audience—yet don't take kindly to having their work edited. However, writing clearly and working with editors to polish and refine your prose is part of a writer's job. If you take that job seriously, editors will find you a joy to work with, and will come back to you again and again—and let *you* handle the difficulties of talking to experts!

- **Flexibility.** Experts, by definition, are specialists. An editor won't be able to ask an expert on dermatology for an article on obedience training. You, on the other hand, may be able to cover both subjects (and you'll be able to find experts to interview for the information you lack).

USING EXPERIENCES WISELY

Once you've decided what experiences to write about, you must decide how. While there are many ways to use experiences effectively, these four are perhaps the most common:

- **As a framework** to support the factual information you wish to present. Use your experience as a vehicle to carry the information you've gathered from expert sources, such as interviews or research. Show how that information affected, or is reflected in, your own experience. Use phrases like "we learned" or "we discovered" instead of "experts say."

- **As anecdotal material** to illustrate the factual information. Use the factual information as your framework, and highlight each point with an experiential example or illustration.

- **As an anecdotal lead and conclusion.** Some articles begin and end with an experiential anecdote (e.g., "When Mary's house burned down, she had no idea her troubles were just beginning..."). The body of the article, however, may be purely factual, with few personal details.

- **As a sidebar.** You may prefer to restrict your article to the facts, and use the personal experience as a sidebar to illustrate and enhance those facts. Another approach is to use the factual material as a sidebar to the personal story. (This works particularly well when your facts can be presented as a list.)

GETTING THE "I" OUT

Awhile back, I read an article about canoeing in the Alaska wilderness. Here's an example (paraphrased) of the author's account:

After a long day of paddling my canoe through the twisting waterways of the Someplaceorother Delta, I was glad to see the sandbar on which we would camp that night. The sun was setting, and the colors on the river reminded me of a blurred watercolor painting. I watched as a skein of geese descended toward some marsh I could not see, their wild cries reminding me just how far I had traveled from the land of cell phones and car alarms. As I steered my canoe to the shore, I marveled yet again at the magnificence of this wilderness...

What's wrong with this picture? Nothing, if it is intended as a self-portrait. If it is intended as a portrait of a location, however, it fails miserably. Why? Because instead of seeing what the author sees, I am forced to watch the author "seeing" it. Instead of being allowed to react to the images presented, I am forced to share the author's reactions. The author can't get out of the way.

First-person narration isn't necessarily a bad thing. In many articles, it is desirable and appropriate. In many others, however, it is out of place. One of the things an author needs to know is when to be part of the scene—and when to remain invisible, framing the picture without entering it.

When writing an interview, for example, watch out for references to "self" (I sat, I asked, I listened, I turned on my tape recorder, etc.). If you want to describe a location, don't write, "I settled myself in one of Mary's overstuffed chairs" when you could just as easily write that *Mary* settled herself in one of those chairs. Another way to remove yourself from the scene is to choose verbs that do not require an indirect object. For example, instead of saying "Mary proudly showed me her award," choose another verb: "Mary proudly displayed her award."

When writing about exotic destinations, you want to convince the reader that you actually climbed that mountain, slept in that hotel, ate in that bistro. One way to sharpen your focus is to remove "interpretive" or "reactive" statements from your article. If you liked the food in a particular restaurant, don't say you *thought* it was good; just say it *was* good. If the hotel bed was lumpy, don't say it *felt* lumpy, just say it had lumps. Try to avoid telling the reader how you felt or reacted; instead, paint a vivid picture of the experience to evoke a reaction in the reader. Watch out, as well, for "me" phrases—"they told me, it seemed to me, he showed me," etc. Whenever possible, use verbs that can act alone. For example, instead of writing, "The locals told me that a ghost walks those halls at night," try "Locals say" or "Locals claim."

Because self-help and how-to articles often result from personal experience, it is tempting to include hefty doses of that experience in the article. Such an article really isn't about you, though; it's about the reader. Thus, the easiest way to stay out of it is to consciously shift from a "me" perspective to a "you" perspective. Whenever you find yourself writing in the first person, consider whether you could express the same information in another way, such as second person ("you can do this"), third person ("many people do this"), or directive ("do this!"). Each of these approaches shifts the viewpoint of the article away from the narrator and toward the reader.

Writing, by its nature, is an "invisible" occupation. Consequently, it can be tempting to try to stand for a moment in the spotlight of our own creations. The bottom line is simple, however: The less editors see of *you,* the more they'll want to see of your *work.*

SOME FINAL TIPS

Besides asking yourself how the experience relates to the reader, you must also ask yourself how *you* relate to the experience. For example:

- **You must be "over" the experience.** If you don't know how the story ends, you're not in a position to write about it. If an event is painful, you need sufficient time to have gained some "closure" before you're ready to write about it for others.

• **You must offer a solution.** Readers want to know how to change things, fix things, make things better. If you see no hope for improvement, write about something else.

• **You must offer the reader an attainable goal.** If your idea of the perfect vacation is to climb Mt. Everest, that's fine—but the experience may find a rather limited readership. Offer readers an experience they can attain, and offer specific steps to help them attain it.

• **You must offer evidence that your suggestions work.** If, for example, you're describing "Ten Ways to Get Your Novel Published," you must have published a novel!

Whatever approach you choose, it's the "been there, done that" element of your story that will bring your article to life. Editors hunger for articles that combine useful, factual information with the warm, human touch of experience. Turning your story of "what I did" into an article on "how you can do it" is one of the best ways to save your material from the slush pile.

PART 3

Finding the Right Markets

❧ 13 ☙

Exploring the Markets

I have to smile at listings in *Writer's Market* that advise would-be contributors to read "five or six back issues." Yeah, right! I don't know about you, but I can hardly keep up with my own subscriptions, let alone the sample copies I tend to order in abundance. At an average of $4 per back issue, the cost of ordering more than one issue of anything would be prohibitive.

At the same time, those publications make an important point: If you don't know anything about a publication, you'll find it difficult to target an appropriate article or query to its editor. How can you understand the needs and interests of the audience? How can you match the style or tone of the publication? How can you catch the editor's eye? How can you avoid submitting an article on a topic that was covered two months ago?

Fortunately, there are ways to explore the marketplace without breaking your bank account. Consider the following possibilities:

1) **Start with magazines you know.** What magazines do you read on a regular basis? Chances are, these publications reflect your interests and expertise. Look carefully at the craft, hobby, or special interest publications on your list. Most likely, you buy these because you pursue that interest, and could develop an article for that market. A word of warning, however: If your subscriptions or purchases include only the top general interest or women's magazines, and you're a beginning writer, this advice does not apply.

2) **Visit newsstands.** Bookstores like Borders and Barnes & Noble offer newsstands featuring magazines you won't find in your local grocery store. You will also find publications that aren't listed in *Writer's Market.* If you can find a "real" newsstand—a store devoted entirely to magazines—so much the better! (Many of these carry international magazines as well as domestic publications.) Newsstands are treasuries of new markets, and the issues usually cost less than special-ordered "back issues" (for which you may have to pay shipping as well as the cover price of the magazine itself).

3) Check *Writer's Market* for free back issues. I usually rank the listings in *Writer's Market* by price: Free, available for return postage, less than $3, and more than $3. I send for the free copies first, then those that ask only for postage costs. Then I order those that cost less than $3, and finally, after careful consideration, I order the most interesting of the rest. When ordering a back issue, save yourself a SASE and ask for the writer's guidelines at the same time.

4) Ask for writer's guidelines of any publication that interests you. Some guidelines are excellent, giving you far more information than a *Writer's Market* entry. Others, however, mention nothing about rates or rights or other vital information. Others are simply vague: "We want sharp, well-written articles that will appeal to our audience." (Well, *duh!*)

5) Research guidelines online. Many magazines are now posting their guidelines on their Web sites. This makes life easier for everyone: You don't have to send a SASE and wait six weeks for a response, and they don't have to print hundreds of copies of their guidelines. When you locate a magazine's Web site, look for such options as "guidelines," "submissions," "tips for writers," "write for us," or "contact us." Also, explore some of the guideline databases online (you'll find a list of these at *www.writing-world.com/ links/guidelines.shtml*). You can search databases not only for a specific magazine, but also for certain categories, such as subject area or payment rate.

6) Research back issues online. Many publications post article archives on their Web sites. These archives are often the "best of the best," which will give you an idea of what excites the editor. Read a few articles carefully to get an idea of their tone, style, content, and depth of coverage. Are they written for a technical audience or for the layperson? Do they offer overviews of a subject, or in-depth reporting? Do the authors have special credentials, or can "anyone" write for this publication?

7) Look for back issue indices. Even if a magazine doesn't publish articles online, it may offer an index of back issues. This will give you an opportunity to determine what has already been published in the past year or two, so you don't waste time with an article that duplicates past effort. (Once a magazine has covered a particular topic, it will usually wait two or three years before considering that topic again, even if your article offers a different angle or focus.) Many magazines also publish an annual index that you can obtain with a SASE.

8) Look for new markets online. Many online newsstands offer links to magazines not only in the United States but throughout the world. You can search these listings topically or geographically, and you're certain to find publications you've never heard of. Also, explore each publication's Web site for additional magazines; for example, while *Writer's Market* lists two

or three pet magazines belonging to "Fancy Publications," that particular company actually produces more than 30 monthly and annual publications.

9) **Subscribe to a marketing newsletter.** Several excellent e-mail newsletters offer market information, including:

- *WritersWeekly* – *www.writersweekly.com*
- *Writing for Dollars* – *www.awoc.com*
- *Writing World* – *www.writing-world.com*
- *WorldWide Freelance Writer* – *www.worldwidefreelance.com* (focuses on non-U.S. markets)
- *WriteMarketsReport* – *www.writersweekly.com* (a monthly e-mail newsletter available for a paid subscription)

Whenever you see a listing for an interesting publication, follow up for more information—visit the Web site, write for guidelines, or request a sample copy.

Many of these resources also cover online markets; the rules for evaluating a market and breaking in are generally the same.

FINDING FREE (AND ALMOST FREE) MAGAZINES

Here are some ways to locate sample copies without paying a penny:

- **Visit the library.** Most libraries have extensive magazine sections, and you can either browse back issues there or check them out and take them home. Many libraries can also order other publications for you through interlibrary loan, though this can take awhile.

- **Check your library for a "magazine exchange" corner.** Many libraries allow patrons to drop off unwanted magazines, and on some days you can find lots of interesting titles. Check the dates, though; a pile of magazines from the 1980s is not going to help you determine what a publication is covering today. (Some libraries are also catching on to this resource, however, and now charge for such magazines.)

- **Check the magazines at your doctor's office.** If you find something that interests you, ask the receptionist if you can borrow it—or bring along unwanted magazines of your own to exchange. (Some offices also offer free publications; I've found free regional baby magazines at women's clinics.)

- **Keep your eyes open when visiting bookstores or specialty stores.** I've just sold an article to a country crafts/collectibles magazine I found in a craft boutique. I've also found interesting tabloids in the Barnes & Noble foyer.

- **Respond to "free issue" offers.** Many publications send out offers for a free issue. (I recently received offers for a free issue of Britain's *Realm* magazine and *Scottish Life*; needless to say, I've said "yes" to both.) If you don't want the subscription, just write "cancel" on the invoice. Many magazine sites have free trial offers on their Web sites. You can also find free trial offers through general magazine subscription and "free stuff" Web sites. These sites often offer free three-month trials. You'll have to provide your credit card; you then have 90 days to cancel the subscription before your card is charged. Here are some sites that offer 90-day trials:

- All Free Magazines - *www.all-freemagazines.com/*
- All Mags 4 Free - *www.allmags4free.com/*
- Free2Try - *www.free2try.com*
- FreeSiteX - *www.freesitex.com/magazine.html*
- MagsNow.com - *www.magsnow.com/?source=overture*

- **Check Amazon.com.** It's possible to subscribe to a variety of magazines via Amazon.com, and you can often find trial offers there as well. You can also find individual back issues for sale on Amazon.com, usually from third-party "new and used" vendors.

- **Use airline mileage credits to pay for subscriptions.** If you accumulate only small amounts of frequent flyer miles (not enough to add up to free travel), find out if your program offers magazine subscriptions. It's a great way to use up a few hundred miles here and there.

- **Ask magazines if they provide a free sample copy.** Approach them as if you were a would-be subscriber, not a writer!

- **Exchange magazines with friends, relatives, and writing buddies.**

- **Ask for gift subscriptions to magazines that interest you.**

- **Ask to be added to a publication's "complimentary copy list"** once you've begun to write for them (even if you've just sold them a single article).

Finally, don't hesitate to order a sample copy of a publication that looks like a valuable market. There is no substitute for actually being able to see a publication before you write for it—so if you have to pay, do so. Remember that the cost of sample copies is a business expense, and can be deducted from your taxes.

EVALUATING A MARKET: IS IT RIGHT FOR YOU?

Finding publications is only half the battle. Once you've found a publication, how can you determine whether it is a good market for you? What clues can you glean from a magazine about how to break in? When I review a new magazine, I am looking for answers to four sets of questions: Demographic, Technical, Personal, and Business.

Demographic Questions

"Demographics" simply means "audience": What type of person will be reading your article? The answers can be found not only in a magazine's editorial pages, but also in its advertisements and illustrations. For example, are all the photos of glamorous models, or does the magazine include "real" people as well? A close look at any publication should give you valuable clues about the following audience characteristics:

- **Gender.** Is the magazine aimed at men or women or both (e.g., a fitness magazine with tips for both sexes)? Or would it appeal to a certain type of person regardless of gender (e.g., *Smithsonian* or *National Geographic*)?

- **Age.** Most magazines target specific age brackets, such as "youth," "twenty-something," "adult" (20-50), or "senior." Sometimes that target audience is obvious from the magazine's title or content (e.g., *Seventeen*); sometimes it can be determined from the advertising (e.g., *Reader's Digest*). Don't try to pitch an article on "planning for early retirement" to a magazine that targets twenty-something executives!

- **Ethnicity.** Except for publications that actively target a specific ethnic group, most general interest magazines still focus on the interests of white readers. Some, however, are actively trying to break that pattern by seeking more diverse, multicultural material (particularly around the holidays).

- **Economic Bracket.** How much is a reader prepared to spend? This can make a big difference when writing about, say, collecting exotic antiques or taking a dream vacation. Advertising is a good way to determine the audience's economic bracket. I recently reviewed two country lifestyle magazines that looked similar on the surface; one, however, contained ads for expensive antique reproductions, while the other contained ads for cheap collectible frog figurines.

- **Religion.** In some markets, religion is unimportant; in others, it is. Religion may be implied rather than overtly stated. For example, while *Reader's Digest* is not a "religious" publication, it clearly assumes that most of its readers prefer material with a conservative Christian slant. Other publications may assume just the opposite, and reject material that even hints of a traditional religious viewpoint. Within the religious marketplace itself, one must also be aware of the differences between (and even within) denominations.

- **Geography.** Does a magazine focus on city pleasures or country delights? Does it focus on active recreational activities available in the region, or on more intellectual pursuits? Even a magazine that is distributed nationwide may have a larger readership in certain parts of the country, and will be most interested in articles that will appeal to readers from that region.

- **Lifestyle.** Lifestyle issues (including interests, activities, and values) cut across all other demographic groups. Two magazines that target young women, for example, may have very different audiences: Does a woman's magazine assume its readers spend most of their time in the office, the kitchen, or the bedroom? Values are also important: You won't find an article on "how to cheat without getting caught" in *Woman's Day*, and you don't find many pieces on "fidelity" in *Cosmopolitan*.

These demographics can give you a picture of your target audience. But is that all you need to know? Just because a magazine targets young, upwardly mobile professional women doesn't mean you necessarily want to write for it. You may also wish to consider:

Technical Issues

The technical aspects of a magazine include:

- **Physical presentation.** What is the quality of the publication? Is it printed on glossy paper or newsprint? Are articles laid out effectively, or are they pasted up by hand (and not too carefully)? Are the photos clear, or do they look like someone's Polaroids? A magazine that is poorly produced usually has a low budget—and that means it probably doesn't pay well.

- **Writing style.** Magazines that appear to address similar audiences may, in fact, have very different editorial styles. Read one or two articles carefully. Do you like the way they are written? Can you imagine writing in a similar style? If the style seems jarring to you, or violates your personal sense of taste, you may not be able to write for that magazine, simply because your style is at odds with the tastes of the editor.

- **Depth.** How much research, investigation, or analysis is involved in a magazine's content? Don't bite off more than you can chew: Some magazines demand more than you can provide. If you don't have the connections to get the right interviews, or the experience to provide the level of analysis required, or the budget to visit five different locations to get the story, don't sweat it. That doesn't mean you'll never penetrate that market; it simply means you may not be able to break in today. Meanwhile, there are hundreds of other publications that can offer the experience and clips you need.

Personal Issues

When I evaluate a magazine, I want to know not only what it says to a reader, but also what it says to me. For example:

- **Does the magazine interest me?** Often, when I try to study a magazine, I find my eyes glazing. I find myself skipping and scanning rather than actually reading. The material doesn't "hook" me, and I may reach the end of the magazine without finishing a single article. Can I write for a publication whose editorial focus doesn't keep my attention? Probably not. The editor's tastes and mine clearly do not mesh, and I doubt I could change my own style to match the editor's preferences.

• **Does the magazine share my values?** A writer is also an individual, with his or her own set of demographics—values, ethics, background, etc. The question of ethics is no different in the business of writing than in any other business: Are you willing to compromise what you believe in just to earn a paycheck? If the answer is no, don't struggle to write for markets you don't agree with, or to produce articles that violate your own values or viewpoint.

• **How will my material be presented?** If a magazine suffers from poor presentation—bad editing, poor design, or inappropriate illustrations—your work may look worse when it comes out than when you sent it in. No one stops to ask whether the bad grammar was the result of poor editing; most people will assume it was the fault of the writer. And while no one will blame you for a bad paste-up job, it certainly won't present your work in the best light. If my review of a magazine indicates that clips from this publication would do me more harm than good, I'll try elsewhere.

• **Would I be proud to be featured in this publication?** I recently examined a woman's magazine that looked like a potential market for a health article I wanted to write. A look at the magazine, however, gave me second thoughts. Most of the advertisements seemed to be for sexual aids (and most of the articles focused on this topic as well). While I might have sold the article, did I really want to show off clips of my work displayed next to a four-color, half-page ad for vibrators? If a magazine makes you uncomfortable, angry, or disgusted, move on; you'll feel happier about your checks.

Obviously, many of these decisions are highly individual—which is why I clustered them under "personal." Your decisions might be different from mine, and neither of us would be "right" or "wrong." The point is that as writers, we are individuals, and our tastes and values are as important as those of the markets we are trying to penetrate. If those tastes and values don't mesh, we could waste a lot of time trying to break into markets that will never be right for us—and "success" may not taste so sweet. By learning to evaluate markets across a broad spectrum of issues, however, you'll find those that you can not only work with but thrive with—and to which you'll become a valued contributor.

Business Issues

There is no excuse for a writer to get the acceptance stage and only then ask, "Oh, by the way, what do you pay?" If you haven't already obtained this information, you're hardly in a position to start negotiating your way out of a bad contract. Plus, you've probably invested a lot of energy and emotion into getting that article out the door and accepted—and if you suddenly discover that the publication pays poorly or demands all rights, it's hard to pull out once you've so nearly achieved your goal. It's also unprofessional. Before you approach a market, therefore, find out the following:

1) **What does the magazine pay?** Most magazines post a range of payment rates in their guidelines. Some pay flat rates (e.g., $200 per feature); others pay by the word (e.g., 5-10¢); others pay by the printed column or page.

Some magazines that pay by the word will pay for the actual number of words you submit, regardless of editing. Others pay only for the number of words they actually *publish*. Thus, if you submitted a 1,500-word article, but the editor trims 500 words, you'd only be paid for 1,000 words. Find out which basis of payment is being used. If you're asked to submit an invoice, you should generally submit it for the number of words in your original article. If you're given a contract, it should indicate the actual payment, not just a per-word figure.

Magazines that pay by the printed column or page generally can't give you a precise payment rate until the article is typeset and laid out. Generally, such magazines pay "on publication," since they can't calculate a payment until the magazine is ready to go to press. However, an editor will generally be able to give you an estimate based on the length of your article.

Magazines that pay a flat rate generally have a range of rates, depending on the difficulty of the article (e.g., the amount of research required), the expertise of the writer, and how much work the editor has to do to whip the article into shape.

Keep in mind that almost all quoted rates are (a) ranges and (b) represent the *lowest* range that a publication is willing to pay. Many publications offer higher rates to regular contributors, and to "better" contributors (i.e., folks who do lots of research and whose work needs little or no editing). I generally don't recommend asking about higher pay on your *first* submission to a publication, but if you expect to be working for that publication on an ongoing basis, or if the editor comes back to you with new assignments, *start asking how to get a higher rate.* Even if you don't get one, it never hurts to ask.

2) **Does the magazine pay extra for sidebars or illustrations?** Editors often try to get away with paying a flat rate for text and photos. However, if you don't provide photos, the editor will have to pay another photographer extra—so there is no reason why *you* shouldn't receive that compensation. If you're submitting photos, find out what a magazine pays for artwork alone—e.g., $25 per b/w photo. Find out how much it pays for articles, e.g., 10 ¢/word. Then, discuss getting paid for *each* item rather than a "package deal." Offer the editor a "deal," if you wish—e.g., $15 per photo instead of $25—but try not to let the editor pay you the same amount for "text and photos" as for text alone. (Keep in mind, too, that cover photos generally pay very handsomely; if you're a good enough photographer to get a cover, you should be paid for it.)

Some publications won't pay extra for sidebars, but others will. Sidebars can be a good way to sneak in extra material over and above your assigned word count. Thus, if you're writing a 2,000-word article that pays 10¢/

word, add on a 500-word sidebar and see if you can't boost the payment up another $50!

What if you can't find out what a magazine pays? Some publications don't like to share that information. Instead, they ask you what *you* expect to receive for your article. This doesn't mean that the sky's the limit and you can set your price. What it really means is that if you come in with a figure that's lower than the magazine's regular price, they will be more than happy to pay you the lower amount—and you'll never be the wiser.

If you run into this type of situation, one solution is to look for help in the writing community. One option, for example, is to check the magazine for the names of some of its contributors—and then send a polite e-mail to one or two of these writers, explaining that you are negotiating an article with the publication and as it's you're first time working with them, you would appreciate some insight into their regular pay range. When this happened to me, for example, I realized that a writer I'd worked with more than once also wrote regularly for this particular publication—and by talking to him, I was able to set a price of several hundred dollars more than what I might otherwise have asked.

3) **When does the publication pay?** There are two basic payment schedules: "On acceptance" and "on publication." A publication that pays "on acceptance" will pay you once the article has been received, approved, accepted, and contracted for—regardless of when it is actually published. A publication that pays "on publication" will pay you only after the material has been published—and not necessarily *soon* after!

Most markets that pay "on acceptance" will pay you only after you have signed a contract. Here's where it can get a bit sticky: Some editors can be *very* slow to actually send that contract! One of my regular markets, for example, takes as long as a month to send out a contract, and another month to pay after the contract has been signed and returned. Thus, "pays on acceptance" in this case means "pays 60 days after acceptance." Another regular market recently managed to delay the contract for so long that my check didn't arrive until after the article was printed—effectively turning their stated "pay on acceptance" policy into "pay on publication."

4) **What rights does the publication require?** This question can be even more important than the question of payment, because it determines what you can do with your material in the future. Print publications tend to demand far more rights than electronic publications. The reason is simple: A print publication can easily (and inexpensively) launch a Web site, and might have a future need for electronic rights. An electronic publication, however, cannot easily launch a *print* publication—so it is less likely to need your print rights. Thus, while most e-pubs *don't* ask for any form of print rights, most print publications *do* ask for some (or all) electronic rights. (See chapter 21 for more information on rights.)

Don't make the mistake of thinking these issues don't matter when you're starting out, or that you don't care what a publication pays or what rights it asks for as long as you can get your name in print. It *does* matter—and you'd be surprised at how often you want to resell an article you thought you'd only use once. Professionalism is something you need to practice from the very beginning—because the only person who can protect yourself in the marketplace is *you*.

SHOULD YOU WRITE FOR FREE?

Many writers believe that one's career must begin with nonpaying markets, and that this is the best way to build clips (and experience). If, however, you have a choice between offering your material to a paying or a nonpaying market, there is no logical reason to choose the latter. The nonpaying market will always be there if you fail to sell the piece—but it needn't be your first choice, or even your second or third.

Does this mean you should never write for free? Not at all! There are many excellent reasons to do so; being new just isn't one of them. Here are some better reasons:

- **For fun.** Sometimes you may want to write something for the sheer enjoyment of it. (After all, someone must be writing all those variations on "how to bathe your cat" circulating on the Internet!)

- **To support a cause.** Instead of contributing money to organizations or issues you believe in, you may choose to donate your writing skills. Your "payment" is often simply the knowledge that you're increasing awareness of an important issue.

- **To help a favorite organization.** You may enjoy contributing to your company, community, or church newsletter. Be careful, however: Once such organizations realize that you can write, you may be flooded with requests for more freebies.

- **To enhance your career.** Many unpaid markets can be career-builders—including your own Web site. Writing FAQs for your site or blog (or others), contributing articles to professional newsletters, or writing for professional journals can be good ways to build your reputation.

- **To help and inform others.** At a certain point in their careers, many writers feel an urge to "give back" some of what they have learned. You may decide to write about "what you know" to help others in your field, or to repay mentoring you received at one time. This impulse seems to be contributing to the growing tide of blogging on the Internet.

Just as there are good reasons to write for free, there are also bad ones:

- **To see your name in print.** Don't assume that the only way to get a byline is to give your work away. If you send your work to a paying market, you might get a double thrill: Seeing your name in print, and seeing it on a pay-check.

• **To find out if you're good enough to get published.** Nonpaying markets are not a good place to test your abilities. Many such markets are stuck with whatever they can get, which means they often don't have the luxury of rejecting mediocre writing.

• **To polish your skills.** Nonpaying markets don't appreciate being dumping grounds for bad writing. If you want to polish your work, do so through a class or critique group.

• **Loyalty.** It can be difficult to abandon an editor who accepted your work when no one else would. However, recipients of such loyalty can sometimes misuse it. Don't let such a relationship interfere with your ability to move on.

Writing for free is an option, never a necessity. The bottom line is that if your writing isn't good (and you know it), your energies are best spent seeking ways to improve it. If your writing *is* good, and you believe in it, don't sell yourself short by failing to sell yourself at all!

❧14❧

Writing for Special-Interest Publications

No matter what your favorite activity or hobby, chances are that a magazine covers it. Special interest publications make up the largest segment of the consumer magazine marketplace. These magazines are always hungry for new writers, including beginners without a portfolio of clips. One reason is that many such publications don't pay high rates; another is the need for fresh voices and perspectives.

"BUT I'M NOT AN EXPERT"

You don't have to be an expert in your favorite hobby or sport to write for such magazines. Experts often don't have time to write articles about their hobbies, which is why many articles are written by enthusiasts. If you care about your subject, that enthusiasm will show in your writing, and will also engage the enthusiasm of others. As an enthusiast—

- **You know what interests you about a hobby or activity,** so you'll be able to develop topics that interest readers like you.

- **You know the types of questions** someone like yourself would ask.

- **You know what it's like to start with the basics,** and are thus qualified to help other beginners.

- **You know the "language" of your specialty,** whether it's the lingo of fly-fishing or the jargon of the dog show circuit.

- **You have a desire to learn more about the subject,** and can share your knowledge with others.

- **You have experience in the subject area.**

These qualities appeal to an editor as much as a sheaf of clips. Non-writing credentials should be an important part of your pitch to a special-interest publication: "I've been quilting for ten years," or "I've owned Norwegian Elkhounds for most of my life." Even a pitch like "I've always been fascinated by..." can get an editor's attention.

UNDERSTANDING THE MARKETS

Writer's Market offers a host of special interest categories, from "animals" to "travel." Each of these offers an equally large number of subtopics (under sports, for example, you'll find subcategories ranging from archery to wrestling). It's not enough just to find a magazine that covers your subject, however. Your research also needs to determine three additional things:

• **The magazine's degree of specialization.** A magazine titled *Pet World*, for example, is aimed at a very different audience from one titled *Turtle Monthly*.

• **The expertise of the audience.** Does the magazine target beginners, experts, or both? If a magazine is designed for experienced gardeners, for example, you won't break in with "My First Vegetable Patch."

• **The mindset of the audience.** Two magazines on the same subject may take very different approaches. For example, a dog magazine aimed at breeders won't want an article on adopting mixed-breed puppies, while one for pet owners won't be interested in an article on breeding and whelping.

MAGAZINE "MUST-HAVES"

"But what can I possibly say about (pets, fly-fishing, paper airplanes)?" The answer lies in determining a magazine's basic article mix: The "must-have" categories that appear in every issue. To determine this, you'll need to review the contents of several back issues (or search for an index of back issues on-line). You'll find that most special interest publications publish a mix of articles that fit into the following topic areas:

• **How-to Articles.** Most special interest publications are by nature "how-to" magazines: How to repair a car, plant a garden, raise a puppy, catch a fish, knit a sweater. Within that general subject context, how-to articles focus on specific issues: How to do something new or unusual, solve a common problem, develop a skill, or increase one's enjoyment. Don't pitch an article on "how to raise a puppy," for example; pitch a new, effective way to housetrain your puppy, or teach it basic obedience commands at home.

• **Health and Safety.** Many special interest areas (especially sports and recreation) involve health and safety issues, such as how to avoid hazards, handle emergencies, or improve one's health by participating in an activity. Pet magazines always need this type of article (including nutrition and first aid pieces). You don't have to be a doctor or a vet to write these pieces; many markets prefer such articles from the perspective of a typical "participant."

• **Equipment.** What are the tools of your trade? Consider an article on how to choose the right equipment, how to determine the tools needed for a specific project, how to take care of your equipment, how to build equipment (e.g., how to build a doghouse), or how to use equipment safely. (This information can often be built into a how-to piece.)

• **Seasonal.** Some activities are seasonal by nature; others have seasonal concerns. If you love gardening, for example; think about the "off" seasons: "How to add fall color to your garden," or "how to winterize your fruit trees." Pet magazines look for articles on summer travel and winter safety; consider, for example, seasonal-related health issues (such as flea control). Remember that seasonal articles should be submitted four to six months in advance.

• **Destination.** With a little imagination, you can incorporate a "destination" slant into many types of articles. For a fishing publication, you might cover the "Top Ten Trout Streams of Northern Idaho." For a dog magazine, you might cover "The Ten Most Dog-Friendly Parks in the U.S." For a quilt magazine, consider covering an event like "Pennsylvania's Annual Amish Quilt Spectacular."

• **Historical Background.** Though these are low on some publications' lists, a well-written background piece can still be a good way to break in. One way to make this type of article work is to combine it with "how-to" tips: For example, a look at the "history of English pewter" could include tips on collecting or care.

• **Personal Profiles.** Some magazines love these; others don't. Personal profiles usually highlight someone whose work has achieved recognition, who has made a significant contribution to the field, or who is doing something unique or unusual. For example, a woodcarving magazine might be interested in someone whose work has just been featured in the *Smithsonian*, or an immigrant who has "carved out" a new life with a rare "old country" skill. Some magazines prefer to combine "who" with "how," such as an embroidery publication that ran an article on a lacemaker who used traditional techniques, along with information on how the reader could apply those skills.

• **Current Issues and Controversies.** If your interest area is affected by controversy or legislation, a magazine may be interested in such coverage. A pet magazine, for example, may be interested in anti-breed legislation or other laws restricting pets. Be sure the issue has more than regional appeal, however; does it establish a precedent that could affect enthusiasts nationwide? Also, be aware that controversies may be time-sensitive; will this issue still be "hot" by the time it sees print six months from now?

• **Personal Experiences.** These are generally lowest on a magazine's "must-have" list. Most publications publish, at most, one per issue—yet most are flooded with such articles. While it's not impossible to sell such a piece, you must be sure your experience is truly unique and avoids the "been there, done that" factor. ("My first puppy," for example, will be of no interest to readers who have already had several "new puppy" experiences.) Chapter 12 discusses writing personal experience articles.

To improve your chances of a sale, look for categories that overlap. For example, consider a how-to article that includes a discussion of the equipment needed for the project, or a seasonal article that covers health hazards. Editors are always happy to find an article that fills two "must-have" slots at once.

Take a look at your favorite activity, sport, hobby or love. Ask yourself what you could say about that topic that fits into one of the categories listed above. Be creative, and don't limit yourself to the things you already know. Instead, consider what questions you might ask, what you'd like to learn more about. If you have questions, chances are that a magazine's readers will have those questions as well—and by answering them, you could turn your curiosity into a sale.

SHOULD YOU SPECIALIZE OR GENERALIZE?

Writing for special-interest magazines doesn't mean one must necessarily write *only* in that specialty. There are benefits to sticking to one's areas of expertise—and there are benefits to expanding beyond a specific area. Each option has advantages and disadvantages. Understanding them can help you make the best choice for your writing career.

Specialization

Specialization makes life easier: It allows you to focus on developing your writing skills without having to learn new subjects at the same time. Specialization can help you build a reputation as an expert in a particular field. It also helps you build on previous work as you climb from lower-paying markets to better, more prestigious publications. As long as you remain within your specialty, your clips will always be relevant, and editors may be familiar with your reputation even before you begin to work for them. (Keep in mind, however, that in some fields, publications won't accept work from writers who write for competing publications.)

For specialization to benefit you, you must choose a field that allows for such upward mobility—i.e., a field that has a large selection of markets. The first question you need to ask, therefore, is "what is the market for my field?"

A writer choosing to specialize in "dogs," for example, would find opportunities somewhat limited. There are only three high-paying dog publications (i.e., that pay $300 or more for feature articles): *Dog Fancy, Dog World,* and *The American Kennel Club Gazette. Dog Fancy* and *Dog World* are both owned by Fancy Publications; *Dog Fancy* focuses on dogs as pets, while *Dog World* has traditionally focused more on breeding and exhibiting, as does *The AKC Gazette.* Other publications include *The Bark, Animal Fair* and *Dog and Kennel;* moving down the ladder, one will find smaller, more specialized markets, such as *Gun Dog* and *Mushing.* Each publication has specific requirements, and most won't accept reprints from other publications. The market for dog articles outside these publications is even more limited.

On the other hand, the market for articles in an area such as "nutrition and natural health" is considerably larger. Besides a number of high-paying health and nutrition magazines, the market includes general interest publications that regularly feature articles on some aspect of health or nutrition. A writer focusing on this area of expertise might be able to place articles in general women's magazines, parenting publications, fitness magazines, and even more specialized publications such as sports and recreation magazines.

The question, therefore, is not so much whether to specialize, but whether the area in which you wish to specialize offers a wide selection of market opportunities, or only a handful of relevant publications. If you choose the right topic, your area of expertise can help you open many doors; if you choose too narrow a topic, however, you're likely to find yourself "stuck."

Generalization

The benefits of generalization are simple: The more subjects you can write about, the more marketing opportunities you'll find. If you're serious about making a living as a freelance writer, generalization can help ensure that you never run out of markets to write for.

Generalization can be a good approach if you don't want your name associated exclusively with one type of writing. Perhaps you enjoy writing about dogs, but you don't want to be known as a "pet writer," because you fear this label will hinder your ability to convince editors that you can write about other topics. You may also want to build a more diverse portfolio of clips that will reflect your ability to handle a wide range of topics.

Generalization requires good writing and research skills. When you generalize, you won't always be able to rely on your own expertise; instead, you'll have to learn how to ask the right questions about subjects you know very little about. Since you're not an expert, you'll need to find good interview sources. Most of all, you need a willingness to take chances—to say "yes" to assignments that may take you out of your comfort zone.

While this can mean more work, it also means that once editors can rely on you to turn in a well-researched article on any topic, your range of assignments is likely to increase. Nor do you have to worry about the limitations of your niche: The market is wide open. You may write for a dog magazine today, a health magazine tomorrow, and a religious publication next week.

Generalization also has its downside, however. When you generalize, you lose the advantages associated with being recognized as an expert on a particular subject. Some publications prefer writers with subject-specific credentials, whether those credentials are experiential or in the form of a list of publishing credits in the field.

There is no "one size fits all" answer to the specialize/generalize question. Either decision will open some doors and close others (or at least make them more difficult to enter). In this area, as in many others, the answer is "it depends." Never let anyone tell you that you "should" choose one road or the other. You must make this decision for yourself, based upon your interests, your goals, and most of all, upon what will bring you happiness and fulfillment as a writer.

❧15❧

Writing for Newspapers

by Sue Fagalde Lick

Newspapers are often overlooked as a market for freelance writing. Any writer who is serious about writing, selling and communicating with readers needs to consider newspapers as a possible market, however. Here's why:

1) **Most people read at least one newspaper regularly.** According to the State of the Media Report produced by the Pew Research Center's Project for Excellence in Journalism in 2010, just over 1,400 daily newspapers are published in the United States. This doesn't count the many weeklies, monthlies and special-interest papers also being produced. According to the Newspaper Association of America, 75 percent of adults have read a newspaper in the last week. Among those over age 55, the number grows to eight out of ten.

2) **Newspapers come out more often, and there are more of them,** so they require more editorial copy. On daily and weekly general-interest papers, staff writers cover most of the news and many of the main features. The Associated Press and other wire services provide national and world news. But there are many stories the staff and wire services don't cover. That's where freelancers come in. Smaller newspapers generally have smaller staffs. How do they survive? Freelance writers!

3) **Special interest papers are everywhere.** Go out for coffee, and you'll probably see a rack with entertainment newspapers and papers put out by special interest groups: gays, Hispanics, coffee aficionados, and others. Go to the library, and you'll find even more papers. Visit an antiques store, and you'll find newspapers on antiques. You may receive a church newspaper. Most religions have local, regional or national publications. And don't overlook newspapers aimed at particular industries, such as *CD Computing News* or *Real Estate Weekly News*.

HOW DO MAGAZINE AND NEWSPAPER WRITING DIFFER?

Many of the tasks involved in writing for newspapers and magazines are the same. But there are differences.

1) **Mission.** The mission of many general interest newspapers is to be the place readers look for news and features about their area. Remember the slogan "location, location, location?" For newspapers, it's "local, local, local." If there's no local angle, they don't want it, no matter how fascinating or well written it might be.

    Other papers center on a particular group or interest. The newspaper put out by the Catholic Archdiocese of Chicago may run some wire stories about Catholics outside of Chicago, but it won't run anything about Methodists. I used to work for a Hispanic newspaper called *El Observador.* The editors made it very clear that if the subject did not have a connection to the Hispanic community, it would not get in.

2) **News Peg.** Timeliness is often a factor in getting an article published. Editors may ask, "Why write this story now?" A feature on an artist is more likely to sell if it can be tied to an upcoming gallery show. A school program may be deemed worthy of a feature if it's new, being considered for budget cuts, or just won an award. Stories that can be tied to holidays or anniversaries of major events have more chance of getting published. Stories on chocolate sell for Valentine's Day, religious stories abound as Easter approaches, skiing sells in January.

3) **Timing.** While most magazines are put together at least two months in advance, news and sports sections of the newspaper are written, edited and laid out less than 24 hours before publication. Feature sections are generally planned a little farther ahead. This may be a week or, in the case of holidays or other special events, a month or two. For weekly newspapers, get your queries in at least two weeks ahead, and for monthlies, allow at least two months.

4) **Pay.** Many newspapers pay less than magazines; I have seen local papers that pay less than a penny a word. Five to ten cents a word is more common for community weeklies. This won't make you rich, but can help if you need experience and clips. The big dailies generally pay at least $100 for columns and opinion pieces, and as much as $500 for feature articles. *The Chicago Tribune* pays up to $500 for travel pieces. *The Christian Science Monitor* rates start at $200-$225 per article.

5) **Writing style.** Most of us have heard of the "inverted pyramid," the traditional style for newspaper stories. In essence, you start with the most important information and work your way down to the least important so that if the story is too long, the editor can cut it off from the bottom.

If you wind up writing news stories, you will still need to employ the inverted pyramid. However, most freelancers write features (non-news stories) where the style is similar to that of magazine articles.

6) **Words vs. Inches.** Some editors will ask for a number of inches rather than words. You can ask them how many words or characters that includes, or you can figure it out for yourself. With a ruler, measure an inch of type. Count how many lines there are per inch, most commonly six, then determine the average number of words per line and multiply that by the number of lines. Do this for several column inches to come up with an approximate number of words per inch. (Some editors use the number of characters to determine column inches. Some computer programs will give you the character count as well as the word count.)

FINDING FREELANCE OPPORTUNITIES

Now the fun begins. Gather up all the newspapers you can. Set aside the ones that don't interest you, because you don't want to write for a publication you don't want to read. (Trust me.) Now start reading. Go for the big paper first. If you don't subscribe, buy one at a newsstand or go to the library. You should go there anyway; you'll find newspapers you didn't know existed.

You're looking for two things: sections with articles written by freelancers, and subjects that seem to fit the paper's mission but aren't being covered. For example, if your daily newspaper rarely touches on your neighborhood, maybe they need a freelance correspondent. If nobody seems to be covering your city council or school board—or your local churches, artists or sports teams—there's an opening for you.

For most dailies, the feature sections are your most likely freelance outlets. These include sections on food, home and garden, travel, entertainment, arts and books, religion and business. There is also generally a "living" or "community" or "our town" section. There may be a special Sunday magazine or feature section. Big papers covering large areas may have weekly sections focusing on particular neighborhoods. Read these sections especially carefully. Look at the bylines at the end of stories. Are the writers identified as staff writers or are they listed as "special writers" or some other category that lets you know they're not part of the staff? Those are freelancers.

Look in the paper for names of the editors. Each section usually has a separate editor. You can often find them on the editorial page. Sometimes newspapers run lists of editors in the front or local section. If you can't find the name in the paper, don't give up. Most papers have Web sites now. One way to find a newspaper online is to search for its title through a search engine; another is to use one of the many newspaper-list sites (see *www.writing-world.com/links/magazines.shtml*). Worst case, make a phone call and ask for the name of the editor. Make sure you also ask how to spell it.

The same method goes for specialty newspapers. Read the paper, look at the masthead, look at the bylines, look for blurbs in the paper asking for submissions.

Or, call the newspaper. Ask if they use freelancers and whom you should address material to. The worst they can say is no.

TYPES OF NEWSPAPER ARTICLES

• **Personality profiles** are standard in newspapers as well as in magazines. You interview someone of interest to the local community or special interest group because of what he does or his history. A profile may include research from other sources, including interviews of friends, family and co-workers.

• **Human Interest stories**—Jill Dick, author of *Freelancing for Newspapers,* writes, "Study the 'ordinary ' stories told by 'ordinary' folk and you'll soon realize... that there is a huge depth of warm-hearted humanity that doesn't make the front pages and is often obscured by the constant daily dirge of evil, death and destruction man everywhere wreaks on his fellow man. Thousands of 'good' stories are just waiting to be told—and when they are, they touch many hearts."

• **Business features** are big in local papers, partially because they help sell advertising, but they also let the community know what's available. Look for a news peg, such as a business just opening, selling a new product, moving to a new location, or planning to close. Maybe your favorite lunch place is about to start serving dinner. Time for a story.

• **Reviews** come in many forms. The bigger newspapers may run reviews of books, plays, concerts, restaurants, movies, or computer software. See who writes these stories. If you don't see reviews of the thing you're interested in, query and see if they'll let you do it. It helps to have some sample reviews ready. Try one just for fun.

• **Roundup pieces** are popular with many editors. I have written everything from where to get a good hamburger to a survey of services offered by local funeral parlors. Travel sections may run "best cruises" or "best playgrounds to take the kids." The food section might do a roundup of local wineries or culinary schools or places to eat pancakes. In the spring, papers look at wedding-related topics, such as the most romantic places to get married or the best places to hold a reception. These are not terribly creative to write, but they are lucrative, and editors love them.

• **How-to** articles help a reader solve a problem, whether it's how to build a birdhouse, how to clean the scuzz off the bathroom floor, or how to buy a digital camera. You don't always need to be an expert on the subject. You just need to interview someone who is.

• **Opinion pieces** allow you to sound off on a subject. These usually go on what is called the op-ed page, meaning it's the page opposite the one with the staff editorials. Dailies sometimes run a whole opinion section on Sundays.

These are rarely just one writer's opinion with nothing to back it up. Such pieces require some research or knowledge, a bit like the essays you wrote in high school or college.

• **Personal experience** articles appear in many feature sections, especially travel stories. Here, using the first person, you tell of something that happened to you, using sights, sounds, smells, colors, moods, and physical description to help the reader experience what you have experienced. A news peg would help you get it published. Your experience as a temporary Santa Claus would be perfect at Christmas.

• **Investigative articles** delve into a subject, ferreting out information that has not been made public before. Often they unmask government wrongdoing, expose a health issue, or look into a crime or disaster. These require a lot of work, using multiple sources to go below the surface and tell a complete story. Usually staff writers do the investigative pieces, but it is possible in some markets for freelancers to contribute.

• **News stories** are covered by staff and wire services on large newspapers, but community newspapers may hire stringers to cover city council, school board, special events, and other news. The term "stringer" comes from the old custom of using a string to measure the number of inches a writer should get paid for. In many cases, you'll have less than 24 hours to attend the event and write the story. It's a rush, but it is exciting to be there when news is happening and present it to the readers right away.

DO YOU NEED PICTURES?

Editors also look for "art," the newspaper name for photos, drawings, maps, charts or any other entity that can dress up the page. Without art, your story may wind up below a less interesting story that has pictures. Larger newspapers usually use their own photographers exclusively, but if you're an artist or a good photographer and can provide your own art, you have a huge advantage when writing for small and medium-sized publications. Not only will editors be more inclined to buy your stories, but you will also get paid extra for every photo or drawing.

Not long ago, freelancers had to worry about whether a newspaper wanted black and white photos, color slides, or digital media. This is not an issue anymore. Digital photos are the norm, and are usually e-mailed to the editor along with the article.

QUERYING A NEWSPAPER

Magazine and newspaper queries are virtually identical, so check chapter 17 for details on how to write a query. The real difference lies in how (and when) editors *respond*. Newspapers are notorious for the non-response. This also applies to e-mail queries.

The delay at newspapers stems from the extreme workload most editors have. If your manuscript arrives while editors are on deadline, they probably won't see it for a few days. By then, it might be completely buried in an avalanche of letters, faxes and e-mails. This means you need to be gently proactive. Wait two weeks, then contact the editor.

Follow up with a short note, telephone, or e-mail the editor. (Do not drop in at the office. Chances are the editor will be busy or not even there, and he/she will definitely resent the intrusion.) A mailed note runs the risk of getting buried along with your query. A telephone call is direct and often works best. In fact, it could open up a dialogue that leads to other things. However, do not expect the editor to remember your piece or know where it is. Chances are he or she will have to make a note and get back to you.

Before you call, find out the best times to talk to the editor. Usually that's shortly after the paper comes out. For a daily morning newspaper, editors start work in the afternoons, finishing late at night. The best time to call is early in the afternoon before the deadline crunch hits. For an afternoon paper, reverse the process. For a weekly paper, or for weekly sections of a daily paper, call the editor after the paper goes to press. Sometimes this is the day before publication, sometimes it's several days before. Check the paper for deadlines—if not for copy, then for advertising. Assume that's when the editor will not want to talk to you.

However you approach it, be polite; don't whine and don't be critical. Try to be as helpful as possible. "I mailed you a story idea about warts on June 3, and I was wondering if you had decided yet." If the editor says no, don't throw a hissy fit and don't push. Say "Thank you very much for your time." You might calmly ask what you might have done to make the idea more likely to be used, but don't press too hard.

If you still want to write for that newspaper, come up with another idea and get it out there. You might even mention it while you're calling about the first idea. Chances are the editor will ask for something in writing, but it wouldn't hurt to say, "Would you be interested in a story on…the new bakery that makes donuts without holes?"

Simultaneous Submissions

While it's never a good idea to send the same stories to *competing* newspapers—newspapers that serve the same market area—you can often sell the same story to *noncompeting* papers. For example, newspapers published in Florida and New York may have completely different readers and contents. Papers that are owned by the same newspaper chain, such as Gannett or Tribune Media Services, often share stories. This can be a boon for the writer if their story is chosen not only by the local daily or weekly but by its counterparts in the same company.

You're safe offering the same story to non-competing newspapers as long it fits their mission in some way. Travel articles are particular adaptable to multiple sales because they're not tied as tightly to the local area. Columns, how-tos, roundup pieces and features of national or international interest can be submitted to multiple publications. It is also possible to reslant the same idea, taking the same basic facts and connecting them with a local person, place, or organization. If the newspapers are in completely different markets, I wouldn't mention your multiple queries, unless you have actually sold the article. Then you may need to give credit to the paper where it appears first.

Ideally you want to sell only First Serial Rights or One-Time Rights (see chapter 21 for more information). That means you can resell the article again and again. Some publications will buy the rights to a story for a specified time, i.e., six months or a year. Some papers will insist on buying all rights. Then you need to decide whether or not the pay and exposure are worth it. Sometimes they are. Often on smaller papers, the editor doesn't have a firm policy about rights and will let you keep them just for the asking. Know what you're selling. Get it in writing. If the editor doesn't send you a contract, send the editor a letter or e-mail describing the assignment and your understanding as to the rights you're licensing. Also find out if the paper is going to publish your story online as well as in print. Ask how long it will be there, and whether you will be paid extra for this.

WRITING THE ARTICLE

We've all heard the saying "Just the facts, ma'am," but if all we provided were facts, our stories would be so dry no one would want to read them. Like fishermen, we need to hook the readers and keep them reading.

Consider your audience when writing your article. Are they young, old or a mixture of all ages? Are they college-educated or not educated at all? Do they live in the city or the country? Are they rich, poor or somewhere in between. Are they likely to know anything about your topic or must everything be explained?

Keep in mind that you're writing for the masses, for your families, your friends, for doctors, lawyers, construction workers and the teenager who bags your groceries. We don't need to "write down," but we do need to make sure no one is left behind. That means we cannot assume they know things most people would not know.

Writing the Lead

Start with a headline, probably the same one you used for your query. This is your theme and your story should never stray too far from it. Then move into your "lead paragraph." In a news story, the duty of the lead is to tell us in a nutshell what happened. An easy way to develop this paragraph is to think of what you would tell your spouse or your best friend if you had to quickly summarize what this is all about. You rush in excited about what you just found out and you say: "A boat just ran aground at Lost Creek. That's the third one this month. Luckily nobody was hurt this time," (a true story that happened practically outside my door) or "Wow, did you know that whales eat 500 tons of food a day?"

In a news lead, it is important to spill the most important facts immediately, moving down the story to the more minor elements. For a feature story, you have more leeway. You definitely need to get to the point soon, preferably by the third paragraph, but you can start in many ways, such as:

• **A startling statistic.** "Last year, 10,000 junior high school boys brought knives to school despite increased security and the installation of metal detectors." [I made that up.]

• **A scene:** "Jake Barnes leaned against a bale of hay, tore off a wad of chewing tobacco with his teeth, and stared out at the sun setting over the cow pasture, ignoring the government officials standing by the road talking about running a freeway right through his ranch. "Ah, I heard all that before," Jake said.

• **A quote:** "Up until I adopted Charlie, I didn't think I ever wanted kids. One look at his big blue eyes changed everything."

• **An anecdote:** "Peter will never forget the day he caught his first fish…"

After the Lead
The lead should draw the reader in. It should also set you on the path for the rest of your article. Your second or third paragraph grounds the reader by explaining what's going on. "Now that I have your attention, here's what I want to talk about." The statistics on kids and weapons would probably lead to a paragraph introducing the main topic of your article, how school security programs have failed. The ranch scene might move into a paragraph about how this time it was really happening and the new freeway would disrupt a whole way of life for Jake and others like him. The adoption quote could move into a story on unusual adoptions. The fishing story could move into a feature on Peter's work as a commercial fisherman or his crusade to save his favorite fishing spot.

With any luck, from here, the story should flow from one point to another, until you have covered each topic in your outline. In a feature, you will want to complete the circle by harking back to the quote, the scene, the statistic, or your thesis statement used in the beginning

You may want to close with information on how to contact the person you're profiling, places to find more information, where to make reservations, etc. Check the newspaper to see how they format this information and plug in the names, phone numbers, e-mail addresses or Web sites.

Quote Correctly
Newspaper articles use lots of quotes from people or printed sources. Number one rule: Write it the way they say it. It's okay to correct minor grammar errors, but in general you need to transmit exactly what your source said. If quotes are too jumbled or awkward, paraphrase them, giving the source credit for the thought if not the exact words. Don't take things out of context just to make your story work better. Our job is to write the truth, even when it's clumsy.

With written material, you need to give credit to the source. Newspaper articles don't come with footnotes, so incorporate the attribution into your prose, as in, "Roger Wilco wrote Dec. 12 in the *New York Times*. . ." or "*Webster's New Collegiate Dictionary* says…" Try not to use a lot of quotes from written material (and if you must, paraphrase as much as possible rather than quoting directly.) Getting someone to actually say it is much more convincing.

Beware of making statements without attribution. If you say the sun rises in the east and sets in the west, no one will challenge you. If you say man is going to land on Jupiter by 2022, you'd better have a source to back that up. Anything odd, startling or that claims to be the best, biggest, first, last or only needs to be attributed to a source.

Stylistic Considerations

Newspapers have their own style, which can be very different from that of magazine feature articles. Here are some stylistic issues to consider:

- **Point of View:** Most newspaper articles are written in the third person, which means you never say "I" (except in columns and opinion pieces" or "you" (except in how-tos). Look at the paper for which you're writing to see how they handle voice and do likewise.

- **Tense:** Most newspaper articles are written in past tense. Use "said" instead of "says," "walked" instead of "walk" etc.

- **Newspaper Style:** Most newspapers use the *Associated Press Stylebook* for issues of capitalization, hyphenation, dates, times, addresses, and other picky matters. If you don't have the book, at least study the newspaper you're writing for to see if you can detect trends. For example, do they write out percent or use %? Are dates Dec. 25, December 25 or 25 December? These styles enable editors to present more information in less space, and they'll bless you if they don't have to change every date in your story.

- **Short Paragraphs:** Looking at a newspaper page, you can see that the stories are set up in columns, usually five or six to a page. When forced into that format, a single sentence can take up several lines and a paragraph can go on forever. Therefore, newspaper articles are generally written in short paragraphs. A good rule is that if you've gotten to the fourth line, it's time to think about ending that paragraph and moving on to another.

- **Active Language:** Active verbs are much more engaging than passive verbs and generally take up less space. Instead of "The whale was fed dead fish every morning" say "Chuck fed the whale dead fish every morning." Or better, "Every morning, Chuck dumped 10 gallons of raw fish into the pool."

- **Include Sensory Details:** Tell us how it looked, how it felt, how it smelled, how it sounded. Put us in the place and take us beyond mere quotes and facts.

- **Look for questions the editor might have.** Did you define any abbreviations, acronyms, technical terms or foreign words? Have you double-checked sources' names and titles? If there is something you're not sure of, do some more research or take it out. You should be able to back up every word.

DON'T OVERLOOK THE INTERNET

If you only look at the print version of a newspaper these days, you're missing a big part of what its staff produces. Over the last few years, newspapers have grown thinner and some have gone out of business while others have moved completely online. Today major newspapers not only publish most of their print content on their Web sites but offer a wealth of other material, including news updates, audio and video features, blogs, forums, and endless links. These offer additional opportunities for freelancers to get involved, and they should not be overlooked. In the same way you would study a newspaper, study the Web site and pitch your ideas to the appropriate editor. Keep in mind that most online stories are short, include lots of links and frequently provide a space for readers to comment. Newspapers are not dying; they're adapting to the 21st century. As freelance writers, we need to do likewise.

ONCE YOU HAVE YOUR FOOT IN THE DOOR...

Although the world is full of would-be writers, most editors have trouble finding writers who can actually deliver a well-written article on time. If you're one of them, you will soon be golden to those editors.

Follow-up is the key to getting more assignments and becoming a regular contributor. If an editor says no to your first idea, come up with another one. If an editor says yes to your first idea, come up with another one. Once you've sold a couple of articles to the same editor, there's nothing wrong with typing up several ideas and trying to get assignments for them all at once. Over time, you'll develop the kind of relationship where you can secure a go-ahead with a quick phone call or e-mail and where the editor calls you with assignments. Once you make the list of proven freelancers, the editor will turn to you again and again.

If you really want to write for a particular newspaper, the worst thing you can do is disappear. If they encourage you in any way to try again, do it before your name fades from memory.

PART IV
Queries and Submissions

❧16❧

The Submission Process

Developing a marketable article is only half a writer's battle. The other half is getting that article *to* the market. In this process, the *appearance* of professionalism can often count as much or more as your actual credentials; even if you've never published a single article, you can impress editors simply by providing a professional-looking submission package.

Your first step is to review a publication's guidelines. These will tell you what type of material a publication is looking for, the preferred word-count, whether the publication prefers (or requires) queries or complete manuscripts, the payment rates and rights required, and whom to contact. The guidelines may also specify a publication's "response time"—which basically indicates the amount of time a writer is expected to wait before following up on a submission. Needless to say, you will demonstrate your professionalism best by following these guidelines to the letter!

WHOM TO CONTACT

While the *Writer's Market* provides a good overview of a magazine's requirements, these listings can often be out of date, particularly with respect to contact information. Before you submit, therefore, I recommend checking an online source; many publications post guidelines on their Web site. The "contact us" section of the Web site will usually list the appropriate editorial contacts (including e-mails).

Generally, a publication's guidelines will specify where you should send submissions. If you're not sure, you can also check the masthead of a publication (either in print or online). Often, you will be asked to send material to a publication's *Managing Editor,* who usually makes the initial decision to accept or reject an article. If there is no managing editor, you should send material either to an *Associate Editor* or to the *Editor,* unless the guidelines say otherwise.

For a publication with lots of departments, you'll generally send submissions to a *Features Editor* or *Articles Editor.* Or, you may have to send a piece to a specific *Department Editor,* such as a health editor, food editor, fitness editor, etc. If you can't tell from a publication's guidelines or masthead, don't hesitate to contact the publication and ask!

Don't send material to an assistant editor, editor-in-chief, or contributing editor, unless the guidelines specifically say to do so. Assistant editors usually have no authority over decisions; they are often little more than glorified secretaries. An editor-in-chief generally supervises a group of publications, but doesn't handle the day-to-day management of any one publication. A contributing editor isn't even a staff person; this is a title given to a freelance writer who is a regular contributor (such as a columnist).

WHAT TO SEND

A publication's guidelines should tell you what to submit—and what *not* to submit. In addition to the question of whether to send a query or completed manuscript, you may also be asked to send the following:

Clips. Many publications ask a writer to "query with clips." This strikes terror in the heart of unpublished writers, who fear they can't get published without clips—or get clips without being published.

Clips are simply photocopies of published articles. Note that "published" doesn't have to mean "paid"—clips from reputable nonpaying publications are often acceptable. (This does not include high school newspapers, company newsletters, church bulletins, or self-published materials.) If possible, try to match your clips to the subject matter of the market. If you don't have "relevant" clips, use those from your most prestigious publications.

If you've been published online, a printout of the article is acceptable as a clip. If you're sending a query by e-mail, you can also reference the URLs of online publications. (Never send a clip as an attachment, unless requested.)

Unless a publication specifically states that it won't work with unpublished writers, don't let a lack of clips discourage you from approaching a market. Even publications that ask for clips will often accept other forms of credentials in their stead (see chapter 17).

Resume. While it's not very common, some publications ask a writer to "query with resume." Generally, this means the publication is looking for writers with relevant credentials who can be offered assignments generated by the editor. Such a market is usually not open to beginning freelancers.

Publications List. Sooner or later, you'll need to develop a publications list to send with queries. This is simply a list of the articles you've published, where they appeared, and when. You can prepare it on your regular letterhead, or create a separate sheet with your name and address and other contact information centered at the top. I recommend starting your list as soon as you publish your first article; it's easier to keep track as you go along than to try to rummage through your records later to locate article titles and publication dates.

List publications chronologically, with the most recent first. Include the article title, the publication in which it appeared, and the date of publication. If an article appeared online, you can also include the URL if you wish. Your list will look something like this:

"My Latest Article," Dog Fancy Magazine, *June 2010*

"My Other Article," Entrepreneur, *February 2010*

"Another Great Article," Newport News Gazette, *December 2009*

Eventually (yes, it will happen!), your publications list will grow too long to fit on a single page. At that point, it's a good idea to break it up into several smaller lists, focusing on particular subject areas (e.g., garden publications, pet publications, etc.). It's still advisable to keep a master list for your own records. You may also wish to subdivide your list by *type* of publication—e.g., books, magazines, newspapers, online publications, etc. You may also wish to include a section for awards and prizes.

SASE or return postcard. Most publications still expect a writer to include either a self-addressed, stamped return envelope[1] with submissions. Some, however, prefer a return postcard with "check-off" options. Most use a postcard for rejections, and will send an acceptance letter on their own stationery. A return postcard should look something like this:

Date: _____
RE: Article Title

____ We have received the article [or query] listed above and will give you a decision by (date) _____.
____ We have decided to accept the article/query listed above, and will send you a formal letter of acceptance/contract shortly.
____ Sorry, we can't use this material.
Editor's Name: _____

You can obtain prestamped postcards at the post office. If you expect to use only a few, it's easy enough to type each one individually. (If you have an electronic typewriter with a memory function, it's easy to store your postcard text and print the message automatically.) If you plan to send lots, however, I'd recommend having them printed at a copy shop.

Bio. Usually, you won't be asked for a bio until an article has been accepted. You don't need writing credentials to produce a bio. Instead, consider what you

---

[1]Many people wonder how to *pronounce* this term: Is it "sayse" or "S-A-S-E"? The answer is: pronounce it whichever way you want. In writing the term, however, it's generally considered correct to refer to a "A SASE" rather than "An SASE" (which people tend to write when they pronounce the letters individually).

could say about your experience or expertise that relates to your article. For example, if you've written about hiking with dogs, your bio might read:

> *LilyAnne Rizzetta has hiked with her dogs in nearly 24 state and national parks, including Yosemite, Yellowstone and the Grand Canyon. Rizzetta is also an accomplished backpacker and "family camper." She lives (and writes) in Alpharetta, Georgia, where she shares her home with a husband, two cats and four Samoyeds. [You might also include a Web site URL or e-mail address, if desired.]*

Most publications ask for a bio of between 50 and 100 words. The bio above is 50 words—as you can see, you can pack a fair amount of information into a short space!

Publicity Photo. Again, you usually won't be asked for a photo until an article is accepted. However, it's wise to prepare for this request in advance. While you can use a snapshot in a pinch, I recommend having a professional photo taken. Keep in mind that you're trying to create a professional image; a professional photo is part of your overall business package, like your letterhead.

A publicity photo can be formal (e.g., a head-shot) or candid (a shot of you at your desk, for example). It can be color or black and white; I recommend color simply because it can be reproduced either way, according to the magazine's preference. Make sure the photographer has experience with publicity photos; I don't recommend using a mall or department store photo salon. Keep in mind that most photographers won't give you the negatives of your photo(s), so buy several prints; then use a scanner to create electronic files and additional copies. In some cases, you may need to provide the photographer's name for copyright purposes.[2]

SIMULTANEOUS AND MULTIPLE SUBMISSIONS

One source of controversy among writers is whether or not to send "simultaneous submissions" (or "simsubs"). This simply means sending the same query or manuscript to more than one publication at a time. Since a publication can take weeks (or even months) to make a decision, many writers feel that sending out simultaneous submissions is a way to bypass the delays that would ensue if one sent out a submission "sequentially."

The problem is, most publications do not like simsubs, and many refuse to accept them. This means one must either limit simsubs to publications that *do* accept them—or lie to those that don't. Either way, simsubs can put a writer in the awkward position of having to say "yes" to the *first* offer that comes in, since you can't ask an editor to wait until you hear from all the other publications you submitted to. Plus, if you *do* get multiple offers, you won't look good to all the editors that you have to refuse.

Editors don't object to simultaneous submissions just to be grouchy. Many don't assign articles until they can fit them into their publication schedule. If an author

---

[2]For more information on publicity photos, see "Your Publicity Photo," by Patricia Fry, at *www.writing-world. com/promotion/prphoto.shtml.*

comes back and says, "Sorry, I sold it somewhere else," this often leaves the editor with a hole in an upcoming issue that must be filled some other way—often on a tight deadline. Rather than putting yourself, or your editors, in this position, I recommend sending submissions to your top markets first; then, you only have to worry about accepting an offer from a less desirable market if your first choices say no.

"Multiple submissions" simply means sending more than one submission (usually an article) to an editor at the same time. Some publications don't accept multiple submissions; others place a limit on how many they will review.

WAITING FOR AN ANSWER

Once you've sent a submission, the next step is to wait. Typical response times range from four to eight weeks, though some publications (particularly online publications) promise to respond in two weeks—and I've seen one magazine that lists a response time of six to eight *months*. Response times apply regardless of whether you submit by surface mail or e-mail.

A published response time is not a *promise* that an editor will get back to you within that time. It is simply the amount of time a publication expects you to wait before following up on your submission. In the past, editors tended to respond more quickly with rejections than with acceptances; unfortunately, more and more editors today simply don't bother sending out rejections at all. This has prompted many writers to cease sending SASEs, reasoning that there is no point in wasting postage; however, I still recommend including at least a postcard.

Dear Editor,

I am writing to inquire whether you received my query for an article on [TOPIC/TITLE], dated July 27? In case you did not receive it, I have enclosed another copy of the query. If you did receive it, could you let me know when you might be able to make a decision on the piece?

Sincerely,
Moira Allen

Once you've waited the appropriate length of time without a response, it's time to follow up. I recommend using the same medium (surface or e-mail) that you used for your original query or submission. Your follow-up should be very polite:

If you're following up on a query, include the original with your follow-up letter. If you're following up on an article, however, it's generally not considered acceptable to resend the manuscript (unless the editor asks you to resubmit it).

If you still don't receive a response after, say, another two weeks, follow up again. In this case, a polite phone call is acceptable. If you still don't get a firm response, or simply don't want to wait any longer, you have the option of withdrawing your submission from consideration. This is particularly important if you've submitted a manuscript; you don't want to send it somewhere else and *then* have the first editor decide to accept it. Just send a short letter to the editor, like this:

> *Dear Editor,*
>
> *On July 27, I sent you a query [submission] regarding an article on XXXX [titled XXXX]. As ten weeks have passed without a response to my query or to my follow-ups (dated September 27 and October 10), I have decided to withdraw this article/query from consideration. [In the case of an article submission, I would add, "Please remove this article from your files."]*
>
> *Sincerely,*
> *Moira Allen*

Writers often wonder whether editors are annoyed by follow-ups. The answer is no. As long as you remain professional, following up on a submission will not harm your chances of acceptance.

THE EDITOR RESPONDS...

You might imagine that there are only two possible responses to a submission: Yes or No. Actually, each has several variations. A rejection, for example, might take the form of "no response," or a form letter, or a "check-list" letter on which the editor can check off one or more reasons for rejection (e.g., "something similar on file"), or a personal rejection. As I mentioned in chapter 5, a personal rejection is good news: It means that you impressed an editor enough to merit a direct response. Sometimes a personal rejection will consist simply of a few words of encouragement ("liked your style, but unfortunately, this wasn't for us"); sometimes it will include feedback on your article, and sometimes (the best news of all), it will include an invitation to submit something else. If this happens, do so!

Acceptance also comes in a variety of flavors. The simplest is a straight "yes"—either "yes, send the article" in response to your query, or "yes, we'll take it" in response to a manuscript submission. This type of acceptance letter may include the terms of purchase—e.g., the amount that will be paid, the rights to be transferred, and possibly a date of publication.

When you send a query, you may receive a direct assignment—a guarantee that the editor will buy your article. More often, however, the editor will say "yes on spec"—that is, "on speculation." This means the editor wants to look at your article, but won't commit to buying it sight unseen. This is usually the case when an editor has not worked with a writer before; often, your first two or three submissions to a publication will be "on spec," after which (if the editor likes your work), you may start receiving firm assignments.

In some cases, if an editor gives a firm assignment and then decides *not* to accept your article, the publication may offer you a "kill fee"—usually 20 to 30 percent of the amount that would have been paid for the article. (This is one reason editors usually won't give assignments to new writers.) Not all publications offer kill fees, however.

An editor may also respond to a query (or even an article submission) with a request for revisions. The editor may want a shorter piece, or a longer one, or a different focus. While it's perfectly appropriate for an editor to ask for changes to an article *proposal,* it's less acceptable to ask for drastic changes to a finished article without a fairly firm commitment to purchase the piece once those changes have been made. If an editor asks you to revise an article more than once (especially if the revisions are substantial) without committing to an acceptance, you may wish to think twice before doing the requested work.

Finally, an editor may reject your submission—but ask you to write something different. Such a request is evidence that you've made a strong first impression; often, it will come as a firm assignment, and may lead to others. In this case, don't feel bad that your original piece wasn't accepted; you have your foot in the door!

AFTER THE ACCEPTANCE

Once an editor has accepted your manuscript, the next step is usually the contract. Chapter 22 discusses the types of terms you're likely to see in a contract, and how to negotiate contracts. If you've reviewed a publication's guidelines, a contract should generally not come as a surprise; however, publications *can* change their terms without notice, so be sure to read *every* contract carefully (including contracts with publications you've already worked with).

While contracts can often be negotiated, this is *not* the time to ask for more money. For example, if you already know that a publication pays 5 cents a word, don't send in an article and then ask for 10 cents. Not only is it not likely to happen, it's likely to prevent you from ever working for that publication again!

If a market pays on acceptance, you should receive a check within 30 days of signing and returning the contract. (This is a good reason to have a fax machine, which can shave a couple of weeks off the process!) If you don't get paid within a month, contact the editor and ask (politely) when you can expect payment. You may also be expected to send an invoice; chapter 23 covers issues of payment in more detail.

If the market pays on publication, you won't see a check until your article is actually printed. While this may not be long when dealing with newspapers or online publications, it can be months (or even years) before a magazine publishes your article. If possible, therefore, try to get the editor to set a firm publication date. Generally, pay-on-publication markets issue checks within 30 days of the *issue* date. This means that if a magazine is published in October, checks may not be issued until the end of November, so you may not see payment until sometime in December.

Your involvement with your article often doesn't end just because you've signed the contract and gotten your check. Often, editors simply file accepted articles until they come up for publication. *Then,* an editor may decide that your piece needs revision (e.g., "please cut 500 words"), and send it back to you for more work.

You may also be asked to review and correct "galley proofs." These are copies of your article exactly as it will appear in the magazine. (Today, editors often send PDF files of galley proofs by e-mail.) At this point, you may discover that the editor has made some drastic changes to the piece—but unless those changes have resulted in actual inaccuracies, or have damaged the integrity of the article, there really isn't much you can do at this stage. (Your contract will probably state that the publication has the right to edit the article as it sees fit.) Your input on galleys is generally limited to correcting factual errors and typos.

If you feel that an article *must* be changed at this point, call the editor and discuss the issue. I once found that an article of mine had been significantly rewritten simply to shorten it; rather than accept the butchered version, I quickly rewrote the piece to the desired length—and the editor was happy to run my new version. Not all editors are this accommodating, but it never hurts to ask!

Finally, once your piece has been published, you should receive at least one complimentary copy of the issue in which it appears. Most magazines will provide two (or more) if asked; I always ask for a second copy, so that I can use one for tearsheets and file the other "whole." Newspapers will also generally send a copy of the issue, or the section, in which your article appears, while electronic magazines will send you the URL where the article is located online.

TRACKING SUBMISSIONS

Once you start sending out queries and manuscripts, you need a way to keep track of them. Otherwise, it's easy to forget that an editor hasn't responded to your query for six months.

While you can buy submission-tracking software, I find that a simple spreadsheet works fine. My spreadsheet includes the title of the article (or query), the publication to which it was submitted, and the date of the submission. Subsequent columns indicate the action taken on the article (was it accepted, rejected, or am I still waiting for a response), the payment due if any, and whether or not payment was received. Figure 16.1 shows a sample submission tracking spreadsheet; yours might include different columns depending on the information you wish to track. (Some writers, for example, also like to note the rights sold.) This type of system helps you monitor what submissions need follow-up, what articles have been submitted multiple times without acceptance (which may indicate they need retooling), and what actions you need to take (such as following up on payment).

Some writers create tracking sheets for every article they write, recording what publications each piece has been submitted to, and the results of each submission. Some do this on spreadsheets; others create a file of 3x5 cards (or larger) to track individual articles. Here's an example of an individual tracking sheet:

Another way to track submissions is to keep a "pending correspondence" folder. Print off a copy of every query or cover letter you send out (including e-mail submissions) and place it in this file. Keep the file organized by date. When you receive a response, pull the appropriate letter and attach it. If further information is needed (such as a contract), put the letter back in the pending folder; otherwise, transfer it to a "completed correspondence" file. Every so often, go through the "pending" file and follow up on those letters on which a response is overdue. At the end of the year, just file your "completed" folder in your permanent storage (i.e., take it out of your desk drawer and stuff it in a box in the closet).

Figure 16.1: Submission Tracking Sheet

ARTICLE TITLE	PUBLICATION	DATE	ACTION	DATE	ACTION	PAY	STATUS
Smithfield Hist.	VA Hist Monthly	1/10/10	Submitted	3/15/10	Accepted	$25	Paid
Writing Synopsis	The Writer	1/30/10	Queried		Pending		
Cancer in Cats	Whole Cat Jrnl	2/15/10	Queried	3/30/10	Rejected		
Victorian Christmas	Victorian Home	2/25/10	Submitted	4/15/10	Accepted	$300	Paid
Herbal Skin Care	Herb Monthly	4/5/10	Submitted	6/10/10	Rejected		
5 Detoxifying Herbs	Herb Lovers News	4/16/10	Queried	5/30/10	Rejected		
Sea Shell Angels	Country Crafts	5/15/10	Queried	7/25/10	Accepted	$175	Pending
Natural Xmas Decor	Country Sampler	5/15/10	Submitted	6/10/09	Accepted	$250	Paid
Newbie Writer Column	Byline	6/20/10	Proposed	7/15/10	Rejected		
Herbal Skin Care	Your Herb Garden	7/15/10	Submitted	9/30/10	Accepted	$250	Pending
Traveling with Cats	Cats & Kittens	7/30/10	Queried		Pending		

Figure 16.2: Individual Article Tracking Sheet
Article Title: Traveling with Cats

PUBLICATION	DATE	ACTION	DATE	RESPONSE	PAYMENT	STATUS
Cat Fancy	*6/15/10*	*Queried*	*7/15/10*	*Rejected*		
Whole Cat Jrnl	*7/20/10*	*Submitted*	*8/30/10*	*Rejected*		
Cats & Kittens	*9/15/10*	*Submitted*	*10/20/10*	*Accepted*	*$300*	*Pending*

WILL AN EDITOR STEAL YOUR IDEAS?

One concern of many new writers is that if they send a query or manuscript to an editor, the editor will simply "steal" the idea and write it up in-house or pass it off to another writer. This fear keeps many writers from even sending their work out.

Authors are also often dismayed to pitch an idea, have it rejected, and then see a similar article in the publication a month or two later. Such an occurrence often convinces them that their idea has been "stolen." In reality, however, this proves just the opposite: Since magazines work three to six months or more in advance, if the article "like yours" appeared that quickly, it had to have been on file long before yours even arrived.

What writers don't realize is how many similar ideas and manuscripts editors actually receive. If you've researched a publication and come up with the "perfect" topic, chances are that several other writers have done the same. For example, a pet magazine is going to receive lots of similar pieces on training, health care, seasonal material, and more. Nor do topics have to be identical to cancel each other out. If a travel magazine has recently accepted a piece on France, for example, it may not accept another for quite awhile—even if yours is completely different from the one on file.

I was once started to see what I thought was an article of mine under another byline. What had happened in this case, though, was that the other author had used the same *sources* I had used—thus producing an almost identical article! (The magazine had a new editor, who didn't know my article was already on file.) This can happen when writers rely on the Internet for research; two writers researching the same topic are likely to find the same sites.

Keep in mind that neither ideas nor information are protected by copyright. All that is protected is your article itself. Thus, even if an editor *does* "steal" your idea, this is not a case of copyright infringement (though it's generally considered unethical).

I won't state categorically that idea-theft *never* happens.[3] I will say, however, that such theft is extremely rare. Nor is it a reason to avoid the marketplace; your goal is to be published, and you won't be published if you're afraid to send your material to an editor.

---

[3]See "How to Protect Yourself from Editorial Theft," by Kyle Looby, at *www.writing-world.com/rights/theft.shtml*.

❦17❧

How to Write a Successful Query[1]

As editors become swamped with inappropriate submissions, more and more publications are closing their doors to unsolicited manuscripts. Thus, a query letter is often the only way to break into a market.

Queries benefit both editors and writers. Editors much prefer to review a one-page proposal than a ten-page manuscript, so queries usually spend less time in the slush pile. They also enable editors to determine whether you:

- Write effectively
- Have a well thought-out idea that fits the publication
- Have a grasp of grammar and spelling
- Have read the publication
- Have the necessary credentials to write article
- Are a professional

Queries save *you* time by ensuring that you don't waste energy writing an article that won't be accepted. As I said in chapter 5, articles are often rejected for reasons that have nothing to do with quality. If an editor already has a similar piece on file, a query will help you find this out *before* you spend time on interviews and research. (It's also easier to *get* interviews when you have a solid assignment.)

Queries also give an editor a chance to provide feedback on your idea. The editor might like a longer article, or a shorter one, or a different approach. He or she may suggest sidebars or artwork. By finding out what the editor wants before you start writing, you won't have to revise the piece later.

A query may also result in assignments you didn't expect. If an editor is impressed by your query but can't use your idea, she may offer you a different assignment. This can be the beginning of a rewarding relationship!

---

[1] An expanded version of this chapter, along with a variety of sample queries, can be found in my book, *The Writer's Guide to Queries, Pitches and Proposals* (Allworth Press, 2010).

ELEMENTS OF A QUERY

A successful query generally includes five basic components: The hook, the pitch, the body, the credentials, and the close.

The Hook

Your very first line must grab an editor's attention. It must demonstrate that you can write effectively, and that you understand your market. There are several ways to approach the "hook:"

1) **The problem/solution hook** defines a problem or situation facing the publication's audience:

   For anyone who enjoys decorating with antique or delicate quilts, care is a vital concern. Most of us realize that we can't just pop Granny's handmade quilt into the washing machine or douse it with bleach, but what are the alternatives? How can we protect fine fabrics from further dirt and damage? ("Caring for Quilts: How to Preserve a Perishable Heirloom," sold to Traditional Quiltworks.)

2) **The informative hook** presents two or three lines of information (e.g., facts, statistics), followed by an explanation of how this applies to the target audience:

   Thanks to a translation glitch, Microsoft was forced to pull its entire Chinese edition of Windows 95 from the marketplace. Microsoft recovered—but that's the sort of mistake few small businesses can afford! ("How to Localize Your Web site," sold to Entrepreneur's Home Office.)

3) **The question,** which is often is a problem/solution or informative hook phrased interrogatively, such as:

   Did you know…?

   What would you do if…?

   Have you ever wondered…?

4) **The personal experience/anecdote hook** is useful for a publication that uses more personal stories, or to establish a writer's credentials:

   Last summer, our beloved 15-year-old cat succumbed to cancer. Along the way, we learned a great deal about this disease and how it affects cats. ("Answers to Cancer," sold to Cats Magazine.)

5) **The attention-grabber** is designed to make the reader sit up and take notice—hopefully long enough to read the rest of the story. This might be a good "hook" for a query about parachuting in Yosemite:

   As I fell from the top of Yosemite's El Capitan, I wondered if my life would truly flash before my eyes—or if I would stop screaming long enough to notice.

HOOKS TO AVOID

Certain hooks are guaranteed to speed a query to the rejection pile, including:

- **The personal introduction.** Never start with a line like "Hi, my name is John, and I'd like to send you an article about..." Don't offer irrelevant information, such as "I'm a housewife and mother of three lovely children."

- **The "suck-up" hook.** Don't tell editors you've been reading their publication for 20 years; prove it by offering an appropriate proposal.

- **The "bid for sympathy."** Don't tell an editor how much it would mean to you to be published in his publication—or that your children will starve if you don't sell an article!

- **The "I'm perfect for you" hook.** Don't inform the editor that your article is "perfect" for his readers. Never declare that your article is "wonderful" or "fascinating." Prove it.

- **The "I'm an amateur" hook.** Never announce that you haven't been published before, or that your article has already been rejected by 20 other magazines, or that your friends/writing teacher/mother suggested that you send your article to this magazine. Act professionally, even if you haven't sold a single article.

The Pitch

Once you have an editor's attention, move on to the pitch. Usually, this is your second paragraph, and its purpose is to explain exactly what you're offering. If possible, your pitch should include a working title for your article, a word-count, and a brief summary. For example, the pitch that followed the "Microsoft" hook went like this:

> *I'd like to offer you a 1,500-word article titled "Internationalizing Your Online Market." The article would discuss how small businesses can take advantage of "localizing" agents to tailor their products and market strategies to the international marketplace."*

How can you estimate word-count if you haven't written the article? Simple. Find out what the magazine's preferred length is, and use that as your guide. When you write the article, you'll know how long (or how short) it has to be, based on those guidelines and what you've already pitched.

The Body

The body of your query should be two to four paragraphs that present the details of your article. Be sure you can tell the editor *exactly* what the article will cover; if you don't know yet, go back to the outline and research stages!

A good way to present your topic is to break it into logical subtopics—e.g., the types of subheads that might appear in the finished piece. The longer the article, the more subtopics you can include (though it's usually not advisable to have more than four or five). For example, a 700-word article on cancer in pets might only cover "The ten warning signs of cancer," while a 2000-word article on the same topic might cover "common types of cancer, warning signs, and current treatment options." A good way to determine whether you have the right number of subtopics is to divide your word-count by the number of topics: a 2,000 word article with five subtopics gives you a budget of 400 words per topic. Here's how I described the article on quilt care:

The article covers techniques of hand-cleaning delicate quilts to avoid damaging fragile fabrics and prevent fading and staining. It discusses ways to remove spot stains (including blood spots and rust stains from needles and other metal contact). It also discusses ways to mend damaged quilts without destroying the integrity of an heirloom piece. Finally, it discusses the best ways to store or display quilts in order to preserve and protect them.

Some writers like to use block paragraphs; others like to use bullets—as I did in my "Cancer in Cats" proposal:

My article will cover:

- *The types of cancers most common in cats (including mammary tumors and cancers of the mouth, lips and gums—some of which are preventable!).*

- *How to recognize the signs of cancer early (what is that lump?).*

- *The symptoms and progression of various types of cancer (weight loss, diminished appetite, coughing and wheezing can all be signs of cancer).*

- *The types of treatments available, pros and cons of different treatments, how treatments can affect a cat's life expectancy and quality of life, and how to find treatment (not every city has an animal cancer clinic).*

There's no rule on the best style; choose a style that makes your query visually appealing and easy to read.

The Credentials

Editors want to know why you're the best person to write the article you've proposed. The most obvious type of credential is a list of relevant publications. Note that I said "relevant:" if you're proposing an article on gardening, your articles on computer maintenance might not impress an editor. If you don't have relevant publications, cite your most prestigious publications, or cite the titles of the publications rather than the titles of the articles. (For example, you could write, "My work has appeared in *Good Housekeeping, Maine Parenting,* and *USA Today,*" bypassing the question of exactly *what* you wrote.) Cite only four or five publications, not your entire resume. Never cite unpublished credits, except for articles that are accepted and "forthcoming." Never cite non-professional credits—such as articles published in your office newsletter, letters to the editor, self-published materials (including materials you've posted on your Web site or blog), etc.

If you can't provide a list of publication credits, don't despair. Some editors prefer other types of credentials, including:

- **Education.** A degree or other educational background in the field you're proposing is always a good credential, as long as it can help establish you as an "expert."

- **Work experience.** One of my writing students planned to write an article on how to avoid building safety hazards into one's landscaping. His edge: He was a lawyer, and knew what advice to offer do-it-yourself landscapers.

- **Personal expertise.** Your hobbies may also give you the background you need to impress an editor. Another student sold her first article—a lovely piece on forget-me-nots—based entirely on her own gardening experience.

- **Personal experience.** Sometimes, simply having "been there, done that" is enough to make you an "expert." Just make sure your experience sets you apart from the crowd; offering a parenting article simply on the basis of "being a parent" may not be enough.

- **Interviews.** You can often sell an article on the basis of the experts you've chosen to interview. Just be sure you *can* get the interviews if you get the assignment! List your credentials in your next-to-last, or last, paragraph:

  My husband and I spent 15 months in England, and became adept at photographing inside dimly lit cathedrals and similar buildings. I have been a freelance writer for more than 30 years, and am the host/editor of the popular writing site "Writing-World.com" (which attracts over one million visitors per year) and the British travel site TimeTravel-Britain.com. ("The Chichester Cathedral Flower Festival," by Moira Allen, sold to British Heritage*).*

The Close

Use the final paragraph to thank the editor for reviewing your proposal—and nudge the editor to respond. I usually include the amount of time in which I can deliver the article if it's accepted:

I hope this topic interests you, and look forward to your response. If you would like to see the article, I can have it on your desk within two weeks of receiving your go-ahead. Thank you for your time!

FORMAT

The presentation of your letter can be as important as your content. A traditional (paper) query should include the following elements:

- **A decent letterhead** that includes your name, address and other contact information at the top (don't type it under your signature). (See chapter 2 for more tips on designing a letterhead.)

- **A business-style body.** If you aren't familiar with terms like "block" or "modified block," see the sample query at the end of this chapter. Always include a blank line between paragraphs, and don't indent more than five spaces.

- **A formal salutation.** Don't address the editor by first name unless you know him/her personally.

- **Clean, proofread copy.** Don't rely on your spellchecker; review your query yourself.

- **Quality paper.** Use at least 20-lb bond paper for queries. Some writers like to use neutral-toned parchment or linen bond (I do) on the theory that it will stand out. Don't use colors, however; pink or blue paper scream for rejection.

- **A SASE** (self-addressed stamped envelope). This should be a #10 (business-size) envelope, folded in thirds. Be sure it includes adequate return postage. You *can* use a "return address label" for your SASE, but I recommend printing out a larger mailing label. If you're sending a query to another country, include at least one and preferably two international reply coupons (IRCs), unless you can obtain that country's postage. (Writers outside the U.S. can order U.S. postage from *www.usps.com*.)

Needless to say, e-mail queries break nearly all of the rules listed above; the next chapter explains how to send a professional-looking e-query.

MULTIPLE-PITCH QUERIES

A multiple-pitch query offers an editor a selection of several article ideas at once, usually with a brief paragraph describing each. Such a query can often result in more than one assignment (though an editor will rarely accept *all* the topics on your list.) Since this type of query won't provide much detail about any topic, the editor needs to know that you're capable of fleshing out those topics in an article—so this is usually *not* appropriate for an editor you haven't already worked with. Here's a multiple-pitch query I submitted to an online publication:

Dear Debbie,

We've talked about several articles recently, and I wanted to find out whether you're interested in any/all of these:

1) Author chats—are they useful? I've talked to several authors who have given "chats" online. This article would discuss whether an author chat is worthwhile and how to make the best of one.

2) Teaching writing classes offline. This piece would discuss how to teach a writing class in a "real world" environment.

3) Teaching writing classes online. The follow-up to the previous article would discuss how to teach a successful online writing class.

4) Giving a talk—this would fall under the category of "promotion." I'd like to include information on how to prepare for a talk, and also information on the technical side—how do you give a good presentation? What will your listeners want to hear? What about handouts, outlines, charts, etc.?

An editor may respond to a multiple-pitch query with a request to pitch one or more ideas in more detail. In this case, you won't need to worry about a "hook" or "credentials" (assuming the latter have been established); instead, concentrate on explaining exactly what will be covered and how the article will be organized.

COMMON QUERY PROBLEMS

Queries fail for many reasons; here are some of the more common:

1) **You're trying to cram too much into an article.** An editor will immediately be able to tell if you have too many ideas, subtopics, subjects, etc., for the type and length of article you're proposing. For example, I often get queries offering to explain "how to become a writer" in 700 words or less! In this case, you'll need to focus in and define the central core of your article and write around *that*, and save the other stuff for other articles (or sidebars).

2) **You have too little to say.** Perhaps the topic is interesting, but you haven't found enough information to fill up 2000 words. In this case, the solution might be to offer a shorter feature or department piece.

3) **You have questions but no answers.** Beware of a query that includes phrases like "I'd like to explore whether" or "I will find out if," etc. If you don't know what the answers to your article's questions are, don't query until you've found out.

Queries can be sent by surface mail, e-mail, or (less often) by fax if a publication's guidelines specify that this is acceptable. Rarely is it acceptable to call a magazine editor to query (this is sometimes acceptable to newspaper editors—see chapter 15). Magazines work months in advance, so no idea is so "hot" that it needs an instant telephone response—and if an editor thinks you're trying to "auction" an idea by pitching to multiple editors, you'll get an even less positive response.

Sending an editor an inappropriate idea may not make that bad an impression (unless it's so far off that it demonstrates that you're *completely* clueless as to the content of the publication). Sending an editor a poorly written, badly organized, misspelled query, however, will convince that editor immediately that he doesn't want to work with you—ever. Think of your query as a letter of introduction, your first and (perhaps) only opportunity to get your foot through that particular door. If you make a good impression, you're likely to be invited back (even if your original pitch is rejected). If you make a bad impression, you may find that door forever closed.

Figure 17-1: Sample Query

Noelle Sterne
(address/city/state/zip/phone)

December 17, 20--

Ron Kovach, Senior Editor
The Writer
21027 Crossroads Circle
Waukesha, WI 53187

Hello, Ron—

Many children's authors may not recognize that they can draw on more publicity opportunities for their works than can mainstream authors. I became aware of this fact through the publication and extensive publicity, much of which I initiated, for my children's book *Tyrannosaurus Wrecks: A Book of Dinosaur Riddles* (HarperCollins).

The book was in print for eighteen years, has been widely used in schools, and was featured on the first dinosaur show of the award-winning PBS-TV series for children, *Reading Rainbow*. This episode continues to be aired nationwide on public and cable television networks.

Using illustrations from my experience with *Wrecks,* my proposed 2500-3000-word article "Let Them See Your Title! Publicizing Your Children's Book" describes over fifteen avenues children's authors can use to broadcast their names and titles and extend the lives of their books. These methods apply equally to commercially- or self-published authors.

The following venues will be discussed:

1. Schools, teachers' groups, PTA groups

2. Public libraries, malls, bookstores

3. Church and synagogue children's groups

4. Book fairs

5. Announcements and postcards

6. Websites and links

7. Book reviews in newspapers and magazines

8. Book donation to a local school or public library, with writeup in local paper

9. Parent- and child-oriented talk radio and television shows

10. Relatives, friends, neighbors, acquaintances, strangers

11. Article about the book for newspapers and magazines

12. References in textbooks for teaching reading

13. Excerpts in children's magazines and other media

14. Spin-offs (e.g., puppet show, t-shirts, stickers)

15. Sequels

As this list shows, children's authors can choose from a wide range of publicity possibilities, some of which have been little written about. If you are interested in this article for *The Writer,* I'll gladly send it.

Sincerely,
Noelle Sterne, Ph.D.

❧18❧

E-mail Queries

Today, e-mail is rapidly becoming the preferred method of approaching editors. Among electronic publications, that preference is nearly universal; many electronic publications don't even post a mailing address.

Both editors and writers find that e-mail queries save time and money. The writer doesn't have to spring for paper, ink and stamps—and when you hit the "send" button, you know your query will reach the editor in seconds rather than days. Since the editor doesn't need to draft a formal response on official letterhead, you may also receive a reply more quickly.

Don't assume, however, that just because nearly instantaneous communication is possible, that means that you *will* hear from an editor immediately. One common complaint amongst editors is that writers now start "following up" within hours of sending their original query, rather than weeks. Regardless of how a query is sent, a publication's posted response times still apply—and if that response time is "three months," don't start nagging an editor in three hours!

Another editorial complaint is that the instantaneous nature of e-mail queries seems to encourage many writers (particularly amateur writers) to spend less time actually *composing* those queries. Many e-mail queries seem to be dashed off with little attention to style or presentation—as if the speed of the medium inspires haste in the writer. Many are not proofread carefully (and not all e-mail programs offer spell-checkers). Editors also find that e-mail queries often tend to be less formal, more chatty (and sometimes even "cutesy"), than traditional queries—qualities that are rarely endearing in a query in any form. Just because a query can be transmitted instantaneously, that doesn't mean a writer should consider this an invitation to "dash off a quick note" to an editor and hit "send."

While e-mail queries contain many of the same elements described in the previous chapter, none of the format rules that are so essential to hardcopy queries apply. Instead, e-mail queries have their own format issues, which one ignores at one's peril. E-mail queries also contain unique elements that need special attention. Understanding these elements can mean the difference between an assignment and a very fast rejection.

ELEMENTS OF THE E-MAIL QUERY

The Header

With e-mail, you can't impress an editor with nice paper or a snappy letterhead. Instead, you must rely on a few lines within your header to provide vital information about yourself and your query. Your header is your "first impression;" make sure it's a good one by putting the right information in each of these sections:

- **To:** As with a surface-mail query, it's important to address your query to the right person at the right address. Try to locate the exact e-mail address of the editor you wish to contact. Some publications may have a specific address for submissions, such as "submissions@"—check the guidelines to be sure.

- **From:** You probably wouldn't think of signing a traditional query with a name like "Crystal Windsinger" or "Rafe Moondragon." If you use such a nickname to communicate online, make sure it doesn't slip into your professional correspondence. Similarly, if your personal e-mail address is something like "2hot2trot@wowser.com," consider setting up something a little more professional for editorial correspondence. (A simple first and last name typically works best; editors have seen too many variations on "WriterLady" or "PenWoman"!)

- **Subject:** Include the word "Query" in your subject line, along with a brief (two- to three-word) description of your proposal—e.g., "Query: Cancer in Cats" or "Query: Writing for Pet Magazines." Never leave this line blank. Avoid cuteness or excessive informality. A subject line like "May I have a moment of your time?" looks too much like "spam" and could cause your query to be deleted. (Granted, one writer did send me a query with the subject line "Of Confetti and Green Sunsets" and got published anyway—but not until her second try!) Never use words like "urgent" or "important" or "read right away"—these will certainly get your query booted to the spam folder.

The Text

The safest way to handle the text of an e-mail query is to treat it just like a traditional query, with all the "essentials" (hook, pitch, body, credentials and close) described in chapter 2. Such an approach will rarely go wrong.

However, one of the advantages of e-mail is its ability to save time—and many editors find that they prefer e-mail queries to be shorter and more concise than surface-mail queries. One reason for this is that an editor likes to be able to read an entire letter without having to scroll through a long onscreen "page." The less scrolling an editor must do to read your query, the better.

Consequently, many writers are turning to brief, one- to three-paragraph e-mail queries. The hook is often eliminated entirely; writers often begin directly with the pitch, followed by a single paragraph of description, and closing with a summary of the writer's credentials. Here's an example of a short but successful query to the UK women's magazine *My Weekly*. The author, Abby Williams, notes that this was her first successful pitch—and that she went on to write fifteen more articles for this publication!

```
Dear (editor name)

I am currently researching the growing environmen-
tal nuisance of plastic bags. I wondered whether you
might be interested in an article about this, firstly
advising readers of the global problem, its effect
on our natural world, what alternatives readers can
use (including photos) plus useful contacts, and if
governments/supermarkets are actually doing anything
about this problem. I was interested to learn that
turtles often mistake upturned plastic bags in the
ocean for jellyfish which they eat, causing either a
blocked digestive tract, or worse!

I look forward to hearing from you if you feel an
article of this type might be of interest to your
readers.
```

When crafting an e-mail query, therefore, give serious thought to ways that you can "condense" your information into a compact summary that the editor can view within a single screen. Just be sure that your summary actually covers all the points that you wish to make!

Credentials and Clips

It's perfectly acceptable to list your credentials in an e-mail query just as you would in a traditional query. Many writers, however, also use this opportunity to provide a link to a Web site where editors can learn more about the writer's qualifications, or perhaps view writing samples. Others list that information after their signature, or in their signature block (see below). You can't be certain, however, that an editor will actually check the sites you list, so it's wise to state your credentials explicitly, and offer Web sites as a source of additional information.

One frustration many authors feel with electronic queries is the impossibility of including "clips." (Never send copies of your published articles as attachments to an e-mail query!) Once again, URLs are usually the best answer. If you haven't developed an author Web site yet, consider doing so, if only to post samples of your published work where they can be viewed by editors who are considering your proposals.

The Address Block

In a traditional query, your name and address and other contact information would go at the top of the page (or be incorporated into your letterhead). In an e-mail query, it should go at the bottom, below your typed signature:

```
Jane Smith

1042 Gloriana Lane
Whippet, IL 60606
(555) 123-4567
(555) 123-4568 (fax)
janesmith@isp.com
```

By the way, do not assume that you no longer have to include this information on your submission itself! As an editor, I receive far too many e-mail submissions with no contact information (sometimes the author even omits a byline), necessitating backtracking through e-mails to locate that information. Your contact information needs to be included not only on your query but on *anything* that you submit.

The Signature Block

You may wish to use a standard "signature block" to include your Web site and any special credentials you'd like to list. This is a good place, for example, to list a book title that you've published. It's not a good idea, however, to include your mailing address and other contact information in a signature block, as you don't want that information to accidentally be transmitted or forwarded in other types of e-mails.

Avoid overly cute signature blocks, or blocks that involve graphic elements. Save the cats, dancing weasels, and emoticons for personal correspondence.

Format

There is little you can do to improve the standard, boring format of an e-mail query. What you can do, however, is ensure that your attempts at "style" don't make an e-mail query even harder to read! If, for example, you type your query into a word-processing program (like MS Word) and use certain types of characters (e.g., long dashes, "smart" or "curly" quotes) that you would use in a normal (non-electronic) query or submission, your text may come across looking like this:

Yet I'm not alone˜every writer I know struggles with "writer's anxiety‰. "First you're anxious if you don't have work, but then when you do, you're anxious about making it the best you can,‰ says fulltime St. Louis freelancer Kris Rattini, who's written for Family Money, Family Circle, and Boy's Life. "If it's a new editor, it's just intensified because you want to make a good impression and get more assignments.‰

To avoid this type of gobbledygook, be sure to observe these basic guidelines:

• Single-space your text.

• Double-space between paragraphs; don't indent.

• Avoid long blocks of text. Use short to medium-length paragraphs.

• Don't use bullets; they rarely show up as bullets on the receiving end.

• Don't insert any "format" commands (such as bold, italics, or underlining). Use asterisks to indicate *boldface*, and underscores to indicate _italics_ or _underlining_. (In a query, there should be little need for either.)

• Go into the "AutoFormat" menu and turn off smart quotes, m-dashes (—) and any other special formatting in both the "AutoFormat" section and the "AutoFormat as you type" section. If your text already includes smart quotes, you can then do a search-and-replace by simply typing in a quote-mark and/ or apostrophe in both the "find" and "replace" boxes and doing a "replace all." (For users of Word 2007, check the "Help" index to find out how to add the AutoFormat icon to your Quick Access toolbar, at the top left of your screen, as this function is no longer included in the regular drop-down menus.) Replace m-dashes with a pair of hyphens (--).

• Don't use any other special character keys—including accents, tildes, etc.

• Avoid emoticons, such as :) or <g>. Save these for personal correspondence.

• Never use HTML or other special types of formatting. Don't insert graphics. Don't use colors (either in your fonts or your background.)

• Use a readable font—at least 10pt. or, preferably, 12pt. Arial and Courier are good fonts for e-mail queries. Make sure your font size is set to "normal." If you're not sure how your font looks to others, e-mail a test message to a friend and ask for an evaluation.

• If you're copying and pasting text from Word into an e-mail program, mail a copy of the message to yourself first. I've often noticed that Word text, when pasted into an e-mail, may mysteriously lose line breaks, causing paragraphs to run together. By mailing it to yourself first, you can catch any inadvertent glitches before sending it off.

Attachments

In a word, don't. Many editors will simply delete unsolicited attachments unread—and with the number of viruses circulating on the Internet, attachments are becoming more unwelcome than ever. Your query should be contained entirely within the body of the e-mail itself. The same applies to submissions; never send an attachment unless you have cleared it with the editor first, and determined what type of file to send. Also, turn off any functions in your e-mail program that generate automatic attachments. (It's also a good idea to periodically check your e-mail program for viruses, so that you don't inadvertently pass along unwanted problems with your queries.)

The ability to contact editors electronically has made life much easier for writers around the world. To retain this ability, however, we must make sure that we make life as easy as possible for our editors as well!

❧19❧

Formatting Your Manuscript

Manuscript format should be a fairly simple issue. Yet from some of the questions I've received, it would seem that people like to make it complicated—from editors who prefer a particular style and therefore declare that *all* editors want the same style, to writers' groups who insist that one must use this font and that layout and so forth.

If conflicting advice on format has left you confused (and wondering if your manuscript will be rejected unread simply because you put your address in the upper right corner instead of the left), the following tips should help clarify the issue.

PRINT MANUSCRIPTS: THE BASICS

Most editors in any genre (articles, short fiction, long fiction, etc.) want a manuscript to conform to the following basic requirements:

- Good paper (20-lb. bond minimum, never erasable)[1]
- Double-spacing
- 1-inch margins all around (at least)
- A clear, readable font (more on this later)
- Paragraphs indicated by indents (tabs), not by an extra line space

Articles should begin about halfway down the page (some folks say two-thirds). Your name, address, and other contact information (phone, fax, e-mail, etc.) should be placed in the upper left corner of the manuscript, in a single-spaced block. The word-count of the article (rounded to the nearest 10 or 50) should go in the upper right corner. Your title should be centered on the page at the halfway point, in a larger font than the text (boldfacing is fine). Skip two lines, and center your byline (either your real name or your pen name) in a slightly smaller font. Skip another two lines and begin your article.

---

[1]Outside the US, look for a paper that is heavy enough that one can't read through it.

Running Headers are expected on articles, short stories, novels and nonfiction book. A running header should appear at the top of every page (except the first), and include the following information:

- Your last name
- The title of the article, book, or story—or a keyword from the title if the title is long
- The page number

For example, a running header for an article titled "A History of Feline Chiropractic Care" might look like this:

Allen/Feline Chiropractic/...2

Contest Submissions are formatted much like regular article or story submissions, with one exception: All your contact information should be included on a cover sheet. Do not put your name or any contact information on the first page of the story/article itself, and do not include your name in the running header. The cover sheet will be removed from your submission, so that the judges do not know anything about the author of the piece. (If you see a listing that asks for work to be submitted in "contest format," this is what it means.)

FONTS AND FORMAT

People get into heated discussions over what types of fonts editors prefer. Some claim that all editors want manuscripts in Courier (which looks like a typewriter font). Lately, some editors and writers have come to prefer Arial. So what do editors really want?

The truth is, most editors really don't care, as long as the font is readable. (In a survey I conducted of over 500 editors, 90 percent expressed "no preference" with regard to font.) Very few editors will reject your manuscript because it happens to be in New Century Schoolbook, Palatino, or Times Roman. Generally, it's best to use a 12-point font size, and to choose a font that doesn't squish letters together too closely.

The rationale for Courier dates back to the days when editors did an eyeball "guesstimate" of line lengths to determine exactly how much space a piece would fill in on the printed page. Courier is a "fixed-space" font, meaning that each letter takes up exactly the same amount of space. This made it easier to estimate how an article would appear when typeset. Today, however, very few editors need to do this.

Arial is a nice, readable font—but it is also a sans serif font, which many editors don't like. (To see the difference between a serif and sans serif font, compare Arial to Times.) Before you use this font, be sure your editor really, really wants it.

The bottom line on fonts is simply this: If your editor expresses a preference, or if you've heard through the grapevine that this editor is obsessive over fonts (some are), use the font the editor prefers. But if your editor has no preference, don't assume that he or she has one—and don't agonize over the issue of font.

ELECTRONIC SUBMISSIONS

Again, electronic submissions break nearly all the rules listed above. Many editors do accept electronic submissions, and some have complex guidelines as to exactly how these must be formatted. Some accept attachments (most commonly in MS Word—and it's a good idea to check which version of Word the editor is using); others prefer that the submission be embedded within the text of the e-mail.

If you're sending a submission as an attachment, you can format it just as you would to print it. If you are asked to include it within your e-mail, you'll need to follow the same guidelines for "removing the gibberish" mentioned in the last chapter. Here are a few more pointers for submissions within e-mail:

- Don't try to double-space your text; it won't work. Just double-space between paragraphs.

- Include your contact information (name, address, etc.) and word-count at the beginning of the e-mail, before the title.

- If the submission is very long, consider mailing it in two parts; some e-mail hosts truncate long messages. (At least check with the editor to make sure the entire message arrived.)

- E-mail the piece to yourself first to make sure it came out properly (that no paragraph breaks were lost, etc.)

COUNTING THE WORDS

Another issue that confuses writers is how to estimate the word count of a manuscript. You will still occasionally read some complex formula ("count the number of lines on each page, divide by X, then multiply by…")

These formulas are left over from the days when we had no easy way to count the words other than ticking them off with a pencil. They are also left over from the days when editors estimated the printed length of a manuscript based on such formulas. Today, using the word-count feature of your word-processing program is perfectly acceptable. You also don't have to be precise. If your article is 1562 words, call it 1550. If it's 1975 words, call it 2000.

OTHER FORMAT ISSUES

One space or two? Those of us who are old enough to have taken typing classes in high school remember the two-space rule: Put two spaces after periods and colons. Today, we are told to leave only one space, as modern typesetting programs don't need this extra space (which was helpful when type was "nonproportional").

While many editors today prefer that you leave only one space after all punctuation, the reality is that it doesn't really matter. If you're "old school" and automatically hit that second space, it's not going to result in a rejection. It's also perfectly easy, after you've finished your manuscript, to do a global search-and-replace and replace every double space with a single.

Should tabs be five spaces or less? Again, in the "old days" of typing, we were taught that tabs should be a standard five spaces. Most word-processing programs have default tab settings at every half-inch. To many writers (and editors), however, such tabs look far too large. There's no longer a hard-and-fast rule on tabs; just make sure that the editor can tell that a space *is* a tab. (I set mine at one quarter of an inch.)

To underline or italicize? The practice of underlining words to indicate italics also dates from the age of the typewriter. Word-processors enable one to indicate italics and bold-face type directly. However, many editors still prefer underscoring (it often makes text easier to read), so I recommend that one use underlining to indicate italics, but bold-face formatting to indicate bold-face text. However, I've never known a writer to lose a sale because he or she used italics instead of underlining.

One area that is particularly confusing is when one is indicating "thoughts" rather than dialogue. Although this tends to be an issue primarily in fiction, it deserves a mention. Thoughts are typically italicized in the final print version of a story or article (rather than placed in quotes); however, in your manuscript, you may wish to indicate them with underlining.

For more information on manuscript format, I recommend *The Writer's Digest Guide to Manuscript Format,* which covers different types of manuscripts, including poetry, essays, books, scripts, etc.

~*20*~

Do You Need a Cover Letter?

When you submit a hard-copy manuscript to an editor, should you include a cover letter? The answer isn't always obvious. On the one hand, a manuscript stuffed into an envelope all by itself seems so—well, naked! On the other hand, stating the obvious (e.g., "enclosed is a manuscript..." or "I hope you find this of interest") almost seems an insult to an editor's intelligence.

Cover letters can serve a purpose, however—and sometimes several purposes. Here are some tips on when to use them, what to include, and what to leave out.

WHEN TO USE A COVER LETTER

Under certain circumstances, a cover letter can be an important addition to your manuscript. Those circumstances will also dictate the content of that letter. Such circumstances include:

• **When the material has been requested.** It doesn't hurt (especially if you're a new writer for the publication) to remind the editor that this is requested rather than unsolicited material. Simply state something along the lines of "Enclosed is the manuscript you requested in your letter of (date) [or "that we discussed in our conversation/e-mail/whatever of (date)], titled (title)."

• **To provide supplementary information.** You may wish to note that you can provide photos, illustrations, contacts or sources of additional information. If a publication wishes to "fact-check" your article, a cover letter is a good place to list your sources.

• **To provide information about yourself.** If the article is unsolicited, use your cover letter to list your credentials, expertise, or other qualifications for authoring the piece. Or, you may wish to list the credentials of the experts you've interviewed for the article.

• **When you write under a pseudonym.** A cover letter is the place to provide your real name and address, along with the pseudonym you wish to use as your byline.

- **To provide a biographical sketch.** Usually, your bio sketch should be no more than 300 words (and more likely around 100 words), and relate to the content of the article if possible. (See chapter 16 for information on creating a bio.)

- **To provide a record of your name, address, and article information.** Your manuscript may be passed from one editor to another, and cover letter gives an editor an easy way to find your name and address even when the manuscript isn't on his/her desk.

- **To indicate whether the manuscript should be returned.** While the size of your SASE should be an indication of your intentions (a large SASE indicates that you want the manuscript returned, while a #10 envelope indicates that it can be discarded), some editors prefer an explicit statement of your preferences. (Editors have received angry notes from authors who wonder why their 20-page manuscript wasn't returned in their #10 envelope.)

- **When you have been referred to the editor.** If you have been referred to an editor by someone that editor knows (such as a regular contributor), mention this in your cover letter. For example, you might say, "Sue Jones, your nutrition columnist, suggested that I send this piece to you."

- **To offer supporting material that isn't included in the package.** For example, I recently submitted an article to a UK market, and promised to provide a sidebar listing various resources mentioned in the article—*if* the article was accepted. Since the task would have required extra time and research, I didn't want to provide it until I knew it was wanted.

If none of these circumstances apply to you, but you still prefer to include a cover letter, just keep it simple and professional and don't worry about redundancy. Your cover letter should be prepared in a standard business format (block or modified block), as follows:

Moira Allen
_____

1234 Mystreet • Mytown, MD 21111
(XXX) 555-1234 • (XXX) 555-1235 (fax)
editors@writing-world.com

March 15, 2011

Editor's Name
Publication
Address
City/State/Zip

Dear Mr./Ms./Editor Jones:

Enclosed is a manuscript of XXXX words, titled (whatever) for your consideration. A SASE is enclosed for your response; the manuscript itself need not be returned. Thank you for your time and consideration; I look forward to hearing from you.

Sincerely,
Moira Allen

Encs. (optional)

TEN THINGS TO LEAVE OUT OF YOUR LETTER

While a professional cover letter usually can't hurt you, an unprofessional letter can. Avoid, at all costs, a letter that might prejudice an editor against you, or convey the impression that you're anything less than a professional writer. That means avoiding the following topics:

• **Irrelevant personal information.** One of the cover letters that has stuck in my memory from editing days is the one that began, "Dear Editor, I am an unpublished mother of three..." Don't offer information about your age, gender, family status, or anything else that does not relate to your article. (If it *is* relevant, it should be part of your credentials.)

• **Announcements of your unpublished status.** If you have never been published before, that's fine—but the editor doesn't need to know this. Don't try to play on an editor's sympathies by explaining that this is your first article, or that you hope it will be your first publication.

• **Hype.** Don't tell the editor that your article is brilliant, thoughtful, exciting, inspiring, or "sure to please." Editors prefer to make these decisions for themselves.

• **Apologies about your article (or yourself).** Some writers actually apologize for flaws they perceive in their articles or in themselves: "I realize I'm not a professional wordsmith, but I hope you will like this piece," or "I'm sorry if my style doesn't exactly match your publication, but I hope you'll take the time to read this." If your article is flawed, don't send it—fix it! If your article is fine, but you have doubts about your abilities anyway, keep them to yourself.

• **Explanations of why you're sending material that doesn't match the publication's guidelines.** If your article is 2,000 words longer than the stated word limit, or written from the first-person POV of your dog, or typed on pink paper, don't explain. Rewrite.

- **An explanation of why the article differs from your assignment or proposal.** Sometimes a change is appropriate (you find new information, or you can't contact an expert you hoped to speak with). These changes should never come as a surprise, however. If you must change the focus of an article after it has been assigned, discuss this with the editor in advance.

- **Demands.** Don't tell an editor what you expect to be paid, or what terms you will offer—especially if those differ from the payment or terms specified in the publication's guidelines. (One of my favorite cover letters was a 3x5 card with the typed phrase, "I am a professional and deserve your HIGHEST RATES!") If you wish to negotiate payment or contract terms, do so before you submit the finished article (or after you become an established contributor).

- **Opinions of your family, friends, or writing teachers.** Editors really don't care what these people thought of your work!

- **A list of prior rejections.** Never tell an editor that a submission has already been rejected five times. Editors are likely to assume there was a good reason! And *never* imply that you hope this will be the "smart" editor who is able to see the merit of your work that others have overlooked!

When submitting a manuscript by e-mail, you should always include a "cover e-mail" that provides a basic introduction to yourself and the subject area of the manuscript. This cover e-mail should be short and to the point, just like a print cover letter. Be sure to include your contact information in the e-mail *and* on the manuscript itself; I can't count the number of electronic submissions I've received with no identifying information on the manuscript (including, even, the author's byline). One more tip: If you're submitting a manuscript directly to an editor electronically, do not put "Query" in your subject line. It's a submission, not a query—and an editor expects you to know the difference.

A good cover letter won't sell your manuscript, but it also won't hurt your chances of acceptance. A bad cover letter, on the other hand, may shoot down your submission before the editor even reaches the first page. So by all means, cover your work—and yourself—by keeping your letter short, sweet, and professional.

PART V

Rights and Contracts

❦21❧

Understanding Rights and Copyright

One of the most common questions I hear is "How do I copyright my work?" Copyrighting your work is actually the easiest part of writing, because your work is automatically protected the moment you write it down. Under current law, copyright on any work you've created since January 1, 1998 is good for your lifetime plus 70 years.[1]

I also get questions along the lines of "I have this great idea for a story; how can I copyright my idea so that no one else will write it?" The answer is, "You can't." Ideas cannot be protected by copyright. Copyright covers your "intellectual property," which means your actual written material. Similarly, the information that goes into your written material—dates, facts, figures, etc.—is not protected by copyright; anyone else has just as much right to use that same information in their own work.

You do not have to register a copyright for your work to be protected, and most writers do not register copyrights for their articles before submitting them. Copyright registration *is* necessary prior to filing an actual copyright infringement suit[2]—but the chances of needing to do this when sending your work out for publication are extremely slim. (Most such suits result from infringements of work that has *already* been published.[3])

---

[1] Copyright terms for materials produced prior to January 1, 1998 vary. Material written before 1923 is now in the public domain; in addition, some materials written or published between 1923 and 1998 may also be in the public domain, depending on various factors. (Anything published between 1923 and 1963 on which the copyright has not been renewed, for example, is now in the public domain.) For more information on when copyrights expire, see "When U.S. Works Pass into the Public Domain," at *www.unc.edu/~unclng/public-d.htm*

[2] If one hasn't registered a copyright before filing an infringement suit, one can only collect "actual" damages, which translates into the amount that an infringement actually cost you (e.g., in lost revenues). One cannot collect statutory damages or attorney fees. Statutory damages can range from $500 to $20,000, and up to $100,000 if the infringement was found to be deliberate.

[3] Traditionally, it was believed that a magazine's "collective copyright" notice counted as copyright registration in the case of an infringement suit; however, this is not always the case.

You have undoubtedly seen articles claiming that mailing an article to oneself counts as a form of "copyright protection" (the theory being that the postmark on a sealed envelope "proves" that you wrote the material prior to that date). "Poor man's copyright" is not a substitute for actual copyright registration and has no value in a court of law.

The cost of registering a copyright is currently $35 for online registration and start at $50 for paper registration. You can also register collections of material (e.g., a compendium of all the articles you wrote within a given year) for a single registration fee. For more information or to download registration forms, visit the Copyright Office at *www.copyright.gov/*.[4]

You can post your own copyright notice on your material, by including the following information at the beginning or the end of a document:

Copyright © 2011 by (your name)

It was once common practice for writers to put such a notice on any material they submitted for publication. This is now considered unprofessional; editors are aware that you own the copyright to your work, and consider this notice a statement of a writer's insecurity. However, if you plan to distribute your material to friends, especially by e-mail (and most especially if you plan to send it to an online discussion group or critique group), a copyright notice is highly advisable. While editors understand about copyright protection, average readers may not, and often pass on works they receive by e-mail without realizing that they are infringing upon the author's copyright.

A WRITER'S RIGHTS

"Copyright" refers to your right to claim ownership (and authorship) of a particular piece of work. It also means that no one can reproduce, sell, or distribute that work without your permission. You have the ability to grant that permission through "use rights." Licensing the right to *use* your work does not mean that you give up ownership of the copyright, unless you actually transfer that copyright through a contractual agreement (such as a work-for-hire contract).

Rights are generally transferred through a written contract. In the absence of a contract, a publisher cannot claim any rights beyond first or one-time use. For example, a print publisher does not have the right to post your article online unless you've signed a contract transferring electronic rights. Nor does it have the right to reprint your article in another publication or an anthology unless you've authorized reprint rights. It also does not have the right to sell your material to other agencies, or distribute it via other agencies. (I've heard, for examples, of writers selling material to local newspapers without benefit of a contract—only to find that the newspaper is owned by a larger syndication service that has distributed their material to other papers, without permission or payment.) Most

---

[4]Canadian writers should check with the Canadian Intellectual Property Office at *www.cipo.ic.gc.ca* (click "Copyright" in the left-hand column). British writers are not able to actually register their copyright with a government agency; however, there are private copyright registration firms in Britain.

importantly, a publisher cannot claim to own the *copyright* to your material unless this has been specifically transferred in a contract. (Chapter 22 looks at contracts in more detail.) Copyright law requires that any transfer of an exclusive right of copyright must be written and signed by the writer or by an authorized agent of that writer. (Note that an "agent" in this case doesn't necessarily refer to a literary agent, but rather, someone to whom the writer has assigned the right to handle contractual agreements, such as through a power of attorney.) Any rights that are transferred *without* an actual written contract are deemed to be nonexclusive.

Following are the types of rights most often used by periodical publishers:

• **First North American Serial Rights (FNASR).** This gives a periodical publisher (e.g., magazine or newspaper) within North America (including Canada) the right to be *first* to publish your work. It authorizes a publisher to use your work once only; it does not authorize a publisher to reprint your work in another publication (such as an anthology) or on a Web site. Note that you can only sell this right once (because only one publication can be "first"); thus, this is considered an "exclusive" right.

• **First Rights.** This term is usually used in combination with a specified medium or location—e.g., "first print rights" or "first English-language rights." It indicates that the publication has the right to the first use of your material within the specified medium or distribution area. Note that you can sell different subsets of "first" rights, such as "first print rights" and "first electronic rights" to another. Each sale of a first right (in any medium) is an "exclusive" sale of those rights, but such sales do not preclude the sale of other types of "first" rights.

• **One-Time Rights.** This grants a publisher the *nonexclusive* right to publish your material. This means that you can sell the same material to other publishers at the same time. This right is often used for reprints, and for columns licensed to multiple publications (such as newspapers).

• **Second or Reprint Rights.** Once you've sold first rights in a medium, your next sale of the same material will generally be regarded as a reprint and thus a use of "second" or "reprint" rights. Second rights are generally *not* associated with a specific medium, and are generally considered nonexclusive (meaning that you can market the same reprint to different markets simultaneously).

• **Electronic Rights.** Many print publications now want some form of electronic rights, usually so that they can post material on their Web site. Some try to claim that electronic rights are included in FNASR, but this is not true. Many don't offer additional payment for electronic rights, even though by using those rights, they prevent you from selling "first" electronic rights to an online publication. Some offer a percentage of the original fee (e.g., 25 percent) if the work is used on the publication's Web site. (See below for more details about electronic rights.)

- **All Rights.** This means everything: First rights, second rights, print rights, electronic rights, even movie rights. Once you've sold all rights to a publication, you've lost all further use of that material; you may not even be entitled to post it on your personal Web site. Many writers argue that one should never sell all rights, while others maintain that there are circumstances in which it is acceptable (such as when the material isn't suitable for reselling, when the fee is high enough, or when the publication is prestigious enough to offset the loss of rights). Some publications that require all rights will license back certain rights to authors, such as the right to sell reprints.

- **Work-for-Hire.** Originally applied to work created as an employee, a work-for-hire agreement not only transfers all rights to your material, but also its copyright. Thus, you are no longer legally the "author"—a publication can remove your byline, change the material, or even run it under another name. In addition, if you write a substantially similar or "derivative" article, you could actually be liable for copyright infringement.

- **International Rights.** In addition to FNASR, you can sell rights to other regions, based either on geographical boundaries or on language. For example, you could offer "First British Rights," "First Japanese Rights," etc. You can also sell "First German Language Rights" or "First Japanese Language Rights," which limits distribution by language but not by geographical boundaries. (Note that a license of "First English Language Rights" is actually more inclusive than FNASR, as it would include the right to distribute in the UK and any other English language-speaking country.)

Many writers are confused by the practice of some e-zines of posting a copyright notice at the end of every article or page on their site, and are concerned that this means the publication is claiming the copyright of the article itself. Actually, this type of notice is a publication's announcement of its "collective copyright" over the issue as a whole—*not* over individual articles or other materials within that issue. Each issue of any periodical is covered by the publisher's *collective copyright,* which gives the publisher the exclusive right to publish and distribute that issue *as an entity.* It does not give the publisher the right to use or sell portions of the issue in other ways.

ELECTRONIC RIGHTS

This catch-all phrase can cover anything from publication on a Web site to inclusion in an online database to publication in a CD-ROM or other electronic medium. The term has become increasingly associated with some form of Web publication, however, including publication on a print magazine's Web site, in an e-zine, in an e-mail newsletter, on a "content" or catalog site, or in an online database.

Web publication rights are generally considered to be "worldwide," as a publisher can't control where an online publication is read or "distributed." (Geographical rights refer to where a publication is read, not where it is published.)

Thus, terms like FNASR don't apply to publication online. Nor are you likely to see a contract that asks for "First British electronic rights" or something similar. Common electronic rights clauses include:

• **First (or First Worldwide) Electronic Rights.** This usually applies to publication on the Web or in an e-mail newsletter

• **One-time Electronic Rights.** Like one-time print rights, this is a nonexclusive clause that generally applies to Web or e-mail publication.

• **Web Publication Rights.** This specifically indicates that the material will be used online, not in a CD-ROM or as a download (such as an e-book).

• **Archival Rights.** This gives a publication the right to archive material (such as the back issues of an e-zine or newsletter) online, sometimes for a specified period of time but more often "indefinitely." Some publications grant an author the right to request the withdrawal of an article from the archive after a specified period of time.

• **Electronic distribution rights.** This gives a publication the right to market (distribute) your work to *other* electronic publications. For example, many print publications request this right so that they can sell articles to online databases (generally without passing a penny of the profit back to you!).

• **All Electronic Rights.** This transfers all *electronic* uses to the purchasing publication, but leaves the author free to market print rights.

While a print publication has a specific "lifespan" (e.g., a monthly magazine is deemed "out of print" once the month has passed), material that is posted online remains available to readers indefinitely. Thus, most electronic rights clauses include a specified *duration*. For example, an e-zine might request "first electronic rights for 90 days," which means that the publication will have exclusive use of the material for 90 days after it is published. Thereafter, the writer can offer it to other electronic publications. Some publications specify archival rights for a period of one year; others request such rights indefinitely.

Most electronic rights clauses also specify whether those rights are exclusive or nonexclusive. Print publications, for example, often request *nonexclusive* electronic rights, giving them the right to post an article on their Web site. Archival rights are generally nonexclusive. Most electronic publications may ask for exclusive *first* electronic rights, but do not ask for print rights, which means that you can sell the material to a print publication at the same time.

Exclusivity can be a tricky thing. While a nonexclusive contract can mean that you can offer the same material to other publications, you must make sure that none of *those* publications want exclusivity. For example, if you sell an article to an e-zine that wants nonexclusive archival rights, you could not sell the same article to a print publication that wants any form of *exclusive* electronic rights.

USE VS. PAYMENT

Many authors are confused over what constitutes a "use of rights." I often get questions like "How can a magazine own my rights if they didn't pay me?" or "How can putting something on my Web site be a use of first rights?" The answer lies in the issue of "usage." When you create something (such as an article), you own the copyright to that creation—which means that you have a bundle of "rights" that enable you and others to "use" that material in various ways. You can *sell* or *give* those rights to others, or you can use them yourself.

I always get a laugh out of guidelines that state that "all rights revert to the author after publication." This sounds nice, but isn't precisely true. If you allow another publication to publish your material, you have given up certain use rights—usually "first publication rights"–whether you're paid or not. The only issue here is whether the material has been *published*—if it has, then no other publication can ever be "first" to publish that work. A publication may give up any *future* claim to a piece, but the author can't reclaim rights that have already been used.

Using a piece of writing yourself can also use up certain rights. For example, if you post an article on your Web site, many believe that you're using the "first publication rights" to that article. (Many publications regard this as "prior publication," and treat such material as a reprint rather than a first use.)

Showcasing your unpublished works on a Web site is poor policy for other reasons as well. The main reason is that it can make you appear to be an amateur—someone who can't get published any other way. Contrary to the hopeful opinions bandied about in some writing circles, editors do *not* surf the Web looking for promising material on personal Web sites, and posting your unpublished material online is *not* an effective way to get it "picked up" by a publisher. Nor are editors interested in queries that invite them to read your available articles online—first, they don't have time, and second, such a query makes it clear that you're offering generic articles rather than material tailored specifically for the publication.

It's much better to post *previously published* material on your site, if you retain the reprint rights. (If you've sold all rights to a piece, you won't be able to do this.) Once you've sold an article or story, you can post it on your site with a notice as to where it was previously published, and use this as an online "clip." This can be a useful promotion tool, for it shows that you're a *published* writer—not just a hopeful wannabe.

PROTECTING YOUR RIGHTS

Knowing your rights is the most important step you can take toward protecting your work in today's competitive marketplace. But can you do more?

Some writers' advocacy groups say that you can. Such groups recommend "boycotting" publications that insist on all-rights or work-for-hire contracts, or that demand ill-defined electronic rights or lump those rights under terms such as FNASR. If you're faced with such a contract, such groups suggest that you take your work elsewhere.

Unfortunately, such tactics have little effect. With thousands of freelance writers competing for the same markets, publications have no incentive to change policies just because one or two writers decide to go elsewhere. No editor is likely to lose sleep over the fact that you, or any other writers, are boycotting that publication.

What you can do is negotiate, as tactfully and firmly as possible. If an editor seems unclear on the definition of a particular rights clause, educate that editor—but do so politely. If an editor claims to be unable to alter a contract, don't assume this is a lie; in many cases contracts are developed by a publication's legal department. If you can't persuade an editor to change the contract, attempt to negotiate a higher fee, or a specific "exception" to the rights (e.g., the right to use certain portions of the material elsewhere in a non-competing market).

In the end, it becomes a matter of personal choice. In every contract decision, you must weigh what you stand to gain against what you stand to lose. Don't let another writer (or group) tell you what you must or must not do. Only you can determine what is best for you and your writing career.

✲22✲

Understanding Contracts

A contract does not have to be printed on stiff paper with gilded edges to be binding. Nor does it have to be packed with legal jargon. A contract can be any form of document that spells out the terms of a sale, including:

• A preprinted legal document, with blanks for the name of the author, the title of the material being sold, and the fee.

• A letter of agreement. This may be an original letter tailored for a particular sale, or a standard form letter, or even an e-mail.

• A "fill in the blanks" or "check the boxes" form.

A verbal agreement can also be a contract—but the problem here is that the two parties to the contract may "remember" that agreement differently. Thus, it's always wise to put such agreements in writing.

A contract must be negotiated *before* the ownership of the material actually changes hands. In the past, some publishers attempted to claim rights by stamping a "rights transfer" clause on the back of a writer's payment check, indicating that by endorsing or depositing the check, the writer was transferring the rights indicated. In 1999, a judge ruling on the *New York Times Co. v. Tasini* decision (regarding questions of electronic rights) ruled that such a stamp did *not* constitute a legally binding contract, and could not be used by publishers to claim rights. However, other rulings have supported the use of check endorsement stamps—so if you do receive such a check, in the absence of a written contract that spells out the rights you are granting, it may still be wise to send it back and request a written contract and/or a check that does not include a rights-grabbing endorsement stamp.

Contracts may be transmitted by fax or e-mail. Faxed signatures are generally considered legally binding. E-mail is trickier; it may lack the editor's signature, and you'll have to print it out to sign it. While agreements may be negotiated entirely via e-mail (without signatures), doing so depends on a degree of trust between author and publisher.

UNDERSTANDING TERMS

Any agreement between a writer and a publisher should contain, at a minimum, the following information:

- **The title of the material being purchased.**

- **The rights being purchased**—e.g., first rights, FNASR, one-time rights, reprint rights, electronic rights, all rights, etc.

- **The medium (or media) to which those rights apply,** or in which the work will be published. Some rights apply only to print publication (such as FNASR); others apply to electronic publication; others apply to all forms of publication. Watch out for clauses that attempt to give a right more "meaning" than it customarily or legally has (e.g., by claiming that FNASR also includes the right to publish material online).

- **Payment,** including the exact fee offered for your material and when you can expect to receive it (e.g., within 30 days of acceptance or publication).

- **Your obligations and liabilities.** Some contracts address issues of accuracy, originality, and libel. Make sure that such clauses don't demand assurances that you can't reasonably provide. When in doubt, insert the phrase, "to the best of the author's knowledge" after such clauses.

Most contracts also include the following clauses:

- **A statement that the magazine is entitled to edit the material.** This is standard, and most publications understand that it means "within reason." A publication typically has the right to do any amount of editing as long as the basic substance and meaning of the article remain unchanged. Some editors take this as a license to rewrite your piece from top to bottom; if this happens, there is generally very little you can do about it.

- **An indemnification statement.** You'll often see a long block of text about indemnification issues. These are provided to ensure that if someone wants to file a suit about the article, it is filed against *you* rather than the publisher. Such suits don't happen often, but it's the sort of legal protection lawyers like. Again, if the statements aren't clear, insert the line, "to the best of the author's knowledge."

- **The right to use the material for promotional purposes.** Most contracts give a publication the right to use some or all of an article for promotional purposes.

- **A statement that the article is original and your property.** This protects the publisher from a lawsuit if someone claims that you stole his or her article. Again, this doesn't happen very often!

Finally, consider requesting a clause that states that any rights not specifically transferred under the terms of the contract are deemed to be reserved to the writer.

NEGOTIATING CONTRACTS

If you don't like the terms of a contract, it's always appropriate to ask whether negotiation is possible. Always be polite and reasonable. Before you attempt to negotiate, be sure you know what you hope to achieve. What do you actually want out of the negotiation? What are you prepared to offer? Are you willing to sell the range of rights requested for a higher fee? Or are you simply not prepared to give up the requested rights?

Keep in mind that the editor may actually not be empowered to negotiate a contract. In larger publishing/media companies, the contracts are often drafted by the legal department, and the editors have no authority to change them. If this is the case, you're pretty much stuck—but even then, some editors may be willing to negotiate while others won't. Again, it never hurts to ask—but if an editor says no, and seems firm on this, there is little point in pushing. Never hassle an editor or lose your professional cool; this will only result in costing you a potential market.

If the editor won't negotiate, it's up to you to make a decision. Will you accept a contract you don't like, or will you withdraw the article? Only *you* can make this decision. Don't let anyone else make it for you. You'll read lots of articles by writers who urge everyone to walk away from all-rights contracts. That's easily said, but if you're trying to earn a living as a writer, you may find that you aren't willing to do so. Your choice is your own; do not let someone else pressure you or make you feel guilty for your decision.

Understanding Your Position

• **Do not assume that you have to accept what a magazine offers or demands.** Many new writers feel that their first acceptance is their *one big chance* to make a sale. They don't want to blow that chance by getting picky over a contract. So, if a magazine asks for all rights, they'll take the deal. The reality is that if you're *any* good at all as a writer, you'll have other chances. You do not have to accept the first offer that comes along. If it isn't good, you can always walk away. Remember, if you were good enough to make *this* sale, you are good enough to make another.

• **Do not assume that a publication will blacklist you** (or worse, spread the word that you're a "difficult" writer) if you try to negotiate a contract. Actually, editors are well aware that it is the *more* professional writers who try to negotiate (because they are more knowledgeable)—so politely attempting to negotiate a contract will not harm you. You may not succeed, but it won't make you "look bad."

• **Do not assume that you will never use a piece again.** It's very easy to think that you have no other possible markets for an article, so why not sell all rights? I've done this myself—and every single time I've been convinced that I would never use a piece again, a market has come up for it. Granted, you may be able to rewrite those articles for a new market—but that's extra work.

• **If you don't understand what rights are being requested, ask.** I've seen some weird phrases—e.g., "multi-use rights"—that aren't intuitively obvious. Don't worry about appearing ignorant; chances are, the ignorant person is the one who made up the terminology in the first place!

WHAT *ISN'T* A CONTRACT

Certain things do not constitute a legally binding agreement, including:

• **A stamp on the back of a check** indicating something like "Endorsement or deposit of this check transfers all rights to your material to MegaPublishers Inc."

• **Writer's guidelines,** whether published in a guide such as *Writer's Market* or distributed by the company itself. Guidelines can be changed without notice, and are superseded by a written contract.

• **Your own notation** on a manuscript indicating the rights you're offering. Many writers like to put a notice at the top of a submission stating something like "Rights Available: FNASR." This means nothing; you should know *before* you submit a piece what rights the market requires. If you aren't willing to sell those rights, don't submit the material.

• **A verbal agreement.** In theory, such agreements are binding—but they're hard to enforce in court. It's wise to back up any oral agreement with, at the least, a memo or letter confirming the terms.

• **An altered document that has not been co-signed or initialed by both parties.** If you want to change a contract, you must obtain the agreement of the publisher; it isn't enough to simply mark out or revise unwanted clauses.

In addition, certain rights can be transferred *only* through a written agreement. If you have no contract with a publication, that publication cannot claim that it owns "all rights," or that your work was "work-for-hire." According to copyright law, if no contract exists, the only rights a publisher can claim are first rights (e.g., FNASR) or one-time rights.

Never let a publisher try to bully you into believing that it owns more rights than it does. (I once heard from a writer who was informed by his publisher that "collective copyright"—i.e., the copyright applying to a magazine as a whole—meant that the publisher owned the copyright to the individual articles in that publication. It doesn't.) Many publications offer contracts stating that they are purchasing FNASR—but then post material on their Web sites without any additional compensation for the writer. This is a contract violation; if you find that someone has posted your work online in the absence of a contract specifically transferring some form of electronic rights, you're entitled to ask the publication to remove the work or provide additional compensation.

MAKING YOUR OWN CONTRACT

If a publication offers no contract, it's wise to protect yourself by offering your own letter of agreement. Keep this as simple as possible, spelling out the terms you're willing to offer and nothing more. Such a letter might read something like this:

> *Dear Editor:*
>
> *Thank you for accepting my article, (title). I have received your check in the amount of ($), in payment for FNASR. I look forward to seeing my article in the (date) issue.*

If no publication date has been confirmed (and especially if payment is contingent on publication), you can use this letter to inquire about the anticipated date of publication. While such a letter may not be as binding as a co-signed document, it does provide a written record of the terms you have authorized.

Another good time to send your own contract is when you've been promised a contract by an editor, but haven't received one yet. If the promised contract never materializes, your letter of agreement should stand as the "accepted" contract; if the publisher later tries to disclaim that agreement, you can simply point out that no *signed* contract exists to supersede it.

SOME TRICKY CONTRACT ISSUES

While some contract issues are straightforward, others are more complicated. Here are a few of the more difficult contract questions I've heard:

Is it ever too late to get a contract?

Many writers ask whether it is too late to get a contract *after* a piece has already been published (and, hopefully, paid for). Technically, the answer is yes. However, in this case, the absence of a contract won't hurt you, and may actually be better for you than getting a contract "ex post facto." In the absence of a contract, the only rights a publication can claim (especially once they've already used your article) are "first" or "one-time" rights. Even if a publisher *tries* to claim (or use) additional rights, it has no legal basis for doing so, and you're legally free to re-use or resell your material.

What if the publisher never uses my material?

One frustrating situation that often occurs is when a publisher buys an article, pays for it, but never actually publishes it. Many writers wonder whether they have the right to resell that piece if it is never published by the original buyer. The answer is "it depends"—specifically, on the rights the publisher has bought.

If, for example, a publisher has bought (and paid for) all rights to your work, then you don't have the right to use it elsewhere, whether the publisher ever publishes it or not. By buying all rights, a publisher has also bought the right, in effect, to *not* publish your piece. Sometimes, for example, an editor buys something and then simply can't find a suitable place for it. In other cases, a magazine changes editors, and the new editor doesn't want to use the material purchased by the old one. When this happens, it's frustrating (after all, you want to see your work in print)—but there's really nothing you can do.

A more frustrating situation is where the publisher has bought *first* rights, theoretically leaving you free to sell reprint rights. However, you can only do this once the material has been published the *first* time—and since the publisher holds the right to be the *first* to use the piece, you can't sell it anywhere else until that first use has occurred.

If, however, a publisher contracts for your work but has not actually *paid* for it (e.g., the publisher pays on publication rather than acceptance), then you may have an opportunity to reclaim that work if a significant period of time elapses without publication. Keep in mind that a pay-on-publication market *can* take years to actually print a piece (and pay for it), so don't expect to be able to reclaim your work after just a few months. When dealing with a pay-on-publication market, I recommend asking the editor to include a clause that indicates approximately *when* the piece will be published. (Most reputable pay-on-publication markets now schedule articles before issuing contracts.) If the piece is *not* published on the specified date, you can then (a) ask the editor for a new publication date, or (b) ask for payment in advance, since the contract date has come and gone.

If no publication date has been scheduled and you've waited a year or more for the piece to appear, then you may wish to approach the editor and ask to withdraw the article from inventory. Since the publication has not paid you, it has not fulfilled its half of the contract, and you're within your rights to request to have the article back so that you can resell it. Keep in mind that not every publication will say "yes," but it's certainly worth a try.

Finally, if the publication was supposed to pay you but hasn't done so, *and* it hasn't published the article, then, again, it has not met its side of the contract. In that case, you're again within your rights to formally withdraw the article from the publisher's inventory.

In many cases, however, the sad fact is that you simply *don't* have any recourse when your article isn't published. If you've been paid, and you don't have the right to reuse the article, then often the only thing you can do is sigh and move on.

Can a publisher ask for additional rights to previously purchased articles?

A new, and nasty, tendency in the publishing industry today is to issue retroactive contracts. A retroactive contract is one that claims rights to *previously* published articles that were originally covered under different contract terms. Generally, a retroactive contract is issued when an author submits a new article—and is told that before the publisher will accept the new piece, the author must agree to sign over additional rights to earlier materials. Often, regular contributors are told that if they want to keep working for a publication, they will have to sign a retroactive agreement and give up their rights to older materials.

This trend toward retroactive contracts was launched when Jonathan Tasini, et al., filed suit against several major publications (including *The New York Times*) over the issue of electronic rights. The suit, filed in 1993, stated that the NYT and other defendants had sold electronic rights to various articles written by Tasini and others without their permission or a contractual agreement transferring such rights. The publications had a practice of selling their articles to various electronic databases (or, in one case, of putting out an electronic edition). Tasini et al. contended that this was an unauthorized use of the material. In 1997, a judge ruled against Tasini, but in 1999, an appeals court overturned that decision, and in 2001, the Supreme Court ruled 7 to 2 that newspapers and magazines could not sell freelance contributions to electronic databases without the permission of the writers.

Tasini, who was president of the National Writers Union at the time, heralded this decision as a victory for writers. The effect in the real world, however, was simply to motivate more publications to either institute all-rights (or work-for-hire) agreements—or, worse, to institute retroactive agreements that required writers to sign over all rights to all articles they had previously sold to the publication, regardless of the rights that the publication had originally purchased. In many cases, publishers told their contributors that any future sales were conditional on signing such a contract.

So far, no one seems to have challenged the legality of such a contract, even though it violates the basic principle of contract law—that a contract must *precede* the exchange of goods and services. The issuance of retroactive contracts has proven a major source of controversy for writers. By signing them, writers give up a huge chunk of rights—but by refusing them, writers risk losing important markets for their work. This is another one of those issues where there is no "right answer"—the answer depends on what is most important to you, in your personal situation as a writer.

Can I get my rights back if a magazine folds?

Once again, the answer to this question is "it depends." If an independent publication folds, then chances are that you can reclaim any rights that you originally sold to that publication. A contract ceases to be valid if one party to that contract ceases to exist.

A key question, however, is whether the publisher has actually ceased to exist. Many magazines are owned by a larger publisher—often, a media conglomerate that owns dozens of magazines. In this case, your contract may not be with the magazine itself, but with the publisher of that magazine, who continues to exist (and hold your rights) even if the magazine itself has closed. If a magazine folds, therefore, check your contract to see who actually owns your rights—the magazine, or some larger publishing entity.

If a publisher has bought all rights to your article, it will continue to own those rights even if the magazine it bought them for ceases to exist. However, such a publisher *may* be agreeable to a request to return those rights, particularly if the article has not yet been published. (For example, when *Cats Magazine* folded in 2001, its owner, Primedia, returned the rights to any unpublished articles to the authors.) If the article *has* been published, a publisher may be more likely to hold on to any rights it still owns, as it still might wish to produce a compilation of "best articles," or a CD-ROM of back issues, or some similar product.

If a publisher has not fulfilled its part of a contract—i.e., it hasn't paid you—at the time that a magazine folds, then you're in a much stronger position to request a return of your rights. A publisher is far less likely to want to pay you on behalf of a publication that no longer exists. If the work was to be paid for on publication, and has not yet been published, then the publisher would be unable to fulfill its agreement with you, and you should have little difficulty reclaiming your rights. If the work *was* published, but was not paid for, then the publisher would be in violation of its side of the contract, and should either pay you or return your rights.

In any case, the best approach in this type of situation is to *ask*. Many writers are afraid to ask publishers for their rights, for fear that somehow they will be blacklisted in the industry. This simply doesn't happen, and you won't get *anything* from a publisher that you don't ask for!

What happens to my work when a magazine is sold to another company?

Magazines change hands with frightening regularity these days, especially as the larger media conglomerates gobble up smaller, independent publications. Sadly, many of these buyers are interested only in the bottom line—bringing lots of money in while paying out as little as possible. When a magazine changes hands, its contributors are often left "in the lurch."

For example, when the online publication Allpets.com was sold in 2002, its new owners informed contributors that they would not be paid for any outstanding invoices. Many columnists were owed for two or three back issues, and were left with no means of collecting payment. The new owners claimed that they had purchased only the *assets* of the publication (i.e., the columns that had been published) but not the *liabilities* (i.e., the payments due to contributors).

I don't know if it's legally possible for a new owner to purchase only a company's assets and not its liabilities as well. However, I *do* know from experience that trying to collect payment when a publication changes hands is virtually impossible. In a situation like this, contributors have no leverage over the new owner; generally, the amounts involved don't justify taking any sort of legal action (in the Allpets case, for example, I was owed a whopping $50).

The same is true when a publication goes bankrupt (as Themestream did in 2000): contributors are generally going to be the *last* "creditor" to get paid, if they even manage to file a claim against the company to begin with. In a bankruptcy case, even if a contributor *does* file a claim, one can hope at best to gain only pennies on the dollar.

In cases where a writer needs to take steps to obtain an overdue payment, or to regain a set of rights, a contract can be both an enemy and an asset. A bad contract can be nearly impossible to overturn—but at the same time, having *no* contract can make it virtually impossible for a writer to claim a debt. A writer's best protection is to be able to understand and negotiate a contract—and, when necessary, to cover one's assets by writing one's own.

～23ҁ

Setting Fees and Getting Paid

O ne question commonly asked by new freelancers is "how much should I charge?" The short answer is "It's not your choice." While most forms of self-employment enable one to set one's own rates, freelance writing is the exception. In this business, rates are determined by the market and freelancers have very little control over what they are paid. In addition, most markets are notoriously inflexible. If a magazine pays 10¢/word, don't expect to persuade it to give you 25¢/word.

There are other ways, however, to determine your "preferred" rate of pay, even if you can't convince editors to loosen their purse strings.

BY THE WORD VS. BY THE HOUR

If you've come to freelancing from a "normal" job, you're probably used to a paycheck that was based on an hourly rate. Converting to an accounting system that is based on the word or the project can be confusing.

As you choose and plan your projects, however, it's a good idea to keep that hourly rate in mind. By determining the hourly rate you would prefer to receive, you can determine what publications to approach, what projects to accept, and how much time to invest in each project.

Determining that rate is a highly individual decision. If you're trying to support yourself entirely through freelancing, you'll need to set it fairly high (especially as you must take into account the number of hours spent on nonpaying projects, such as queries, researching markets, basic accounting and administrative tasks, etc.). On the other hand, if you're just trying to break in and don't need to earn a living wage, you can set a lower rate.

The next step is to determine how long a particular project is likely to take. In the beginning, this may not be easy; tasks such as interviewing, research, and revision may take longer than you expect. As you become more experienced, however, you'll be able to estimate a project's requirements fairly accurately. Then, setting your rate becomes a simple matter of dividing a magazine's fee by the estimated number of hours to see if it meets your hourly requirement.

Suppose, for example, that a magazine offers $100 per feature article, and you've decided that you want to earn no less than $20 per hour. In that case, you'd only pitch an article idea to this magazine if you were certain you could complete the entire piece in five hours or less. On the other hand, if a magazine offers $1000 per feature, you'll be willing to invest considerably more time and effort into that market. Similarly, you'll soon realize that a single $1000-article actually "pays" considerably more than ten $100-articles, given the same rate of effort per article.

Another way to look at your rate is by averaging it across assignments. Suppose you accept a $100 assignment, but spend ten hours completing the project. You've earned only $10 per hour, or half your goal. On the other hand, another article may bring you $600 for ten hours' work, giving you a total of $60 per hour. On the average, you're now earning $35 per hour, which exceeds your goal (and also helps compensate for all those hours when you aren't earning a penny). Often, "averaging" is a more accurate method of determining how much your time is actually worth.

WHEN TIME ISN'T THE ONLY FACTOR

Money is nice, but it may not be the only consideration when choosing whether to seek or accept a particular assignment. Some factors may be worth more than cash, including:

- **Credentials.** If you're just starting out, your first goal may be to build a portfolio of clips. In the early stages of freelancing, getting published is often more important than getting highly paid. In the beginning, a track record of success and acceptance can be more important than the actual fee.

- **Practice.** Some writers believe that every word they write makes them a better writer—and is therefore worth the effort. Writing for lower-paying markets can provide an opportunity to build and hone your skills, and prepare you for the demands of the "big time."

- **Reputation.** Some markets pay little, but offer extra rewards in terms of recognition and reputation. This is especially true online, where your work may be viewed by readers from around the world. Writing for a low-paying publication that will put your name in front of thousands of readers (and quite possibly a number of editors) can be worth more than the higher pay-checks offered by comparable print publications, and lead to bigger and better markets down the line.

- **Love.** Sometimes you may choose to write about a particular subject, or for a particular publication, simply because it's what you want to do. In many cases, passion counts for more than cash. Many writers would rather get paid a little for writing about what they love, than get paid big bucks for writing material of no personal interest.

Conversely, you may also discover that some projects aren't worth doing, no matter how much they pay. Some factors outweigh the potential financial benefits of a piece, including:

- **Difficult editors.** Some editors provide unclear guidelines, then expect the author to keep revising a piece until it seems "right." Some are impossible to please, even when you've provided exactly what was asked for. Some drag out the process by constantly asking for one more thing—more information, another interview, another sidebar, another revision, etc. Others won't answer your questions, provide clarification, or even return your calls or e-mail. Whatever the problem, a difficult editor can outweigh the benefit of a check.

- **Unacceptable alterations.** Few things are as frustrating as to write an article, and then find that the published piece bears little or no resemblance to your work. Perhaps it was edited by someone with no concept of basic grammar, resulting in a piece that you'd be ashamed to send out as a clip. Perhaps it was cut to half its length, wasting your work. Or perhaps material has been added— not only material that wasn't your work, but worse, material that actually contradicts the point of your article. If this happens, it's wise to avoid that market in the future, unless you really don't care what appears under your byline!

- **Unfair terms.** Only you can decide what terms you're willing to accept when negotiating a contract. Keep in mind, however, that even a high rate of pay may not fully compensate for the loss of your rights. Be very sure, when giving up all rights or signing a work-for-hire contract, that you have absolutely no chance of selling that material elsewhere.

- **Damage to your reputation.** Will an article make you look good, or bad? Sometimes the very context in which an article appears may damage your reputation in a particular field. If the publication itself is not reputable within a field in which you hope to sell more work, then selling to that publication could damage your career. It's also important to avoid assignments that might cast you in a negative light—e.g., that present an argument you don't actually agree with. What you say in print will be taken as representing your point of view, even if it doesn't. Your good name is worth more than any paycheck, and losing it can make you "poor indeed."

The bottom line is that "the bottom line" for a writer can be influenced by a number of factors, of which money is only one. By considering those factors carefully, you *can* set the rates you desire—rates that not only improve your bank account but also contribute to your ongoing career goals.

HANDLING "PAY ON PUBLICATION" MARKETS

Many writers refuse to write for "pay-on-publication" markets. This type of market pays the writer only when the piece is actually published or printed. However, pay-on-publication markets are often more open to new writers (perhaps because more experienced writers prefer not to work for them!). So it may not be realistic to recommend that you avoid such markets altogether. If you do write for such markets, here are some ways to protect yourself:

• **Try to get a commitment as to when the article will appear.** Ask the editor to specify a publication date in your contract.

• **Ask for a time limit.** If you can't get a specific issue date, consider having a clause inserted into your contract that specifies that the article will be published *within* a certain time limit (e.g., two years). If possible, try to include a kill fee if the material is *not* published within that time—e.g., if it isn't published in two years, rights revert to you and you will receive 25 percent of the promised payment. Not all magazines will do this, but *it never hurts to ask.*

• **Keep following up on the piece if it doesn't appear.** I'd contact an editor at least every six months to inquire about "anticipated publication date." Keep in mind that as long as this article isn't published, not only are you not getting paid, but you're also constrained from reselling the article anywhere else.

• **Withdraw the piece if it remains unpublished.** If your article is not published with a year, you may wish to consider withdrawing the piece from the publisher's inventory. I would give the editor one more opportunity to either schedule the piece, or pay you for it in advance. If the editor is not willing to do either, then you can send a polite "withdrawal" letter stating that you wish the article to be removed from the publisher's inventory, and for all rights to revert to you. Since you have not received any payment for the article, the publisher has not yet fulfilled its side of the contract, which makes it easier for you to cancel your side.

ASKING FOR MORE MONEY

While publications generally quote a specific payment rate in their guidelines, the reality is that most publications offer a *range* of rates—and the quoted rate is often the lowest end of that range. Editors and publishers know that *most* writers will never bother to ask if they can get paid a higher rate. Many writers, indeed, are afraid to ask such a question; they're afraid that it will make them look difficult, or demanding, or unprofessional.

Of course, asking for a raise *can* make you look unprofessional if you do it at the wrong time, or in the wrong way. Here are some *bad* times to ask for more money:

• **When you contribute your first article to a publication.** When you first submit to a publication, an editor expects you to have reviewed the guidelines and to be aware of the pay range. If the publication doesn't offer as high a rate as you want to receive, don't write for them! It's not considered professional to demand a rate higher than the posted range on your very first submission.

• **When you've accepted an assignment and your article is due.** As an editor, I've had more than one experience with a writer who promises to provide an assigned article—only to call on the due date to ask for more money before turning in the piece. Editors have a word for this: It's called blackmail. Essentially, the writer is threatening to hold an assigned (and possibly scheduled) article "hostage" for more pay. Occasionally, a writer may get away with this once if the editor absolutely *has* to have the article for that issue (if, for example, the cover has already been printed with a blurb advertising the article). However, you can be sure that if you try this approach, you'll never write for that publication again!

- **When you find that an article is taking more work than you expected.** When you agree to write an article, you agree to the terms. If you find that an article is requiring more work than you anticipated, that's your problem, not the editor's. Telling an editor that the article is "harder than you thought" simply looks like bad planning on your part.

The time to start asking about higher payments is after you've sold your second or third article to the same publication. By this time, the editor should be familiar with you and your work, and you may even be considered a regular contributor. If you're a reliable contributor, an editor will generally want to keep you happy—and one way to do so is to increase your rate.

Before you ask for a raise, however, take a look at what happens to your work after you submit it. Are your articles printed just as you write them, or are they substantially revised and edited? If an editor has to invest a lot of work in your contributions—particularly if the editor needs to clean up your grammar, spelling, and punctuation—then the editor may not be enthusiastic about giving you more money. Editors generally pay higher rates to the contributors who need the *least* amount of editorial work.

You also need to know the criteria for different rate levels. Some publications offer higher rates for articles that are more "difficult"—i.e., that involve more research, interviews, or in-depth knowledge. For example, a publication may pay more for an article that requires interviews with four or five technical experts than for a light, personal experience piece that you could write "off the top of your head." If you're writing "easy" pieces, start asking for more difficult assignments—and then ask for more money. For example, you might approach the editor with a statement like this:

As you can see, this piece required considerably more research than some of the previous articles I've written for you. It involved several interviews and a lot of fact checking. Consequently, I feel that it might be worth a higher rate than you have paid in the past. I note that your pay range is between XXX and XXX—any chance that you could bump this one up a bit on the scale?

Another approach is to ask the editor to move you from the "new contributor" pay range to the "established contributor" range:

I notice that your guidelines indicate that you have a pay range from XXX to XXX. I assume that the lower end of this range is the rate you offer writers who are new to the publication. As I've now contributed (X) articles, I'd like to think I've moved up to the status of regular contributor. Any chance that my pay could be adjusted to reflect that?

Yet another approach is to ask, flat out, what the criteria are for higher payments:

I notice that your guidelines specify a pay range of XXX to XXX. Can you tell me what the criteria are for the higher rates? I'd like to offer you the best possible product, and knowing exactly what you're looking for will help!

Keep in mind that not all editors control the pay rates. If a range is specified, however, chances are that the editor has a voice in what writers are paid, and it never hurts to ask. Again, don't let fear stand in the way. The key is "professionalism."

GETTING PAID

"Selling" your article is often only half the battle. The other half involves getting your check.

Some publications offer payment once they have received a signed contract. Others, however, require an invoice from the writer. I recommend sending an invoice even if it is *not* required—it provides a good record for you, both in case you need to take further action to get paid, and also so that you can monitor what payments are still outstanding.

An invoice can be a very simple e-mail statement, or a more complicated form. You can purchase invoice blanks at an office-supply store, but the easiest way to create an invoice is to simply design one in a spreadsheet program (such as Excel— see Figure 23.1). This way, you can print off your invoice and mail or fax it to the editor, or you can send it as an e-mail attachment (with the editor's permission).

Here's an example of a simple e-mail or text invoice:

INVOICE
DATE: (Date of invoice)
TO: (Contact name, publication, address)
FROM: (Your name, address)

FOR: (Article title)

(If the person you're invoicing handles several different publications, you might also wish to list the title of the publication the article has or will appear in, and the issue date.)

AMOUNT DUE: $XXX

(If the payment rate is per-word, include the word count here—for example, "2000 words @ 5¢/word = $100")

SSN: Your Social Security number, if this has not already been request-ed on your original contract. This will be required by U.S. publications of any author who is a U.S. citizen, even if you're not resident in the U.S. If you don't want to provide this information by e-mail, then send an invoice by fax or surface mail.

Send the invoice to your editor. Your editor is responsible for getting this information to the accounting department. If you don't receive your payment, contact the editor directly. The editor may tell you to send your invoice directly to the accounting department; if so, do this, but remember that it is *still* the editor's responsibility to make sure that contributors get paid. (Most editors are required to submit a payment list to the accounting department for every issue.)

But what if you don't get paid? If a significant amount of time goes by and you haven't seen a check, start following up. While a phone call is one way to follow up, I recommend *always* following up with a written request—either by e-mail or by surface mail. It's important, at this point, to establish a paper trail that indicates your efforts to obtain payment. Make sure that you (a) have a contract or a letter of agreement indicating what you're supposed to be paid and when, and (b) an invoice indicating that you've made an attempt to collect that payment. Save a copy of any correspondence you send thereafter. Submit regular invoices to the accounting department, and indicate the amount of time that has elapsed (e.g., 30 days, 60 days, etc.) from the date of the first invoice.

Most publications honor their commitments to contributors. Some, however, are slow payers, and respond only after a fair amount of nagging. And now and then, you're bound to run into a publication that doesn't pay at all, no matter how much you follow up. When this happens, and you've done everything you can do, you may be able to get assistance from a writer's organization such as the National Writers Union (*www.nwu.org*) or the Author's Guild (*www.authorsguild.org*). Unfortunately, you have to be a *member* of such an organization before you can turn to their legal department for help, and membership dues for many authors' groups tend to be high. If, however, you're trying to claim a payment of $500 to $1000, a membership fee will be well worth the cost.

Finally, until you're familiar with a market and know that it pays in a timely fashion, never submit a *second* article until you've been paid for the first! I've heard from writers who have submitted five articles or more (and even had them published) before ever getting a check for their first submission (or worse, never getting paid at all). Having a publisher express interest in your work is great—but make sure that interest is backed up with cash.

The sad truth is that there will be times when, even when you do every-thing you can, you will get stiffed. It happens. Sometimes publications change hands, and the new owners refuse to honor the contracts or invoices of previ-ous contributors. Sometimes a publication shuts down or goes bankrupt, and though writers can submit their invoices to the court for collection, they're likely to be the last creditors paid—and may receive only pennies on the dollar. And sometimes you run into a publication that simply doesn't honor its agreements.

When this happens, there is very little you can do. Generally, the amounts are not sufficiently large to justify hiring a collection agency or filing a lawsuit. The one bright spot to consider is that if a publication fails to pay, it has failed to honor its side of your contract—which leaves you free to market the material elsewhere. The best response to nonpayment (after you've exhausted every collection means within your power) is to move on, and to avoid agonizing over the loss.

❧ 24 ❧

Handling Income and Expenses[1]

Any income that you make as a writer is taxable—including article sales, book royalties, advances, etc. This means that you need to know how to keep accurate records of that income, and of your expenses that relate to writing. Generally, this income falls into the category of "self-employment." (The exception is if you work as a contractor for a company—e.g., doing business or technical writing—and receive a paycheck from which taxes are withheld. In this case, you would treat that income as "wages" rather than as self-employment income, even though you may technically be considered a private contractor rather than an employee.)

If you don't expect to do a great deal of writing, or to earn much money from writing (e.g., less than $1000 a year), you have the option of treating your writing income as "hobby" income. Hobby income must be reported to the IRS on the "Other Income" line on your 1040 (line 21). Hobby expenses (e.g., paper, postage, etc.) are deductible only if (a) you itemize deductions, and (b) those expenses exceed the 2-percent-of-income minimum. The only advantage of considering your writing a hobby is that you don't have to worry about such matters as saving receipts, keeping good records, etc. If you honestly don't mind giving the IRS more money, this is certainly an option.

If you consider yourself a "serious" writer, however— if you write frequently, and if you're hoping to increase your skill, your output, and your income— you need to think of your writing as a business. This is in your best interest even if, in the beginning, you do not make a great deal of money. After all, your goal is to make more later—so it's best to get in the habit of thinking (and acting) like a professional as soon as possible.

One way to qualify as a business is to make a profit in three years out of five. Even if you do not, however, you may still qualify if you can demonstrate

---

[1]Note: The information in this chapter applies to writers who pay U.S. taxes. If you're not a U.S. citizen, or liable for U.S. taxes, you'll need to check with the tax agency of your country of citizenship or residence for information on how to handle your writing income.

that you have made a reasonable effort to (a) make a profit and (b) conduct your business in a professional fashion. That means being able to demonstrate that you:

- **Spend a significant amount of time writing,** or engaged in writing-related activities. Your business does not have to be full-time, but you should be producing work regularly.

- **Actively attempt to market your work.** This means seeking appropriate markets and submitting to those markets (even if you're rejected). The best way to prove this is by keeping track of your submissions and responses.

- **Keep accurate and businesslike records.** This includes records of your income and expenses, and records of your work itself (e.g., tracking submissions, time spent, etc.).

Even if you're making no money whatsoever right now, these are good habits to get into, because they'll protect you once you *do* begin earning an income.

TRACKING YOUR BUSINESS

In the "business" of writing, good records are important in two areas: To track your work, and to track your income and expenses. Tracking your work means keeping copies of your submissions, cover letters, queries, and responses (see chapter 25). It's also a good idea to keep a running log of submissions that notes what the item was (e.g., query or article), when it went out, to whom, when a response was received, and what the response was. This log will also help remind you to follow up on items that have received no response.

Tracking your income and expenses can be just as easy as tracking your submissions. No fancy filing system or advanced bookkeeping degree is needed for this. All you need is a few folders or envelopes, and some method of keeping a running account of your financial transactions (see below).

To track your writing income and expenses effectively, you'll need to keep them separate from your personal finances. This means getting into a few simple habits:

- **Purchase writing supplies (such as paper, printer cartridges, and postage) separately from other supplies.** If you're making business and personal purchases in the same store, pay for them separately.

- **Store business receipts separately from personal receipts.** My method is to stuff each month's receipts and canceled checks into an envelope that is clearly labeled with the month and year. When the month is over, I close the envelope and (hopefully) forget about it. If I need an old receipt, I know where to find it. At the end of the year, I move that year's envelopes to a storage box in the closet and start a new set. Record project titles on your receipts, if appropriate. This isn't necessary for office supplies, but is useful for travel and entertainment expenses.

• **Store (and use) writing supplies separately from business supplies,** as much as possible. Granted, you probably won't swap "business" paper for "personal" paper in the printer just because you're writing a letter to your sister, but be realistic. If you attempt to deduct the cost of 50 manila envelopes and you can show that you've sent out 45 manuscripts, no one is likely to ask about the other five. But if you write off 50 and have sent out five manuscripts, that could raise eyebrows in an audit.

• **Open a separate checking account.** This isn't a "must," but it's helpful. It needn't be a business account (which often costs more and may require a business license); your best bet may be a personal account that charges no fee if you maintain a minimum balance. These days, I don't know of any bank that returns your canceled checks, but some provide statements that include images of those checks—or you may be able to access them online. Others provide statements that give a fairly detailed explanation of each expense debited from your account. Be sure to keep copies of your statements, whether you receive them by mail or electronically.

• **Consider investing in a separate telephone line,** especially if you conduct a lot of writing business (such as interviews) by phone. Again, this need not be a business line. If you use a separate line for business, the entire cost of the line is deductible; if you use your single personal line, you can only deduct the cost of the calls themselves.

• **Maintain an ongoing record of your income and expenses.** This can be as simple as a handwritten ledger (though I personally recommend using a computerized spreadsheet). At the minimum, your record should contain four entry categories: Date, Item, Income, and Expense. Whenever money goes in or out, enter the amount in the appropriate category. If you'd prefer to save time and effort at tax time, it's helpful to include additional columns that correspond to the numbered categories on the Schedule C (or at least those categories that you expect to use). If you use this method, it's best to "double-enter" your expenses: Once under the generic "expense" column, which will give you an ongoing total of your expenses, and once under the "category" column (such as "office" or "utilities"), which will give you a total for that particular category (see Figure 24.1).

• **Keep your records (correspondence, tax forms, and income and expense receipts) for at least three years;** some sources recommend seven or ten. While the IRS technically won't go back more than three years unless they suspect fraud, keep in mind that an audit may not be initiated until a year or more after a return is filed. (You can also scan records such as receipts. My personal method is to scan all my business receipts and expenses at the end of the year. At the end of three years, I dispose of the hard copies, knowing that I still have the electronic files in case of an audit.)

WHY ALL THIS TROUBLE?

Why is all this record-keeping important? After all, you got into this business to write books, not keep them! Some writers fancy that "words" come from one side of the brain and "figures" from the other—and those of us who are good with words just don't have a head for figures. That's about as accurate as saying "girls can't do math." Besides, we have computers to do the really hard work for us!

Getting into the habit of good bookkeeping is important for several reasons. Here are the top five:

1. **Good bookkeeping can protect you from an audit.** If your tax figures make sense, your return is less likely to raise a "red flag" at the IRS. When you track your income and expenses over the course of a year, you can recognize areas where your expenses are outstripping your income, and make the necessary adjustments. For example, if you're hoping to show a profit (and thereby demonstrate that you're truly a business), remember that there is no law against *not* claiming all your deductions, even if you're entitled to them. (You can also "postpone" some deductions until the following year.)

2. **Good bookkeeping protects you if you *are* audited.** I know; I've been there. Thanks to the fact that I had all the records I needed to support my claims (and knew exactly where those records were), my audit was neither scary nor particularly costly. I didn't have to worry whether the IRS was going to "uncover" some ghastly accounting or reporting error. Believe me, there's nothing like the confidence good records give you if an audit notice arrives in the mail!

3. **Good bookkeeping can help you determine how successful your various writing ventures are.** By tracking income and related expenses, you can determine which projects are profitable, and which are actually costing you money. (For example, if you pay a $50 phone-interview bill for a $25 article, you may want to rethink your marketing strategies.) Good records will also show you areas in which you may be overspending: If you're like me, for example, you may find that you're spending a lot of money on books about writing that you don't have time to read.

4. **Good bookkeeping is essential if you have to pay estimated taxes.** This occurs if (a) you have a tax liability (you owe money) and (b) no taxes are being deducted from your total family income to cover that liability. (One way to avoid this, if there is a wage-earner in your family, is to increase the amount of tax being deducted from that person's paycheck to help cover your self-employment liability.) When you receive a paycheck, your taxes are deducted each time you are paid; when you're self-employed, however, you have to make that "deduction" yourself—often long before you actually receive the money you're expecting. Good records are essential to help you figure out how much money you're likely to receive in a given quarter, and how much tax you're likely to owe.

5. **Good bookkeeping drastically reduces your stress level at tax-time.** When you've kept a record of your income and expenses throughout the

year, all you have to do is plug the totals into your tax form and you're done. Then you can get back to your real job: writing.

PREPARING YOUR TAXES

Believe it or not, declaring your writing income and expenses really isn't that complicated (most of the time). Let's start with the simple stuff, then move on to the exceptions.

When you operate a sole-proprietor business (such as writing), you declare income and expenses on the Schedule C. (If you have no more than $2500 in business expenses, only one business, no depreciation or amortization, and do not claim the home office deduction, you may be able to use the Schedule C-EZ.) The Schedule C is remarkably straightforward (for an IRS form); it asks a few basic questions, offers a few categories to fill in, and you're ready to go.

First, you'll be asked to fill in your name, address, social security number, and "Principle Business Code." For writers and artists, that's 711510. Your principal "business or profession" is "writing" (or "author"). Your accounting method will be cash; that means you claim expenses when you pay them (by cash, check, or credit card) and income when it is received. Did you "materially participate" in your business? Yes, unless someone else is doing your writing for you!

Next you'll list your income, which is all the money you've received from writing during the year. This includes royalties; don't be confused by Schedule E, which involves a completely different kind of "royalties." You'll almost certainly enter the same amount on lines 1, 3, 5 and 7; ignore the other lines. (By the way, don't assume the IRS doesn't know how much you earned: If you received more than $600 from any single source, that source will file a Form 1099 with the IRS declaring that income.)

DEDUCTING EXPENSES

Now for the fun part: Expenses. Fortunately, you can deduct any expense that is directly related to your writing efforts, including (but not limited to) the following:

* **Office supplies,** such as paper, envelopes, postage, printer cartridges, pencils, pens, computer disks, etc. (You can deduct these under "office" or under "supplies."

* **Printing and photocopying,** such as tearsheets, business cards, etc.

* **The expense of an Internet connection,** if it is used primarily for business. If you "share" your connection with other family members, figure out the percentage of time spent on business and pro-rate the expense accordingly.

* **Telephone calls related to writing,** such as calls to editors, interviews, etc. If you have a separate line, you can deduct the entire cost of the line (under "utilities"); if not, you can only deduct the cost of the calls themselves. If you have extra services related to writing, such as a "distinctive ring" number for your business or fax, you can deduct that as well.

- **Books, magazines, and similar materials** that relate to writing or research. This includes sample magazines for market research, and subscriptions to magazines relevant to your field or to writing in general (within reason). Books are a tricky issue: If a book is for short-term use only (e.g., if it is for research for a one-time project, or if it is an annual such as *Writer's Market*), it can usually be deducted under "miscellaneous." If, however, you keep the book as part of your "professional library," it may have to be amortized.

- **The cost of attending a writer's conference,** including 50 percent of your travel and meal costs.

- **Business fees, bank fees, professional fees** (such as the cost of an accountant or lawyer), fees paid to an agent, etc.

- **Dues paid to societies and organizations** that are related to writing, or to a specific area of expertise that you write about.

- **Taxes,** such as state and local taxes incurred on your writing income, and sales tax on large purchases.

- **Repairs to office equipment,** and rental of office equipment (such as a postage meter).

- **Classes, reference materials, and other resources** that are designed to improve your skills in your existing profession are deductible. Thus, once you have decided to establish yourself as a "professional writer" (even if you have made no sales as yet), you can deduct the cost of writing classes, reference books, magazine subscriptions, etc. (However, if you have not yet begun to do any actual writing, you may not be able to deduct the cost of a course designed get you started as a writer.

These are the simple deductions. Now let's look at some of the more complicated expenses you may incur as a writer.

Mileage

Certain auto expenses are deductible. If you can claim a home office deduction, for example, then you can also deduct the cost of using your car to drive from that office to, say, the office supply store, or on an interview, or whatever. If, however, you do *not* claim the home office deduction, then you can't claim the expense of driving from home to a work-related location. However, you may be able to claim the cost of driving from one work-related location to another. For example, if you drive from home to the office supply store, and from there to the post office, and from there to an interview, you could deduct the cost of driving from the store to the post office and from the post office to the interview—but *not* the cost of driving from home to the store, or from the interview back home again. (The drive to and from your home is considered "commute.")

For those mileage costs that you can deduct, you can either deduct "actual expenses" (by prorating the costs of maintenance, gas, etc.) or "mileage." Check with your account for the current per-mile rate, as this changes from year to year. (Auto expenses are handled on Form 4562.)

Depreciation, Amortization, and Expensing

Some expenses cannot be deducted directly. Items that have a long "lifespan," such as equipment, furniture, autos, etc., generally must be depreciated or amortized. This requires a separate form and some rather complicated calculations. In brief, some of the types of expenses that must be depreciated include:

- **Computer hardware,** including monitors, keyboards, printers, scanners, modems, etc.

- **Office equipment,** such as fax machines, copiers, telephones, answering machines, etc.

- **Furniture,** such as chairs, computer desks, carpeting, lamps, etc.

- **Computer software** (unless updated annually, like a phone disc or tax software); this must be amortized.

- **Books** that become a part of your permanent professional library.

The good news is that you may elect to "expense" many of these items rather than depreciate them over the course of 3-7 years. You can "expense" up to $17,500 of depreciable equipment (but not items that must be amortized) by using Section 179 of Form 4562. The amount you expense, however, cannot exceed your total writing income.

I've heard varying opinions on whether books should be expensed or amortized. My own accountant claims they must be amortized, but others say they can be expensed. When in doubt, discuss the question with an accountant (or two). So far, every accountant I've talked to agrees that computer software *must* be amortized *unless* it is something that you have to replace every year.

Travel

Some travel and entertainment expenses are deductible. However, this deduction is shrinking fast. Also, the IRS frowns on deductions that look like "I took a $5000 dream vacation to France, and now I think I'll see if I can sell a $100 article on it." If you're going to deduct travel, you'll do better if you have an assignment in hand before you leave (then you can claim that you're traveling for business purposes, not trying to wring a business deduction out of personal travel).

The Home Office Deduction

Writers are entitled to take the home office deduction, which is the "cost" of the space you use for an office. You can deduct a variety of home-related expenses in this category, including a percentage of utilities, mortgage interest (though not your mortgage itself), repairs, homeowner's insurance, homeowner's fees, etc. The percentage of these costs that you can deduct is based on the percentage of your home that is dedicated to business use. For example, if your house is 2000 square feet and your office takes up 100 square feet, your deduction is 5%. If you own a home, this deduction may also include a percentage of depreciation on your property.

Taking the home office deduction is *not* an automatic "red flag" for auditors, as many small business owners assume. It can, however, be a complex calculation—and it's not a bad idea to use an accountant the first time you attempt this. To claim this deduction, the following conditions must apply:

- **Your office must be a clearly defined location,** such as a bedroom, an attic, a nook, a closet, etc. You cannot deduct "a corner of your living room" or "10 percent of the kitchen."

- **Your office must be used exclusively for business purposes.** Pay your personal bills somewhere else, and don't use that space for personal storage. Clean the games off your computer!

- **Your home office deduction cannot be used to create a loss.** For example, if your total deduction were to come to $2000 per year, but your writing income is only $1000 and you have $400 in other expenses, the maximum home office deduction you will be able to claim is $600.

If you plan to sell your home, and you have been claiming a portion of it as an "office" on your taxes, you may find that you have to pay taxes on a portion of the income of your home sale. Since you have declared a portion of your home to be "business property," when you sell your home, a corresponding portion of the revenue from the sale is now "business income" (i.e., income that you gained by selling the "business" portion of your home). If you anticipate moving or selling your home, talk to your accountant about this issue before declaring a home office deduction.

ESTIMATED TAXES

While we all dread April 15, the truth is that taxes aren't actually due on that date. They are technically due *when your income is earned.* When you earn a paycheck, your taxes are deducted automatically. When you work for yourself, however, you don't have that advantage—and chances are that you will have to pay estimated taxes not only to the IRS but also to the state.

According to the IRS, you are expected to pay estimated taxes if your anticipated tax liability for the coming year is $1000 or more. For example, if, in April 2010, you were required to pay $1000 or more in taxes for the year 2009 (over and above the taxes, if any, that were deducted from your paycheck), then you will probably be required to file estimated taxes for 2010, *beginning* in April 2010. (In other words, you'll be filing last year's taxes *plus* the current year's estimated taxes for the first quarter at the same time.)

Estimated taxes are due quarterly, beginning in April. The problem, of course, is that you must pay them in advance—i.e., before you actually know what your income will be. As a writer, it's often difficult to predict one's income from one quarter to the next, but that's exactly what you're expected to do. It's better to overestimate than underestimate; refunds are better than penalties.

If your writing is not your sole source of support, or if you or someone else in your household is earning a paycheck, one way to reduce your estimated tax liability is to increase the withholding tax on that paycheck. While that may mean slightly less cash now, it can help offset your tax burden later.

According to the IRS, you can also pay your self-employment tax (another little goody you'll be hit with when you make a profit as a writer) through estimated taxes.

SURVIVING AN AUDIT

The thought of an audit seems terrifying, but in fact they are not that common. Audits are more common in some regions than in others (Las Vegas and Los Angeles are high on the list). Don't let the fear of an audit prevent you from establishing a writing business. And even if you are audited (as I have been), the event is not as terrifying as you might think. Your best defense against an audit is good records.

• Keep all expense receipts; never claim a deduction you can't verify.

• Make sure you know where your receipts are. File receipts by month and by year.

• Keep copies of all writing correspondence, which proves that you are "working."

• Make sure your ledger numbers are accurate.

• Don't make stupid claims, like huge travel expenses that will get an auditor's attention.

• Don't give an auditor more than he or she asks for. Simply provide the requested receipts.

• Don't panic!

GET AN ACCOUNTANT!

When it comes to the more complicated aspects of tax preparation, such as depreciation, amortization, mileage credits, the home office deduction, etc., there is often no substitute for a good accountant. Yes, an accountant costs money. On the other hand, so does an audit (usually), and an accountant is usually far more friendly than an IRS agent. The IRS is also (theoretically) somewhat less likely to audit small business returns prepared by an accountant, because these are (theoretically) less likely to contain errors than returns prepared by the taxpayer.

A somewhat less expensive approach is to use an automated service such as Turbotax. I have moved to this approach myself for the first time this past year—but only after having had my taxes prepared by an accountant for many years, so that I'm not only familiar with the types of deductions that I can claim, but what forms I need and how to fill them out. I would recommend using an

Figure 24.1: Sample Income/Expense Tracking Spreadsheet

DATE	DESCRIPTION	INCOME	EXPENSES	OFF/SUPP	POSTAGE	INTERNET	BOOKS	DUES/PUBS	PROMOTION	UTIL	MISC
2-Jan	Web hosting renewal		$100.00			$100.00					
3-Jan	Article: Tuscarora Times	$25.00									
4-Jan	Cats Article	$225.00									
11-Jan	Sample magazines		$13.29					$13.29			
13-Jan	Comcast		$45.95			$45.95					
15-Jan	Business cards		$25.00						$25.00		
17-Jan	Phone bill		$23.62							$23.62	
18-Jan	Lulu Royalties	$18.82									
20-Jan	Writer Article	$400.00									
21-Jan	Cat care book		$17.74				$17.74				
25-Jan	Paper and envelopes		$43.50	$43.50							
28-Jan	Amazon Affiliate	$75.19									
28-Jan	Domain name renewal		$44.00			$44.00					
29-Jan	ETS	$300.00									
28-Feb	Postage		$9.82		$9.82						
INC	$1,044.01										
EXP	$322.92	(Note: tracking Profit and Loss by month is optional but useful for keeping track of progress)									
P/L	$721.09										

DATE	DESCRIPTION	INCOME	EXPENSES	OFF/SUPP	POSTAGE	INTERNET	BOOKS	DUES/PUBS	PROMOTION	UTIL	MISC
5-Feb	Book		$37.20				$37.20				
10-Feb	Lulu Royalties	$37.52									
12-Feb	Lulu	$6.25									
15-Feb	Computer repair		$80.00								$80.00
16-Feb	Comcast		$45.95			$45.95					
17-Feb	Phone bill		$23.62							$23.62	
21-Feb	Book Royalties	$569.00									
23-Feb	Camera batteries, case, etc		$30.00	$30.00							
24-Feb	Amazon Affiliate	$183.45									
25-Feb	British Heritage	$800.00									
25-Feb	Printer cartridges		$39.95	$39.95							
26-Feb	Bookmarks		$27.76						$27.76		
27-Feb	Postage		$4.99		$4.99						
28-Feb	Google AdSense	$30.85									
	INC	$1,627.07									
	EXP	$289.47									
	P/L	$1,337.60									
2010	PROFIT/LOSS	INCOME	EXPENSES	Editorial	PayPal	Pubs	Postage	Internet	Prof	Misc	Util
	$2,058.69	$2,671.08	$612.39	$113.45	$14.81	$235.90	$54.94	$13.29	$52.76	$47.24	$80.00
		$612.39									

(This "check sum" figure totals the subtotals of each column to make sure that they have the same total as the expense column--this cross-checks for entry errors.)

accountant during your first year or two of business—and then, if you feel sufficiently confident, consider striking out on your own.

Notes on Figure 24.1:

- The categories listed on this spreadsheet are: Supplies, Postage, Internet, Utilities, Dues, Books, Promotional, and Misc. You may find that you need different categories. A good rule of thumb is to create a category for any type of expense that exceeds $10 per month. One place to start is to look at the categories actually listed on the Schedule C; however, many of these often don't apply to writers, and writers may also find that so many of their expenses fall under the "miscellaneous" category (there is, for example, no Schedule C expense category for "postage") that it's easier to develop your own. (If any subcategory of "miscellaneous" expenses exceeds, say, $50 per year, it's wise to spell out the nature of this category rather than presenting the IRS with a large and undefined "miscellaneous" expense deduction.)

- Year-end totals are achieved by totaling each column. The Profit/Loss for the year is, of course, the total income minus total expenses.

- It's not necessary to create a subtotal for each month. However, I find this useful for tracking my progress over time.

- I also run a "check sum" figure at the end of the spreadsheet. This figure is the sum of the totals of each individual "expense" column.

- Compare this figure to the total of the main expense column to make sure they match; if they don't, an item has been entered incorrectly in one of the expense columns.

ঙ 25 ঞ

Keeping Records

One thing you're bound to produce as a writer is *lots* of paper. Forget the concept of the "paperless office"—while you may find that you can store *some* records on your computer, you're still going to amass large quantities of files.

Sooner or later, you're going to start asking yourself how much of that paper you actually need to keep. The quick and easy answer is: every file that relates directly to your writing business. That includes the following:

Contracts and Letters of Agreement
Whenever you sell a "work" (an article, story, poem, book, whatever), you should have some sort of written agreement with the purchaser. Sometimes this will be a formal contract; in other cases, it may be little more than a letter saying, "Thanks for sending this; yes, we'd love to use it." If you don't receive even that much, create your own letter of agreement specifying the rights you're licensing. For the greatest degree of protection, ask your editor to countersign a copy of this letter and send it back to you.

Such contracts and agreements may be your only evidence, in later years, that you sold (or did *not* sell) a specific set of rights. If you have no record of the terms under which your material was published, it will be very difficult for you to prove the terms of that agreement.

Keep these contracts *forever.* You don't need a fancy filing system for them; a simple folder marked "contracts" should be enough. If you have lots of contracts, consider investing in an expanding pocket folder with alphabetical dividers, so that you can file your contracts by publication name. Never assume that you won't need a copy of that contract in later years; stuff of mine is appearing online that I sold decades ago!

Correspondence
Granted, a lot of your writing correspondence looks pretty trivial: "Do you want to buy this article?" "No." Even rejection letters are important, however. If nothing else, they demonstrate to the IRS (in case of an audit) that you really

are attempting to conduct a writing business. Acceptance letters are even more important: Often, they spell out the terms of the sale. If so, put them in your "contracts" file.

While it may be tempting to set up alphabetical files for your correspondence, I've never found this necessary. My own system consists of two folders: "Pending" and "Completed." Once a response arrives to a letter in the "pending" file, I staple it to my outgoing letter and file both in the "Completed" file. At the end of the year, I label the Completed folder for that year (e.g., "Correspondence 2010") and store it in a file box in my closet. If my correspondence becomes too much for a single folder, I subdivide it into "acceptances," rejections," and "everything else"—all of which get stored in the box at the end of the year. You may never have to touch these files again—but you never know! (A note for those who live in wet climates: Don't store your files in a garage, cellar, or other non-insulated room. Keep them where they won't be damaged by damp.)

Invoices

If you regularly send out invoices to editors, you may want to store these separately from your regular correspondence. You may also want two folders: One for pending invoices, and one for paid invoices. If you want to subdivide these alphabetically, fine; otherwise, a single "paid" folder will usually suffice for a single year of invoices.

Clips

Rare is the writer who doesn't preserve copies of everything he or she has ever published! This is your "clip" file, which you can use both as a portfolio and as a way to store and file clips that you want to copy and send with queries. I recommend getting a nice leather binder (which you'll find in the briefcase section of office supply stores) for your "display" portfolio—this will be the place to file your best (and most recent) clips. Eventually, it will overflow, and you can store older and less prestigious clips in regular binders.

Use plastic page protectors—the kind that has an extra strip on the side for the binder holes—to store your clips. If these include newspaper articles, I recommend cutting out the article and arranging it so that it will fit on one or more sheets of regular paper; then, photocopy it. Photocopies last longer than newspaper clippings, and this will make your article easier to read and copy. Then, when you need to make a copy of a clip, you can photocopy it directly through the page protector. (Don't bother with color copies unless the article includes your own artwork or photography.)

In addition, you may want to keep copies of the actual magazines in which your work appears. I always ask publications to send *two* complimentary copies; I pull my clips from one and store the other whole as a backup. Store your magazines in magazine holders, or in a file box; you can also purchase individual plastic magazine-protectors at a comic book shop.

Many writers like to post clips on their Web site. This is fine if you still own the electronic rights; if, however, you've sold all rights, or all electronic rights, you technically no longer have the right to do this. There are two ways to post clips to your site: As HTML files (usually from the original electronic document), or as scanned PDF files. Keep in mind that if you scan a clip from a magazine, it might include elements (such as photos, or portions of other articles) to which you do not own copyright—so you might want to check with the publication for permission before posting a scanned PDF on your Web site. If you wish to post the original document, make sure the published version hasn't been changed significantly from your original, or you aren't really posting a "clip" at all. If the document has been changed, see if you can get a copy of the final, edited version from your editor.

I recommend scanning your clips and saving them as PDF files regardless of whether you wish to post them on your site. Making high-quality electronic copies ensures that you will always have a copy of your clip even if something happens to the paper file. It also makes it easy to simply print out a copy of the PDF file whenever you wish to send a copy of the clip to an editor. Paper copies (particularly of newspaper articles) may also deteriorate over time, and this will ensure that you always have a clean, fresh copy. Finally, eventually (yes, this can happen to you!) you'll have so many clips that you don't want to keep all that paper on file.

Manuscripts

Should you keep your old manuscripts forever? Once, I would have said, "don't bother." That was before I tried to submit a fairly ancient reprint, and realized that I had only the published version of the article available—a version that had been considerably butchered by a grammatically challenged editor. Since I no longer had the original, I couldn't resubmit what I'd actually written; I had to reconstruct the piece from another editor's hatchet job.

Fortunately, most of our manuscripts are electronic these days, so we don't have to worry about saving boxes and boxes of published (or unpublished) works. Just be sure to back up your manuscript files on disk periodically, or a computer crash could wipe out your life's work in a blink of an electron.

KEEPING ELECTRONIC RECORDS

Chances are, most of your writing and much of your correspondence is handled electronically nowadays. That's great from the standpoint of saving trees (and space in the back of your closet). However, it does present a risk: A computer failure can irretrievably wipe out your most important records. It can also be difficult to locate important correspondence in a confusion of e-mail folders.

The key to keeping good electronic files is to resist the temptation to purge them. It's very easy to think that you'll never need a particular e-mail record—only to find, months later, that it had a vital bit of information that is now lost to you forever. If nothing else, keep an "archive" folder in your e-mail system that stores copies of every writing-related bit of e-mail you send or receive.

Did I mention the importance of *backing up* these files periodically? While I often fail to practice what I am about to preach, I cannot emphasize enough the importance of making regular backups of *everything* that might be relevant to your writing records.

Fortunately, these days it's easier than ever to back up your files. I recommend investing in an inexpensive portable hard drive; you can get a 500-GB drive that fits in the palm of your hand, for example, for around $100. Make a habit of backing up your important files at least once a week. Important files include whatever projects you're working on now (i.e., that have changed since your last backup); your income and expense records; correspondence; photos; and anything else you don't want to lose.

While there are programs that you can invest in that will synchronize your folders, or entire computer, to your backup drive, I find the easiest way to back up my work is to create an "archive" folder on my main computer. Whenever I add new files to the computer that I want to back up, or when I make changes to a project, I store an extra copy in the "archive" folder, and then back it up to the appropriate section of my portable drive. Another option is to maintain a "working files" folder that you back up regularly. If I am in the middle of a project, I'll back up my day's work every evening on a flash drive, and then back up my weekly progress on the portable hard drive.

All this is nice, but what if your house burns down? This concern has led me to make a habit of creating backup CDs or DVDs from that same "archive" folder. (I make backup DVDs because I take large numbers of photos; if most of your files are Word or Excel files, you should only need to make backup CDs.) If you have a day job, store them in your office; if your spouse or partner has a day job, ask that person to store them for you. Or, ask a friend or relative to keep them safe; the idea is to keep them "off site" so that if anything happens to your computer and files at home, you'll still have a fairly recent backup. These backups serve an extra purpose: I've often turned to them to find some ancient file that I can't locate anywhere else, or that I've deleted or changed.

Another way to archive material off-site is to store it in a protected directory on your Web site, if you have one. If you don't, there are a number of sites that offer secure online storage. This is a particularly good option if you are working on a major project that you absolutely want to protect, without having to make physical backups every night.

Scanning Files

Another way to protect your records is to scan your paper files. It is acceptable, for example, to save tax records as scanned electronic files—including copies of expenses receipts, payment stubs, and the tax forms themselves. Over time, this can save a lot of closet space. As I noted above, I scan all my business financial records at the end of the year, and then store three years of records in hardcopy.

To scan this type of record, it's a good idea to invest in a sheet-fed scanner, such as a Fujitsu Scansnap. These aren't cheap, but thanks to that scanner, I've sent literally boxes of old records, manuscripts and clips to the recycle bin. Scan correspondence and contracts, so that you'll have an electronic backup if anything happens to the originals. A scanner like this will automatically convert your scans to PDF files, which makes this an ideal way to preserve and share your clips. (If you wish to scan photos, invest in a flatbed scanner.) Then, just make sure that you include your latest scans in your file backups.

Keeping good records isn't just a matter of saving what you're working on today. It's a matter of recognizing that you have no way of knowing what will suddenly become vitally important to you *tomorrow*. It can be so tempting to throw out that e-mail, that unsold article, those old letters. But you never know when you're going to need proof that you sold a particular item for a particular set of terms, and good records are your best (and only) source of protection. When in doubt, *don't* throw it out!

PART 6

The Online Writer

❧ *26* ☙

The Writer and the Internet

Do you need a Web site? Should you be on Facebook? Should you write a blog?

Once upon a time, to become a freelance writer, all you needed (pretty much) was a place to set up your typewriter, a ream of paper, a *Writer's Market,* some envelopes and a bunch of stamps. That day is long gone. Now, the electronic world offers writers a new set of opportunities—and challenges.

Perhaps the greatest change brought about by the Internet is to render the concept of "distance" meaningless. Today, a writer can connect instantly with another writer on the opposite side of the globe. Contacting an editor in another country no longer means spending a small fortune on international postage, and then waiting for weeks while keeping your fingers crossed that the envelope actually reached its destination. Conducting an interview with an expert in another country is a piece of cake. And with programs like Skype, you can do more than just send e-mails around the world; you can actually *chat,* live, with that fellow writer or interview contact.

Similarly, you are no longer limited to critique groups and writing organizations in your physical neighborhood. If you want feedback on your work, or the camaraderie of networking with other writers, you can find a group online that suits your interests and level of expertise. If you want to hone your skills by taking a writing class, there are hundreds of online courses to choose from. There is even the occasional online writer's conference.

There's no doubt that the Internet has made it vastly easier for freelancers to locate, and research, new markets. Most US publications have a Web presence, and many publications post their current guidelines online. Even if they don't, those Web sites make it a lot easier (and cheaper) to research a publication's content and style than by purchasing a handful of sample copies. Non-US publications are sometimes a bit harder to find on the Web (and many only post "subscription" sites as opposed to sites with actual content, let alone writer's guidelines)—but they're still easier to find than they were a decade ago.

Though it's rarely cheap to maintain a high-speed Internet access account, that account can end up saving you money in the long-term. Back when I started freelancing, if I wanted information on writing and markets, I had to go out and buy a book or subscribe to a magazine. Today, there are thousands of Web sites offering tips for writers. While I still recommend that you add some good "how-to" books to your library, on the Web it's possible to find out nearly anything you need to know about the business and craft of writing without spending a penny. Don't want to buy a magazine subscription? There are many excellent newsletters for writers (including my own Writing World newsletter, available at *www.writing-world.com*) that are available absolutely free. I've already discussed the ease with which one can research nonfiction topics online in chapter 9.

The Web can save you money in other ways as well. If you're in the habit of running down to the office supply store every time you need a new print cartridge, try comparison-shopping online first. You may not *always* find a better price, but you will often find basic supplies for less (even counting shipping) than at the local store. You may also be able to find supplies that are more difficult to find locally; my office supply store never seems to stock the size of mailers that I need to ship my self-published book, for example. If you're in the market for a new computer or peripherals, it's definitely a good idea to get an idea of the prices online before making a decision. And in today's economy, who can afford to throw money away needlessly?

Speaking of money, PayPal makes it easy to set up a completely electronic bank account. If you hope to do business with electronic publications and/or international publications, this is essential. If you sell an article overseas and receive a check, you could lose $15 to $20 in fees just trying to get it deposited in your US bank account (and you can also wait six weeks or longer for it to clear). If you receive those same funds into your PayPal account, they'll be available immediately and at a fraction of the cost (particularly as the company paying you can choose to make the payment in *your* currency rather than *theirs,* thus avoiding any currency conversion fees).

PayPal is also essential if you hope to market a self-published book or e-book from your Web site. No longer are writers thwarted from selling their own books by the difficulty of setting up a "merchant credit card account." Anyone with a credit card can pay you via PayPal, from anywhere in the world (well, almost). PayPal also enables you to purchase and print postage from your computer, which can be useful if you're shipping a self-published book.

If you operate a Web site, affiliate programs can help you earn a bit of extra income. Many writers participate in Amazon.com's affiliate program, which lets you post books that you feel would be of interest to your readers or visitors (including your own!). Here's a quick tip, though: Don't use the links that Amazon.com generates automatically. For some reason, these always point to the cheapest (used) copy of the book available, which doesn't help you at all. Instead, download book covers yourself and set them up with the "old-style" Amazon affiliate link (*www.amazon.com/exec/obidos/ASIN/0984249605/youraffiliatename*); this will take your visitors directly to the book's primary sale page.

Besides Amazon.com, there are many other affiliate programs out there (and you can even set up your own through ClickBank if you're marketing an e-book or some other electronic product). Some affiliate programs work well, others don't. I've tested many that led absolutely nowhere; I've tested others that have produced a small but steady stream of income. Look for potential affiliate links on sites like Clickbank, Shareasale, and Commission Junction.

Many writers use Google AdSense to generate a bit of income from their Web sites. I use this as well, on my British travel site (*www.timetravel-britain.com*) and bring in around $100 every quarter—not riches by any means, but again, a nice little extra that helps pay for the cost of maintaining the site. Be warned, however, that you have no control over the content of the ads posted on your site with this program.

Setting up your own Web site or blog is like taking out your own bit of real estate on the Web. It gives you an "address" where people can visit—or more accurately, where people can "find" you. If you're promoting a book (fiction or nonfiction), having a Web site is just about essential these days; readers expect to be able to learn more about your book online, as well as where they can find it and your *next* book. A Web site is also essential if you're hoping to establish a career as a commercial freelancer, editor, book designer, or any other service-related business.

Many writers are turning to blogs and various forms of social networking to increase their professional connections online—to build a following for their work, to connect with other writers, and to connect with editors and others who might wish to offer assignments. Twitter is currently the fastest growing social network online (as of April 2010); writers are also flocking to Facebook, LinkedIn, and MySpace, among other social networking sites. Thousands of writers host blogs, covering just about every topic imaginable (and probably quite a few you hadn't imagined).

Of course, there are perils on the Web as well. Anyone with an e-mail account knows the frustration of being flooded with spam. Viruses and trojans are a perpetual risk; never surf the Web without an effective anti-virus, anti-trojan system in place. (You'd be amazed at the sites that you stumble across that are "infected," often without the knowledge of the site host.)

There are also plenty of hucksters out there who would like to get their fingers on your pocketbook, usually by making the sort of promises a writer most wants to hear: "You'll get published!" One such peril to writers is the infamous agent/book-doctor scam, wherein an "agent" tells the writer that his or her book is "almost" publishable, but needs "work" from a "book doctor." The agent kindly refers the writer to such a book doctor, with the implied promise that if the writer pays to have editorial work done, the agent will then consider taking on the manuscript. In reality, the agent and the book doctor just split the editing fee and the writer is left stranded. Another infamous site, the "International Library of Poetry," has finally closed its doors; this site operated a so-called "competition," in which *every* submission was a "winner" and ended up published in an anthology—the object being to convince the happy writer to buy the anthology. Subsidy publishers still promise writers the moon, for about the cost of getting there.

Covering every opportunity (or danger) on the Web would require an entire volume. This section, therefore, looks at three ways in which a writer can enhance a freelance career online: by creating a Web site, by participating in social networking sites, and by launching a blog. More tips for ways in which writers can benefit from online resources can be found at my Web site, Writing-World.com (*www.writing-world.com*).

❦ 27 ❧

Creating a Writer's Web Site

D o you want to attract more readers and sell more books? Do you want to impress editors and win more article assignments? Do you have a writing-related service (such as editing or copywriting) that you wish to promote? Or do you just have a desire to share information with other writers like yourself?

If you answered "yes" to any of those questions, you need a Web site. In the old days, we handed out business cards; now, anyone who receives a business card expects it to tell them where to find out more about us on the Web.

But wait, I hear you saying... I have a profile on Facebook! I'm on LinkedIn! Isn't that enough? Many writers are turning to social networking sites primarily, I suspect, because they're free and because they offer a sense of "security"—you get to choose with whom you "connect" and interact. However, limiting your online presence to social networking sites is like joining a club—and then telling your readers that if they want to know more about your work, *they* have to join too. If you truly want to promote to the widest possible audience, you need to be where that audience can find you. And that means a Web site of your own.

Before you rush out to post a page, however, take a deep breath. The Internet is flooded with sloppy, unimpressive, cutesy and trivial "writer" home pages. As a professional, you want something that says more than "Hi, my name is Bob, click here to read my stories, click here to read about my dog!" Before you launch, you need to make some important decisions about your site.

FIVE GREAT REASONS FOR A WEB SITE

A professional Web site requires a professional purpose. It should, in some way, advance your career (or at least your dreams). Your first step, therefore, is to determine what writing goal is most important to you at this time. Is it to sell more articles to magazines? To sell more copies of your nonfiction book? To attract more readers to your novels? To market a skill, such as editing? To educate and inform your readers (or anyone else who comes along)?

Keep in mind as well that visitors aren't impressed by sites that are little more than electronic ads for your books. Purpose must be supported by content; content must be guided by purpose. Choose both with care, and you'll give readers a reason to visit—and also to stay, explore, and recommend your site to others.

Following are five of the more common purposes for writers' Web sites, and the types of content that can help support those purposes:

To Post Clips and Attract Assignments

One of the downsides of electronic queries is the impossibility of attaching clips. The easiest solution is to post a selection of appropriate articles on your Web site and provide the URL in your query. If your primary goal is to win more article assignments, a clip site is a good way to impress editors with the work you've already done. Such a site should include:

An introductory home page that indicates the types of articles that will be found on the site. It's often a good idea to organize a clip site around a particular topic (e.g., health articles) rather than "shotgunning" your site with clips on a host of unrelated topics. Another option is to cluster clips in two or three separate categories (e.g., pets, travel, writing). Your home page should help the visitor navigate to the appropriate section of clips, and also give your name and provide a brief overview of your experience and/or credentials. Many writers believe that it's also a good idea to post a professional photo on your home page.

Selected clips of your best work. Before posting clips of published articles, be sure that you own the necessary rights. If you've sold all rights, produced the material as work-for-hire, or do not own the electronic rights, you may need to obtain permission from the original publisher before you post a clip. It's usually best, if possible, to post articles as HTML files, but you can also post scanned PDF files. However, keep in mind that in the latter case, a scanned article may contain copyrighted material that does not belong to you (such as someone else's photos)—so again, you may wish to obtain permission. (If your published articles appear elsewhere online, such as on the Web site of the original publisher, you can simply link to that location rather than posting the article directly on your own site.)

Copyright and attribution information for every clip. Since the point of posting clips is to let editors know where you've been published, be sure to include complete copyright information with each article. In this case, the copyright should reflect the date of publication, *not* the date on which you posted the material online. Include the name and date of the publication in which the material appeared. This notice should usually appear at the end of the article, and might appear like this:

Copyright © 2010 by Imagood Author. This article was originally published in Pet Lover's Monthly, January 2010.

To Establish Your Expertise and/or Educate Readers

One of the most common reasons writers set up Web sites and blogs is because—well, because they're *writers,* and they have something they want to say. Many writers set up Web sites or blogs to talk about the business and craft of writing itself. Others are passionate about some other subject (usually, a subject they write about professionally). Writers who have a particular interest in a hobby, career, area of study, or similar area of expertise often want to tell the world more about that subject. In this case, your goal may not be to convince editors that you're a brilliant writer, but simply to promote a better understanding of your field. However, such a site can also help establish your credentials and expertise! Such a site is likely to include the following elements:

A home page that provides a basic introduction to the subject you want to cover, or that provides the reader with an idea of what the site has to offer. Include a title that will give a clear idea of the subject area when it comes up in a search. (For that matter, include a title that is most *likely* to be searched *for* when someone wants to know more about your topic.) Choose keywords that would be chosen by someone searching on this topic. Make sure that your home page clearly indicates what the reader will find on your site, and how to find it.

An array of information resources. These might include articles that you've published on the topic, a FAQ developed specifically for the site, full-length articles written for the site, a blog, a regular column, a Q&A where you answer questions from visitors, and so forth. If you create a column or blog, be sure to archive back issues so that readers can find them.

A selection of good-quality links. To position yourself as a vital resource in your field, you'll need to search the Web yourself to find other worthwhile sites in that same field. This accomplishes two purposes: It adds to the value of your site, and encourages other sites in the field to link back to you (which not only increases your traffic, but also can improve your search engine ranking). Remember that your visitors rely on you to screen sites, so never add a link that you haven't personally checked. Also, keep your links up-to-date; nothing signals an out-of-date site than one that is full of dead links.

A bookstore. If your goal is to promote awareness of a topic, consider offering a "bookstore" of titles related to your subject or field. If you have a book of your own, it's true that listing *other* books may compete with your title—but it will also show readers that you've done your homework and are familiar with the top titles in your field. If you set up an "associates" program with an online bookstore, this section of your site can also earn money.

Your credentials. Keep your bio short, sweet, and professional. Focus on anything that supports your standing as an expert: education, credentials, job history, personal experience, and so on. Let visitors (and editors) know that they can trust you as a source. It's up to you to decide how "personal" you want to make this section, but for an information site, it's best to try to keep your bio relevant to the topic of the site. If your site is all about pet care, for example, don't spend a lot of time in your bio discussing your love of gardening!

A decade ago, one of the most common reasons writers would set up a Web site was to educate other *writers*. Today, sites for writers have proliferated beyond count. There's still room on the Web, however, for good-quality writing advice. If you'd like to set up an information site for writers, the best approach is to move beyond general "how to write" or "how to get published" tips, and focus on your area of specialty. What can you offer writers that isn't easily found elsewhere? Focus your site on tips about writing for a specific genre, category or field.

For example, if you're a mystery writer, share tips on how to become a mystery writer—or how to become a *better* mystery writer. Be creative: Don't just talk about writing techniques, but tell your readers where to find helpful research information, such as sites that cover forensics or police procedures. Offer links to mystery magazines and e-zines. Offer a bookstore of how-to books for mystery writers.

Like any other "information" site, a site for writers requires an array of top-quality information. Consider posting previously published articles, FAQs, book excerpts, a column, a blog, and anything else that will help writers improve their skills. Be sure that your information not only discusses good writing, but models it as well! Nothing detracts from a so-called "how-to" page for writers like flawed grammar, spelling and punctuation errors, and errors in content. Another factor is article length. I've seen a great many "writing" sites that claim to offer dozens of articles—and each of those "articles" proves to be no more than two or three paragraphs in length. While there are many "expert" articles on Web content that declare that people only skim the Web and don't really "read" articles, when it comes to writing for writers, don't you believe it! Writers, by definition, are people who read—so give them something to sink their teeth into.

To Promote Your Novel(s)

If you've published a novel, the Web is the first place fans are going to look to find out more about you, your book, your *next* book, the world in which your novels are placed, your characters, and more. A Web site is the ideal way to reach out to your current readers and fans—and to attract *new* readers. A novelist's Web site will often contain many of the following elements:

An introductory home page. This should clearly list your name (or the name under which you write, if you write under a pseudonym). Keep in mind that most fans will search for your site by author name, not by book title. Your home page should also indicate what can be found on the site and how, and images of your novels with, perhaps, a brief description of each.

An author bio. Fans will want to know more about you, so satisfy their curiosity with a brief, professional biographical sketch (and a photo, if you wish). This is a good place to discuss how you began writing, why you write the types of books you do, your expertise relating to those books (e.g., how you happen to know so much about coffee or medieval Scotland or whatever), your future writing plans—and, of course, how many cats you have. Keep in mind that fiction readers are often more interested in an author's *personal* life than would be relevant for a site in which you're promoting your professional writing services or a purely nonfiction topic. It's up to you, however, to decide how much personal information you wish to share.

Descriptions of your books. This is your chance to give your readers a better summary (and teaser) than they will find on the backs of your books. A good way to handle this is to display your book covers and a brief description on your home page, with each linking to a more detailed page (or series of pages) about each book. For example, if you wish to include a description of the book, an excerpt, and other information, each book cover on your home page could link to a table of contents of information on your site about that book. You probably have electronic images of your book covers on file; if not, you can download cover images from Amazon. com or BarnesandNoble.com.

Excerpts. Selections from your current or forthcoming novels can be a huge draw for your site, as well as an excellent sales tool. Such excerpts give readers something free to take away, but also leave them hungry for more. Choose an excerpt that the reader can understand without having read the rest of the book—but that ends with a cliffhanger that will make the reader *want* to read the rest of the book. Most publishers are more than willing to allow you to post chapter excerpts.

Background information. Is your novel set in a particular period, locale, or cultural milieu that readers might like to learn more about? Your Web site is an excellent place to answer questions, post background history or details, explain unfamiliar terms and concepts, and provide links to other sources of information.

Writing tips. Many of your readers undoubtedly dream of writing the types of books you write. Give them a hand by offering advice on writing in your field or genre. A section of your site dedicated to writing tips will also improve your chances of receiving links from other writers, writing Web sites and organizations in your field, because your site will now qualify as a source of useful information for writers as well as readers.

A news page. Let readers know when your next book is coming out, what awards you've won, when you'll be appearing on radio or television (or giving a podcast), when and where you'll be giving talks or book signings, and anything else that is newsworthy. Some authors also provide links to fan sites, book reviews, online interviews, podcasts, etc.

A bibliography. Many authors provide a full list of all their writings, including short stories, awards, and any other credits.

Links. No site is complete without a few links. Choose those that relate to the general content and purpose of your site—other sources of background information, or other sites for writers in your genre. You might also seek reciprocal links with authors of related books.

Other works. Some authors use their Web site to archive previously published stories. This works well if the stories are relevant to the novel(s) you're trying to promote. Be careful, however, about posting material that might contradict the image you're trying to build with your fans. If you're currently promoting a line of cozy mysteries full of cats, cottages and afternoon teas, don't confuse the issue by posting those erotic vampire stories you wrote ten years ago.

Ordering information. Make it easy for readers to obtain your books. If your novels are self-published, make sure readers can purchase them directly from your site. If they are commercially published, consider not only providing direct links to Amazon.com or another online bookstore, but setting up an affiliate program with your chosen store, so that you can earn a bit of extra income every time someone buys one of your books through your site. If your books are published through a print-on-demand or subsidy publisher, or through a small press that doesn't have them on Amazon, make sure that your titles link *directly* to the book's sale page on the publisher's Web site.

To Promote Your Nonfiction Book(s)

The primary difference between a site designed to promote fiction and one designed to promote nonfiction is that while fiction readers tend to be author-focused, nonfiction readers tend to be subject-focused. Readers interested in books on Victorian medicine are looking for the next book on Victorian medicine, regardless of who wrote it. A Web site designed to promote a nonfiction book, therefore, should focus on the subject of the book, and include:

An introductory home page that will attract visitors searching for information on your subject area. Your name may be less important here than keywords that describe the subject. To ensure that your site gets good search engine rankings, make sure that your home page includes lots of appropriate keywords, as close as possible to the top of the page. Make sure, as well, that your page has an appropriate title that will let readers know they have found what they're searching for.

Information of value to readers. The best way to promote a nonfiction book is to offer free, useful information. Turn your site into the best possible resource on the Web on your topic. Offer book excerpts, articles (including articles you've already published on the topic, and/or articles you write just for the site), a FAQ, a column, a blog, etc. Make your site a *resource,* not an *ad.* Resources not only attract visitors, they give visitors a reason to come back—and to recommend your site to others (both by word of mouth and through links). Also, avoid giving the impression that you're manufacturing some sort of crisis or hype to sell your book ("Five things doctors don't want you to know about health condition X—revealed in my book!")

Links. One way to make your site a useful resource is to provide links to other sites covering similar topics. This will help convince visitors that you are genuinely interested in sharing information rather than simply trying to peddle a product. It will also encourage other sites to link back to you, which increases your traffic.

Your credentials. Before accepting your advice and information, readers will want to know why they should trust you. Don't spend a lot of time on personal details here; keep your bio professional, listing any relevant information about your education, experience, work-related credentials, personal experience, background, and anything else that will demonstrate your qualifications to write about your topic.

A summary of your book. On a nonfiction site, it helps to keep promos low-key. On your home page, provide a cover image of your book and a brief summary that links to a more detailed "book page" that provides more information. Consider including, on separate pages, a table of contents, excerpts from favorable reviews, book chapter excerpts, etc. Make sure that readers can easily determine how to order your book, whether from an online bookstore, an online publisher, or directly from you.

To Promote a Writing-Related Service

If you operate a writing-related business—such as copywriting, editing, "book doctoring," book formatting, cover design, etc.—a Web site is absolutely essential. In the old days, we handed out business cards; today, anyone receiving your business card expects that card to point to a Web site where they can gather more information about you, your services, and your credentials.

Chapter 36 describes in detail what a "commercial" Web site should involve. For now, suffice it to say that it should tell the visitor who you are, why you are qualified to offer the services you provide, and what those services are. It should *not* include a price list; that's the sign of an amateur (and can easily put off those who aren't familiar with going rates for services like yours). Your site should also indicate your location, even if you don't wish to provide your actual address. While clients in the Internet age are often willing to do business with professionals in a completely different part of the country or even the world, many still prefer to do business locally. Thus, you need to make sure that if you're based in Peoria, anyone searching for "editors in Peoria" will have a good chance of coming across your site. Also, it should hardly need to be said that a "commercial" site should not only list what services you offer, but *demonstrate* those services. I'm always amazed to come across ads for "editors" that are riddled with spelling and punctuation errors.

Needless to say, these aren't the only reasons writers launch Web sites, and in many cases, these reasons may overlap. Feel free to mix and match the items listed above, as well as adding items of your own. Be cautious, however, about trying to develop a Web site that does *everything* I've listed above (e.g., to promote your novel, showcase nonfiction clips, establish your expertise in a completely unrelated area, and market your editorial skills). Many writers have several separate career tracks. If you're one of them, don't try to create a multi-purpose Web site—this is likely to simply come across as cluttered and confused. Instead, create a separate site for each "primary" purpose—one for your novels, another for your nonfiction research, another for your editing business. It's perfectly OK to cross-reference your sites, but don't assume that readers who are interested in one part of your career will be fascinated by every other part.

ELEMENTS OF A SUCCESSFUL WEB SITE

There are hundreds of ways to design an effective Web site, so I won't even attempt to tell you how to design yours. It's also up to you to decide whether you want to do it yourself (there's lots of great software out there to help you) or to hire a designer. Whatever approach you choose, just remember to keep your primary purpose in mind; avoid unnecessary bells and whistles that don't actually contribute to the goal of your site. A good way to decide how you'd like *your* site to look is to spend some time reviewing the sites of other authors, selecting those elements you like and ignoring those you don't. You can find a huge list of links to author Web sites at *www.bookbrowse.com/author_websites/*.

Here are some elements that can contribute to the effectiveness of *any* Web site:

1. **A Domain Name.** A decade ago, many writers relied upon free hosting sites with free templates (like Homestead and Geocities) or sites that catered specifically to writers (such as SFSite). This often meant having a URL like "*www.freehostingsite.com/directory/directory2/myname/*"—a URL that was neither easy to remember nor easy to type into one's browser.

    Today, Homestead and Geocities are no more, and the vast majority of authors are investing in their own domains. Having your own domain name is simply one more mark of being a "professional." Some writers use their own name (e.g., *www.nevadabarr.com*). Those who focus on nonfiction often choose a name that indicates something about the topic of the site (e.g., my own *www.pet-loss.net*). Novelists often use the name of a character (Nancy Atherton's *www.aunt-dimity.com*) or a phrase that relates to the theme of a series (Cleo Coyle's *www.coffeehousemystery.com*—which is, by the way, a good example of "how to do it").

    The cost of obtaining a domain name varies, but usually begins at $25 for one year, with lower rates for longer registrations. If you expect to be promoting your writing for several years, it's worth the investment to register your domain for several years in advance; it also saves the need to renew every year. Try to obtain a .com address if you can, but don't hesitate to use a .net or .org if your first choice is taken. If you can't find the exact domain you want, experiment with different spellings, or with the use of hyphens: "*www.john-smith.org.*" Sometimes, too, a hyphen can make a domain easier to enter, particularly if, without it, you'll end up with three repetitions of the same letter (e.g., "*www.auntbess-stories.com*" is easier to remember than "*www.auntbessstories.com*").

2. **A Site-Wide Navigation Menu.** No matter where readers travel within your site, they should be able to access other sections, or get back to the home page, with a minimum of fuss. To make this possible, make sure that every page on your site features a basic navigation menu that will take the reader to the primary, top-level sections of your site. This menu might appear at the top, the bottom, or in a column on one side of your site—but it should be consistent throughout the site. For example, if your site offers a section of articles, a bookstore, a set of links, a newsletter, and a blog, consider a navigation menu like the following:

Home · Articles · Links · Blog · Newsletter · Bookstore · About Me · Contact Info

3. **A Hit Counter.** It's nice to be able to track how many visitors you receive—and nice to be able to let others see this information as well. There are many sources of free hit counters on the Web; I use Statcounter (*www.statcounter.com*), which enables me to design a counter that matches my Web site design and determine how many digits I wish to display. Statcounter also enables me to log in to my (free) account and get a detailed report of my monthly visitors. (Many Web hosting services also provide visitor Web logs, but may not actually provide you with a hit counter that you can display on your site.)

4. **A site-wide copyright notice.** Make sure your visitors know that your information is protected by copyright. It's amazing how many people still believe that if something's posted on the Web, it's "available." Your copyright notice should appear at the bottom of every page on your site. It should include the year and your name (and should be updated every year, or your site may appear out of date). Here's an example:

Copyright © 2010 by Moira Allen. All rights reserved.
For reprint information, contact Moira Allen.

5. **Contact details.** In the example above, I would hotlink my name so that it opens an e-mail message when clicked. If you wish readers to be able to contact you, make sure that your contact information is clearly displayed. However, you may also wish to *protect* your contact details so that your e-mail won't be picked up by spam-bots. There are several ways to do this. One is to uni-encode your actual e-mail address, and not display it directly on the site (go to *http://infinetdesign.com/temp/unicode/* and enter

your e-mail address in the box to do this). Another way is to mask your e-mail by typing in characters that must be removed by a person who wishes to contact you—e.g., contact "moira (dot) allen (at) mydomain (dot) com." Yet another way is to put a contact form on your Web site that doesn't reveal your e-mail address at all; you can find such a form at *www.foxyform.com*. Your Web host may also provide some e-mail protection features.

6. **A search feature.** If you have lots of information on your site, you can make it possible for visitors to actually search for what they're looking for. One site that offers this capability at no charge is PicoSearch (*www.picosearch.com*). The downside is that you need to keep your search facility updated when you add new material to your site.

MAKING MONEY FROM YOUR SITE

A factor that often discourages writers from developing a Web site is the concern that Web sites cost money to build and maintain. Even if you do your own Web design, you will still end up paying for your domain registration and for Web hosting. While it's possible to get free Web hosting, this usually means that (a) you will get virtually no support if something goes wrong or you need help, and (b) the Web host will plaster *their* ads on *your* site, which will hardly contribute to a professional look. However, it's quite possible to add features to your site that will not only make it self-supporting, but possibly even profitable (over and above its benefits in promoting your writing).

One of the most common ways to earn money from your Web site is to sign up for an affiliate program—and one of the most popular of these is Amazon. com. With an Amazon.com affiliate, any time someone buys a book you've mentioned on your site (and linked to your affiliate program), you get a small fee. In fact, if someone clicks through to Amazon via your site and buys some *other* book or product, you'll *still* get a fee. Barnes and Noble offers a similar program.

There are a host of affiliate programs besides those relating to online bookstores, however. One way to find affiliate programs that might relate to your content is to visit sites like Commission Junction (*www.cj.com*), ClickBank (*www.clickbank.com*) or ShareaSale (*www.shareasale.com*). These sites offer hundreds (if not thousands) of affiliate programs, and will provide you with banners, buttons, and any other tools you need to get started.

Another way to earn some extra money from your site is to sign up for Google AdSense. With this program, you put code onto your site (in a location you choose) that enables Google to automatically generate text ads based on its analysis of your page. You can design the section to match your Web design as closely as possible. However, be warned: the "analysis" of your text is done by computer, and the ads may or may not prove "relevant" to your content. I run Google AdSense on my British travel site, TimeTravel-Britain.com—and because my home page lists articles about churches and cathedrals, one of the Google ads currently displayed is "Become a Pastor!"

Finally, if you wish to sell products from your site (such as self-published books or e-books), you'll need to set up a PayPal account. PayPal has become the standard method for small businesses (like writers) to accept credit cards online. Anyone with a credit card can pay you via PayPal, and their information is kept private; you never actually see their credit card details. PayPal is also indispensible if you expect to make or receive international payments.

The best approach for a writer is to set up either a premiere or merchant account on PayPal, and link your PayPal account to your bank account. This will enable you to transfer funds between your regular bank account and your PayPal account as needed. You can also attach a credit card to your PayPal account; then, if you need to make a payment but don't have enough funds in the account, it will be charged to your credit card. As a merchant account-holder, you'll have access to tools to set up "buy now" buttons, a shopping cart, and so forth. PayPal also gives you the ability to purchase and print shipping labels.

THREE THINGS YOUR WEB SITE CAN DO WITHOUT

In developing a Web site, it's also important to know what to leave out. Certain elements can detract from the professional image you're trying to project, including:

1. **Unpublished writings.** Never use a Web site to try to "market" unpublished writings to editors. Editors do not surf the Web looking for material to publish; they get quite enough of that from other sources. Posting articles "available for publication" on your site simply sends the message that you haven't been *able* to sell that material. And since it obviously wasn't written with a specific publication in mind, it's not likely to interest an editor. Worse, editors may regard such material as "previously published" if you *do* submit it, if it has appeared on your site first.

2. **Too Much Personal Information.** If your goal is to advance your writing career, keep your site as professional as possible. This isn't the place for news about your grandchildren or photos of family pets. That doesn't mean you can't include personal information—but make sure it's relevant to the purpose of your site. Also, with the exception of a site that markets a professional service, it's always best to leave off any contact information other than your e-mail. Don't include your address and phone number!

3. **Irrelevant links.** Today, any Web site owner will be bombarded with link exchange requests. These rarely come from real, live people; instead, there are now a host of "backlink" programs that search the Web for keywords that relate to the site offering the "reciprocal" link. The pitch is always "link to us and we'll link to you," the idea being that such "backlinking" increases search engine rankings. In reality, the links offered will do you no good whatsoever—and linking to such sites won't make you look professional. Only post links to sites *you* consider worth linking to. This also greatly increases your chances of getting *effective* reciprocal links; whenever

you link to a worthwhile site, contact the site owner (if possible), let them know about the link, and invite them to visit your site and consider a link in return.

THE GREATEST DANGER OF ALL...

The greatest danger of a writer's Web site is not what you put on or leave off. It's not spammers or hackers. It is the extent to which such a site can consume your writing time. The temptation to keep tinkering with your Web site is hard to resist. There's always the urge to redesign your pages, add new elements, rewrite your menus, add better graphics, or simply surf the Web for new links or new ways to promote your site. Moreover, it's easy to justify such tinkering as "working to promote my novel" or "gathering important information."

Before you know what has happened, however, you'll have spent the entire day tinkering, without adding a single word to that article or story you need to complete by deadline. (Trust me, I know!) Designing and maintaining a site can be an excellent way to promote your writing and advance your career, but it should not be allowed to *replace* writing. High-tech procrastination is still procrastination. If necessary, ration yourself to only so many hours of site development per month. Otherwise, you may end up with the perfect writer's Web site—and nothing for it to promote!

❧ 28 ❧

How Social Networking Sites Help Writers
by Penny J. Leisch

Would you be interested if I told you that I received two job contacts and a contract within the first week I used Twitter? I did. Do I get that response every week? No. Are there ways to promote yourself and increase your visibility? Yes. This chapter will show you how to use the social networking sites that are most commonly used by professionals at the time of this writing: Facebook, LinkedIn, and Twitter.

Each of these sites allows an individual or business to set up a profile. Think of each profile as a mini–Web site. These services provide tools that allow you to limit who sees your information (called privacy controls), who may contact you, how they contact you, and how much information you share. The biggest challenge for newcomers is that you must define your purpose for the site to be effective.

First, let's talk about each site and what they offer, as well as how they differ.

FACEBOOK

Facebook is a hybrid of personal and business users with over 300 million users (SiteProNews, October 9, 2009). According to Alexa.com, it's the third most trafficked site in the world. It's also the number one social network (Nielson. com). If you want exposure, you can get it here. Set up a basic account and a great profile, at the very least.

The demographic is primarily 35 years old and up (Facebook.com), with high incomes: 51% over $75K and 33% over $100K annually (Jayde 2009). That's a lot of market potential, and it's an international market! I bet those folks with $100,000 annual incomes can afford to hire a writer to help with their memoirs, newsletters, and resumes.

This Web site appeals more to professional and mature audiences than MySpace, partially because the format is cleaner and easier to navigate. It's designed to allow people to communicate through messages, posting to the wall—which is like a bulletin board—sharing photos, news, blogs, and more. There are also fun features, like sending flowers or hugs, to customers, friends, and family.

Business users also add personal touches to their sites. They use logos showing charities the business supports, company picnic photos, and good PR news. It's very important to check the privacy settings carefully, though. You'll quickly annoy friends and family if you send every update to the entire list. It's also not a good idea to send your boss a note that says you sent flowers to your girlfriend or applied for another job. These risks are good reasons not to mix business and personal use.

LINKEDIN

This is the most respected and widely used site for business networking. LinkedIn is where you share ideas and get answers to questions from professionals that you'd never meet any other way. Industry specific professional groups help each other through advice, resources, referrals, and more. Plus, employers post jobs and recruit here.

LinkedIn isn't a fast track to becoming an executive editor at Random House, but it is good exposure that can be focused on your specialty. People get to know you through discussions. They learn about you and your expertise when you answer questions for others by responding to a discussion. Again, it's about others and earning the respect of others in your network who can make referrals.

In addition, customers and employers can post public recommendations on your page, and you can see when people in your network change jobs or location, which helps you maintain a current network with viable contacts. Your network can be as wide or narrow as you want to work to make it.

Because of my LinkedIn profile, I netted a job offer from one of my husband's connections. A former co-worker of his is starting a small business and had no idea that I write professionally. Once that became known, I got an e-mail asking if I would edit their Web site content. I accepted, and two more projects followed, with more to come.

TWITTER

The Twitter phenomenon is still relatively new. It's really a micro-blogging site, and it grew by 1,928% from June 2008 to June 2009 (Nielson.com). As of April 2010, it was the fastest growing social network in the world.

One resource, istrategylabs.com, states that 46% of Twitter users are college graduates, and 31% are between the ages of 35 and 49, with use roughly equal between males and females. According to TechCrunch.com, the 50 millionth unique visitor arrived in July 2009. That's a lot of potential exposure.

The purpose is to create awareness of your presence. Messages should provide helpful tips, entertain, or inform your target market. Yes, there are spammers and hookers here too. It's easy to block the undesirable element though. The big no-no is blatant self-promotion. Like all customer-oriented content, it's about them, not you.

The short message format is also the ultimate test of your ability to get to the point, which isn't a bad thing to practice. You build a following by offering information that people want, solving problems, and engaging in useful conversation, not by promoting your work *ad nauseum*. There is an amazing amount of good research information available by doing simple searches too.

Two job offers appeared within the first week after I set up my Twitter account. First, I searched for writing jobs and followed them. Second, I tweeted daily. I tweeted a couple of writing tips, a coupon for a discount on resumes, a new blog entry, and an entertaining quote pertaining to writing.

One day, I received a DM (direct message) from a manager asking if I'd be interested in writing for her company. She had visited my Web site and seen my writing on other sites. We exchanged e-mail addresses, and a contract followed. The other employer tweeted a job that I saw because I was following writing jobs, and I replied. Many of the jobs posted are SEO [search-engine optimization] content writing and bid-for-work sites. However, there are agents, authors, writers, individuals, and businesses online. Any of them may need a writer or may be looking without advertising. You can easily maintain a presence and monitor your account with simple management tools.

I only spend a couple of hours each week managing my accounts. In fact, the time people spend on Twitter is declining now that the novelty is wearing off. That may bode well for the content becoming leaner and more meaningful.

USING SOCIAL NETWORK SITES

Think of anything on a networking site as public information. If you wouldn't share the information with your boss or your grandmother, don't put it on a Web site that's open to the public. There are privacy controls that allow you to limit access. However, we are talking business here, and you won't get business by hiding your profile.

A recent article notes that 56% of employers say hiring decisions are affected by what an applicant puts on social media sites (SitePro News). This is of significant importance to writers, since many writers have other full time jobs.

Brian Solis of Future Works, a Silicon Valley PR firm, performed a social media gender study and found that women outnumber men by a minimum of 5 to 15 percent on most social networking sites. If women are your audience, social media is where you want to market. How you market in this arena may not be as obvious. In real life and in online marketing, customers don't usually hang out with your peers.

What types of activities engage your ideal customer? Do you write about finance? High net worth clients may be in philanthropic or investment groups. Find a reason to be there. Are you a printer or publisher? Get in front of marketing professionals. Are you a resume writer? Join job search forums and networks where people actively search for jobs. Then, participate in discussions, start discussions, and offer tips to show your expertise.

It's not necessary to advertise everything on every site. Focus on the purpose of each site. Use Facebook to advertise classes, teleclasses, products, services, or webinars. Try to offer some free incentives. To do business-to-business advertising, post workshops, meetings, conferences and articles on LinkedIn.

Search for groups of potential customers that need to be aware of you and join them. Tweet short tips and useful information.

Another thing that builds visibility and credibility are discussions on LinkedIn. Start one. Not only do you learn a lot and gain visibility, you get a wealth of information. I asked the members of several LinkedIn groups this question, "How many of you are using Twitter? Are you networking with others or connecting with customers? Do you have more than one account for different purposes? Tell me your experiences and strategy." I received fifteen responses at last count. Everyone openly shared information. One Freelance Success member tweets twice a day about her editing business and books and tweets occasional social comments. She states that she gets some referrals to her Web site from Twitter, but more from LinkedIn. She keeps Facebook for personal use to connect with friends and former co-workers.

Another writer from the Austin Independent Business Alliance (AIBA) group has used Twitter for about a year and states she has landed a few projects, but she uses it mostly to learn about her industry, "like my own online library of resources."

What else can you do? You can pitch a job to a journalist that followed you back on Twitter. You can share a link with valuable writing tips. You can build your personal brand and create an image that makes you approachable and human.

This is especially important for writers who mentor other writers or teach lifewriting skills, because personal stories are always a sensitive topic. You can even do advanced searches to find people in your area to network with in person. Don't be intimidated. Just take it one step at a time.

GETTING STARTED

LinkedIn and Facebook

Basic accounts are free on both of these services, and it's easy to set up a profile by following the instructions. Both offer a variety of controls that allow you to decide which information you want to show the public.

For example, you may want to display your state of residence but not your birth date. Remember, don't include too much personal information, such as a home phone number, home address, or photos of your kids and where they go to school. Save those things for a site restricted to family.

On the other hand, if you want to do business, you have to accept some form of contact. If you elect only to accept contact through the message feature on that site, you must also remember to log in regularly. Most sites forward e-mail from the site to your personal e-mail if you wish. Gmail or Yahoo e-mail accounts can provide an extra layer of privacy, but you must remember to login and check them.

Be consistent and decide what you want to emphasize before you set up profiles. Business people need to be accessible and personable, without being naive and vulnerable. That's a fine line to walk in the world of the Internet.

However, it's a proven fact that a photo can increase sales by fifty percent. You must be real. Before you set up accounts, pick a photo, write a tagline or short description, decide on several different login and password combinations you like, and draft a statement that describes you, your accomplishments, and your services.

In addition, some password systems don't allow you to use your first name, two letters in a row, or your e-mail address. You may have to come up with one that fits the site specifications. Remember to write all of them down.

Don't use the same login and password for every social media Web site, and don't select one you use for personal banking or logging into your blog. If a company has a security breach, that could leave you vulnerable in other areas. Once you have all of this information together, you are ready to create an account and build a profile. Select groups and contacts based on what you want to accomplish. If you are an author who wants to get to know publishers, follow publishers; join publishing groups, post messages about what you write and how you build your platform. If you work in publishing and want a new job, your messages could be tips you've learned in the trade with subtle information about your accomplishments.

Compliment others on their blogs, Web sites, and successes too. Those entries create an awareness of your presence that can result in referrals and work later.

Twitter

Twitter's profile is limited to 256 characters. With this limit, you definitely want to draft the profile before you set up your account. It must be highly focused to fit and be effective. There are limits in the communication format too.

Your message is a tweet. Tweets have a limit of 140 characters, and your followers are called tweeps. You can also send and receive a direct message, called a DM. The idea is to follow people in your industry and in subject areas where you want to gain information or contacts, e.g., *This Old House* for home renovation tips. Tweeting is where you gain real visibility.

Most people you follow check your profile to decide whether they want to follow you back. That makes them aware of you. The exception is companies. They usually follow back automatically or not at all. While there is a convention that says, "If someone follows you, you follow them," don't take that too literally. We don't all need real estate in San Francisco or a daily update from the BBC in London.

The easiest way to read and manage Twitter is by downloading free software called TweetDeck, which consolidates the messages in one window that's organized in four sections that are easy to scan. For tweeting, the free management tool I use is SocialOomph. This program allows me to monitor mentions of my profile, and it lets me set up tweets in advance, which is essential when I need concentrated time to write. It also allows me to generate a daily digest e-mail of specific people or subjects that I want to watch.

There are tons of paid upgrades available for all of the services, but there isn't any need to pay. The free services work fine. One other caution is to be very sure of the meaning of any shortcuts or abbreviations you use. Many text terms have multiple meanings that can lead to great embarrassment. A good source of clarification is the Urban Dictionary.

Of course, there are disadvantages too. People sometimes complain that too many of the group messages on LinkedIn are spam. It is true many people don't follow the guidelines, and some marketing gurus advocate breaking the rules. Many new users follow these "gurus" blindly. Once you see how annoying it is, you'll understand why it's not a technique to use to build relationships for freelancers and small businesses. You can always drop an annoying group.

One means of control is to set up mail sort folders. Send group e-mails to a separate folder that you read at your convenience or on a set schedule, such as Tuesday and Thursday. That way those messages don't clutter your inbox, and you don't waste time. It's easy to scan quickly through the headings to see whether you've received a DM or an e-mail from an individual that may need attention sooner.

BEYOND THE BASICS

You've set up your account, navigated through the basics, and you're at least familiar with moving around on the sites you've selected. Now, it's time to talk about how to build your contacts and how to use these sites to build your business.

The first thing to understand is that this is a part of marketing yourself as a writer. It's not a magic job magnet. I've read the articles where the author announces instant fame and a book contract within weeks, but that's not what happens for most people.

On the other hand, a writer who doesn't learn to market online loses many opportunities. More and more people search online for all of their services from doctors to carpet cleaning. You don't have to be an Internet guru, but you need a presence.

When you set up multiple sites that describe your work and your services, the consistency of those descriptions establishes your brand. In marketing, it is said that a customer has to see an ad seven times to remember it. Plus, all of these sites provide an opportunity to link back to your main Web site too.

Use your Web site name or your name to customize the link. Select whichever name you use to do business, if it's available. You can further solidify your brand by selecting colors that are consistent with your Web site. Unless you are a programmer, you might not have a perfect match, but you'll have a consistent image on the sites that offer color options.

Next, it's time to start selecting groups to join on LinkedIn. You also need to find people to connect with on Facebook and people or organizations to follow on Twitter. Of all of these, Twitter seems to be the most confusing to novice users, and I understand why. Hash tags (#), address signs (@), abbreviations (U, R, 2, etc), and unique things like follow Friday (FF) make it look like alphabet soup.

Give yourself time and find a good tutorial. (Twitter and Mashable.com, listed below, both offer excellent tutorials.) If you have a friend that is already tweeting, watch and ask questions. It isn't hard. It's just new and different. This article explains what these tools are and how to benefit by using them. There are many very well done systematic tutorials available to teach the rudimentary skills. If the first one you try isn't easy to understand, try another.

Now, go have fun and try something new.

MORE INFORMATION:

LinkedIn — *www.linkedin.com*
Facebook — *www.facebook.com*
Twitter — *www.twitter.com*
Tweetdeck — *www.tweetdeck.com*
Twuffer (a Twitter scheduling site) — *http://twuffer.com/home*
Twitter Contests — *http://twtaway.com*
Social Oomph — *www.socialoomph.com*
Mashable: The Social Media Guide — *http://mashable.com*
FriendFeed — *www.friendfeed.com*

❧ 29 ❧

To Blog or Not to Blog

A recent article reported that there are now approximately 200 million blogs on the Internet.[1] Other estimates are a bit more conservative, but still weigh in with numbers in the millions as of the end of 2009. With everyone and their dog, seemingly, rushing to jump on the blog bandwagon, is this an avenue that you as a writer should be exploring as well?

First, let's take a look at what a blog is. While blogs can obviously come in many forms, the basic concept of a blog is a "type" of Web site (according to Wikipedia) that is regularly updated by the host. Typically, the most recent post will appear at the top, with earlier posts beneath—or in some cases archived elsewhere on the site, with a list of archive topics appearing on the main page. Many blogs incorporate images, links to other sites and blogs, and even video clips. Finally, a blog often includes an interactive component: An invitation to readers to respond to and make comments upon the blog.

Many writers make a distinction between a "blog" and a "Web site." Though it is possible to post your own blog under your own domain, the majority of blogs are posted on sites dedicated to blogs (e.g., *www.blogger.com*). Because the general idea of a blog is that it be updated regularly (often several times a week, if not daily), bloggers often refer to ordinary Web sites as "static"—though there is certainly no reason why one can't post new material to a Web site just as often as to a blog! Many bloggers maintain both blogs and Web sites and cross-promote between them (e.g., a writer may post a full-length article on a Web site and then promote the article in a shorter piece posted to the blog).

While many bloggers will maintain that blog posts should be between 200 and 500 words at most, one will certainly find much longer blogs on the Web. However, many bloggers feel that readers will only read shorter posts—and also feel that this requirement to "keep it short" helps writers learn to write tightly and concisely.

---

[1] "Statistics Show Social Media Is Bigger Than You Think," *http://socialnomics.net/2009/08/11/statistics-show-social-media-is-bigger-than-you-think/*

With 200 million blogs out there, who's actually blogging? Actually, several studies suggest that the total number of blogs being tracked by sites like Technorati (which also operates one of the most popular blog directories) is inflated, as it doesn't take into account "dead" blogs (blogs that are no longer actively maintained) or "splogs" (spam blogs). A 2007 article in *Business Week* showed that of the 70 million blogs being tracked by Technorati in that year, only 15.5 percent were actively maintained (i.e., had been updated within the last 90 days).[2] A study cited by Caslon Analytics indicated that 60 to 80 percent of blogs are abandoned within one month, many after only a single post.

As for who's blogging and why, Caslon Analytics points out that the vast majority of blogs are personal journals aimed at "nanoaudiences"—a small circle of family and friends. *The Blogging Iceberg,* a report by Perseus Development, shows that teenagers create the majority of blogs; more than 90 percent are created by people under age 30, and 50 percent of bloggers are between the ages of 13 and 19. Just over half the blogs in the world are in English, and the U.S. seems to be responsible for most of those; a 2006 survey showed that only 2 percent of UK Internet users posted blogs and only 10 percent viewed blogs as often as once a month.[3]

That still leaves a lot of blogs—and a lot of writers who host blogs. Many writers host multiple blogs and post material to them several times a week. Should you be one of them? Specifically, will hosting a blog (or three) advance your freelance writing career? Will it, for example, attract more readers to your books? Help you earn writing assignments? Assist you in marketing a writing-related product or service? Or, at the very least, make you a better writer? These were the questions I asked in a survey of writers who run one or more blogs on a regular basis.

WHY BLOG?

The writers who responded to my survey blogged on a wide range of topics—health, cooking, homeschooling, current events, politics, books, travel, etc. Fewer than one third actually blogged about writing, per se; those who did used their blogs to share tips, markets, experiences, and insights into the writing life. Two or three reported that they used their blog as a personal journal, to write (or "rant") about whatever they felt like at the time, but this seemed to be the exception rather than the rule.

In fact, most respondents emphasized the importance of having a solid, well thought-out reason for having a blog in the first place. "If you are going to blog, decide why you are doing it and what your goals are," says Nanette Croce. Jan Kozlowski concurs: "Spend some time figuring out how you want to present

---

[2]Green, Heather, "With 15.5 Million Active Blogs, New Technorati Data Shows that Blogging Growth Seems to be Peaking," *Business Week,* April 25, 2007, *www.businessweek.com/the_thread/blogspotting/archives/2007/04/blogging_growth.html*

[3]Arnold, Bruce, "Blog Statistics and Demographics," Caslon Analytics, September 2008 - *www.caslon.com.au/weblogprofile1.htm*

yourself, what the purpose of your blog is and who your audience will be." Alice Wisler advises, "Have some focus. Provide interesting content."

Several writers launched blogs specifically to promote their writing. Roberta Roberti uses her cooking blog to promote her cookbooks and food-related writing. UK author Helen Gazeley writes, "I started partly because I thought I should know something about blogging, partly because I could direct people to my writing, partly with an idea that I might eventually hire myself out as a professional blogger, and partly in the hope that the blog might make some money." Fiction writer Michael Bracken uses his blog to chronicle his writing life and give writing advice; Jan Kozlowski's "But She Keeps a Nice Lawn" promotes her horror writing. Carol Alexander, who blogs on homesteading and homeschooling, hopes to create an audience for books she plans to write on these topics. Alice Wisler expected to *stop* blogging once her own book came out and she developed a Web site, but, as she put it, "Surprise!"

"I have links to a selection of my print and online published articles," says Anne Goldberg, who found it easier to set up a blog than a Web site. "I always give a link to the blog when I write queries. I also decided to set one up in case I applied for writing jobs." Leslie Dinaberg uses her blog to enhance her weekly slice-of-life/humor columns: "Either to promote them, to solicit information from readers about topics of interest, or to write about things I find compelling but that may not be quite right for my columns."

Nanette Croce uses her blog to advertise her editing business. Ronica Stromberg uses a blog to share her experiences as a children's writer. "I had spoken at a conference for children's writers, and several in the audience had expressed a desire... to see what my day-to-day life as a children's author looks like. My blog is an attempt to meet that need. I also visit schools frequently as an author, and use my blog as a Web site where teachers, librarians and conference coordinators can learn more about me, check out my credentials and the types of presentations I do, and my publications."

Many respondents, however, chose to launch a blog not to promote their writing, but to inform and entertain their readers. "I have written two books that I promote on my blogs, but the purpose is more to entertain and to form a community," says Keetha Mosley. Carol Alexander notes, "I try to make it a service-oriented blog... a place to find out how to do things or encouragement to keep on doing what we feel called to do when the going gets tough."

Amy Minchak launched a blog "to discuss the books I was reading that I wasn't doing reviews for. It was a way for me to share my passion for books and find new books by reaching out to other bloggers. The main reason behind my blog was to share book titles and information." Jan Kozlowski writes of her first blog, "I wanted to provide information and links to our members about children's writing." Her next blog was launched "partially to support my other freelance and fiction writing and partially to have a place to share thoughts, information, and other things I feel passionate about."

Yet another reason to launch a blog was the freedom the venue provides to publish whatever one wishes. "I found I missed the freedom of writing on subjects of my own choice, and not having to wait for editors to choose to publish what I wrote," says Nanette Croce. Dory Adams was "getting frustrated with the slow process of submitting work to literary journals, and I longed to connect with readers rather than feel that I was writing alone in a vacuum." She uses her blog to get shorter essays "into the world of readers," as does Vivian Unger, who sought "an outlet for my urge to write personal essays without having to go through the tedium of finding a publisher."

Leona Wisoker found blogging less threatening than seeking "regular" publication. "I hate writing articles, and wanted to learn how. The notion of submitting an article to a publisher scares me silly, so I got around it by writing for myself. And I decided that since I'm writing all these articles for myself, I may as well share them so that other writers can skip all the research I went through... and posting on my own blog didn't scare me a bit, so I started doing that. I still need to learn to cut the word count down, as I didn't realize that blog posts were only supposed to be about two or three hundred words! I moved all the really long articles to my Web site and tried to keep the blog stuff short, and since then the hits—and the comments—have gone up dramatically."

SPEAKING OF NUMBERS...

If one's goal is to attract a following and reach out to readers, how effective is a blog in achieving that goal? One problem with blogging is that there are a wide range of methods of tracking visitors—including regular "followers," page views, subscribers to RSS feeds, e-mail subscribers and more.

Many respondents didn't track visitor rates at all. Of those who did, numbers varied from nine page views per day to several hundred page views per month. One respondent reported three "official" followers and 50 e-mail readers; another reported "four followers and five other people who check it out from time to time." Dory Adams reported 200 hits per week; Leona Wisoker, 100 to 300 hits per month; Nanette Croce, 800 to 1000 page views per month.

Many respondents also took little or no action to promote their blogs, which may account for the low volume of hits. Others recommended an array of promotional techniques, including:

- Put links to your blog in your e-mail signature block
- Post announcements of blog updates to your social networking profiles (e.g., LinkedIn, MySpace, and Facebook)
- Send a Tweet to your Twitter following whenever you post to your blog
- Put your blog URL on your business cards and other stationery
- Add your blog to directories, such as Technorati
- Post your blog to "blog carnivals"
- Visit other blogs and leave comments with a link back to your own blog

- Notify sites whenever you provide a link

- Learn how to use "pings" and "pingbacks"

- E-mail your writing friends and other contacts when you upload a post

Several writers felt that the effort of promoting a blog wasn't worthwhile, however. "I wouldn't want to write for no one," says Nanette Croce, "but as long as someone is reading, I don't care if it's ten people or a thousand. It's the ability to write about subjects I enjoy that keeps me going." Croce also points out that "the time you spend promoting your blog could go directly into promoting your work. Unless you can really, really make your blog stand out, it is hardly going to make a great promotion tool."

A number of respondents have sought to earn money from their blogs using Google AdSense and Amazon.com associate programs, with varying results. Tiffany Jansen uses both, and "while they don't pull in a significant amount of money, it is a nice little bonus!" Tom Botts writes, "The only direct money I receive from blogging has been Google AdSense. It hasn't been all that lucrative, but that may be because I don't have that many people following the blog, or those that do just don't click on the ads." Nanette Croce felt that "Google AdSense is a big dud." She uses Amazon.com Associates on her book review blog, noting, "It seemed like a natural, but that has turned into a big zero as well."

Other writers have been reluctant to attempt to "monetize" their blogs for fear of alienating readers. "I would like to eventually incorporate some sort of advertising but would prefer it to be minimal, since I myself find it distracting and don't want to distract readers coming to the blog," says Amy Minchak. "I also don't want to look like my opinions are swayed by any form of advertising revenue. I don't know how others feel about this, but if a blog is heavily promoting a book, author, etc., and I see ads, I sometimes wonder. With the new FTC rules, this is not supposed to happen, or at least as a reader you are supposed to be told whether or not money was involved, but it still crosses my mind." (In 2010, the FTC imposed regulations requiring bloggers to disclose whether they received any "compensation" for reviews of products or books, including receipt of a free review copy or product sample.[4])

Jan Kozlowski agrees. "Frankly, I don't like reading blogs with ads on them. They turn me completely off, so why risk others feeling that way for the pennies you usually end up with? I tend to think of blogs as career support and a labor of love, not an income stream." Dory Adams also feels "it would be nice to be able to earn some compensation for my time, but I don't want to clutter up the design with ads. It's extremely important to me that the blog be visually appealing and that ads not detract from the images on the posts. For now, my purpose is to attract a loyal audience and not blast them with ads."

---

[4]Paul, Ian, "New FTC Blogging Regulations: Forcing Transparency on a Culture of Full Disclosure," *The Huffington Post,* October 6, 2009 - *www.huffingtonpost.com/ian-paul/new-ftc-blogging-regulati_b_311851.html*

BLOGGING VS. "WRITING"

One downside of blogging cited by several writers was the amount of time it consumed. "I spend a minimum of two hours on each entry, often longer," says Roberta Roberti. "This involves not just writing the blog, but research on the subject, copying and pasting passages or quotes, and finding the right artwork." She also finds it time-consuming to monitor for trojans and spammers. Ronica Stromberg notes, "It's work without a paycheck attached. The time spent on it might have been used to write a paid article or book." Leslie Dinaberg agrees: "Since I am a professional writer, it's always tough to balance the things I get paid to do versus the projects that are purely mine."

"Readers expect new material pretty frequently," says Tiffany Jansen. "A blog becomes your very own column, and as we all know, columns are not easy to come by. Caring for your blog can become an obsession. I try to spend no more than 1½ to 2 hours per day blogging, through that doesn't always happen. Another trick is to use blog posts to direct traffic to your other writing. For example, as soon as a new article or interview of mine is published, I write a blog post linking to the newly published material. Those posts take about five minutes *and* my new article gets instant hits."

Ronica Stromberg and Leona Wisoker, however, have found ways to make their blogs serve double duty. "I often field questions from beginning writers, and I can sometimes refer questioners to my blog or Web site for answers instead of having to respond with an extensive e-mail every time," says Stromberg. "I also don't blog every day. If I don't have anything particularly useful to say, I'm not going to waste my time." Wisoker writes "the same bit for my bimonthly writer's group newsletter and the blog, with a few modifications to suit the different audiences. It saves me a ton of time and effort." Also, she notes, "committing to a biweekly post forces me to settle for 'good enough' instead of perfection."

Herein lies one of the hidden benefits of blogging, according to several writers. Far from being a hindrance to their writing time and careers, they feel that blogging has made them *better* writers. "It's difficult to introduce a topic and come to a worthwhile point in under 500 words," says Jack Dunigan. "Blogging forces you to be a tight writer and to edit brutally." Maureen Anderson agrees: "It takes discipline to come up with something as fun to read as it is useful, and to do that four times a week." Michael Bracken notes, "Blogging has allowed me to more closely examine my own productivity and methods of writing. The need to post on a regular basis... prevents me from slacking off."

Amy Minchak feels that blogging has improved her writing discipline. "I feel it has given me a reason to write because I now have a schedule to follow. In the past, I would put off writing since it was only for me and no one else. Now that I have an audience, I have a reason and a want to sit down and put words on paper." Peter Buckton feels that "it is an ongoing process that is good for my writing experience and practice. The more I write, the better I get at the craft. The practice of writing for your blog is a great writing discipline." Pina Belperio feels her writing has "greatly improved because I am writing on a weekly basis." Cathy Hall believes that blogging "can make you a better, tighter writer, improving your skills in the long run. And it will make you a more disciplined writer, getting you in the habit of writing regularly."

In short, as several respondents pointed out, blogging *is* writing. "It obviously isn't fiction writing," says Penny Ehrenkranz, "but there have been times when my blog posts have sparked an idea for a writing-related article." Keetha Mosley feels that "blogging seems to be a warm-up for writing on my novel and working on pieces for the newsletter."

TAKING THE PLUNGE

There may not be precisely 200 million blogs on the Web—but there are enough to make it difficult for a new blog to stand out amongst the crowd. If you're considering launching a blog, here are some tips to keep in mind before (and after) you begin:

"Don't do it because you feel you have to. Only do it if you want to."

—Nanette Croce

"Make sure you have a clear idea of what you want to talk about. I don't think you should start a blog if you don't have a deep interest in your topic. Otherwise you'll be bored trying to find things to write about, and it will show. Also, let your personality show. I spent a few weeks blogging and felt like I was missing something, and one day I realized what was missing was me. You need to let yourself show in your posts. You don't have any other way to draw people in. All they see is your words. You need to make them count. You need to make them interesting."

—Amy Minchak

"Don't forget the passion factor. Readers know when you're just blogging to sell something, or to further your brand or for some other asinine obligatory reason. Blogging is writing and the best writing comes from the heart, not the head. Have fun and your readers will too and reward you with their time, attention and support."

—Jan Kozlowski

"Make a list of topics you want to cover and write about ten posts before you ever launch. That way you know how much you can say in 300 words or less, you have some time to parcel out posts, you can adjust based on audience reaction, and you're not panicking for stuff to say over the first few weeks."

—Leona Wisoker

"Keep posts around 200-300 words. People won't take time to read anything longer. Read everything you can online to educate yourself about blogging, about building a blog, and about attracting followers, before beginning. Post regularly. You want to keep your name in front of people."

—Carol Alexander

"Make it easy to find. Update it regularly; if you don't, people will stop coming to it. Make it visually interesting, but don't overload the page too much. Write well. Just because it's a blog doesn't mean it's OK to have bad spelling, incorrect grammar, incomplete sentences and dumbed-down language. People will assume that if you write like that on your blog, you write like that elsewhere. And who wants to read bad writing?"

—Roberta Roberti

"It's very important to remember that a blog is not going to make you instantly famous. Nor is it going to guarantee your success as a writer. Ever since Julie Powell got a publishing contract for her blog (which then became a movie), writers think that all they have to do is launch a blog and fans and publishers will come to them. That's not the way it works for most people. You should blog because you love the topic you're writing about. Don't have major expectations because you will be sorely disappointed."

—Roberta Roberti

"Don't post in haste, especially if you're in a bad mood when you write something. If there's any concern that what you're writing might be offensive or might simply make you look like a dork, sleep on it first. You might go back and remove it later, but by then it could already be cached, in which case it's there forever."

—Carol Penn-Romine

"You have to keep it fun and remember that you're doing it for fun. If it becomes one more thing on your to-do list, that zaps all the fun out of it. Remember why you began to blog."

—Keetha Mosley

"Remember, you run your blog; don't let the blog run you."

—Dana King

And that's perhaps the best advice of all. A blog is a tool—and the purpose of a tool is to make it work for you, not the other way around. If a blog proves useful to your writing career, then by all means use it. But if you feel that it's getting in the way of what you really want to do, let it go. The world will survive without it!

TOOLS FOR THE BLOGGER

There are a host of tools online for the beginning blogger; here's a sampling of some sites that can be helpful:

Blog—*en.wikipedia.org/wiki/Blog*
An excellent overview of what blogs are, including definitions of commonly used terms.

Starting a Blog—*www.startingablog.com/*
A variety of how-to articles on getting your blog set up.

Starting Your First Blog? 29 Tips, Tutorials and Resources for New Bloggers—*www.problogger.net/archives/2009/01/30/starting-your-first-blog-29-tips-tutorials-and-resources-for-new-bloggers/*

How to Make Money with a Blog – *www.christianpf.com/how-to-make-money-with-a-blog/*
A good overview of blogging techniques in general, plus tips on how to earn income through AdSense and affiliate programs.

Weblog Matrix—*www.weblogmatrix.org/*
Compares the features of a variety of weblog tools, including Blogger and Wordpress.

Seven Blogging Tools Reviewed – *www.techsoup.org/learningcenter/webbuilding/page5516.cfm*

Blogger – *www.blogger.com*
One of the most popular sites for developing and posting blogs.

Technorati Blog Directory – *http://technorati.com/blogs/directory/*
Search for blogs by category, and have your own blog listed in the directory.

PART VII

Expanding Your Writing Business

❧ 30 ☙

Selling Reprints

You've probably read articles on the wonders of selling reprints. A lot of them sound something like this: "I've sold the same article 462 times, and netted thousands of dollars!" Such pieces tend to make one feel like a total slouch for having sold a piece only once.

Are reprints really an untapped goldmine for writers? Can you make your fortune reselling work you've already published? The answer often depends on who you ask—and also on what you write. The following questions and answers will give you an idea of the basics of the process.

Q: What is a reprint?

A: Publications consider an article to be a reprint if it has been previously published and remains substantially unchanged from that previous publication. Many publications do not accept reprints at all. Others pay a lower fee for reprints than for original material. Within these broad guidelines, however, you can find a host of variations and exceptions.

Q: When is a reprint not a reprint?

A: When you sell simultaneous, nonexclusive, or one-time rights to a piece of material. "Reprint" terms apply when you're marketing to publications that use "first" or "second" rights. When you sell first rights to your article, typically any subsequent sale would be of "second" or "reprint" rights. However, in some markets you can sell the same material to several different publications, either simultaneously or sequentially, by offering "one-time nonexclusive" rights. This gives every publication who buys your work the right to use it once, but not the right to use it "first," and not the right to be the only publication to use it. A good example of this type of use would be a column distributed to several newspapers or similar publications.

Q: When can I sell a reprint?

A: If you have sold first rights to an article, you generally cannot offer (or sell) reprint rights until that material has actually appeared in the original publication.

"First" rights means the publication has the right to use it first, so if you were to sell reprint rights before the first article appeared, you could be in violation of your original contract. Once the article has appeared in print or online or wherever, however, you're generally then free to offer reprint or "second" rights to other publications.

Q: Do all articles make good reprints?

A: Some articles have good reprint potential; others don't. If you have tailored an article toward a specific audience and publication, it may be difficult to remarket that material elsewhere without doing a substantial rewrite. If you're writing for a very narrow market niche, you may not find many markets for reprints. If a small number of publications are competing for the same market share (as is common in the pet magazine market), you may find it difficult to find a "noncompeting" market to buy a reprint.

Time-sensitive articles generally don't work well as reprints. If the subject you're covering will be old news once the article hits print, if the material is outdated, if things have changed substantially, or if interest in the topic has waned, your chances of reselling the material are low. Similarly, material of purely local interest may be difficult to resell to a different regional market. The focus or slant of your article may also hinder its resale potential.

Q: Where should I market reprints?

A: The most important rule to follow when looking for markets for reprints is to look for "noncompeting" publications. If two publications serve the same market or audience, each is unlikely to accept material that previously appeared in the other. For example, the magazine *The Writer* is not likely to purchase an article that formerly appeared in *Writer's Digest,* and vice versa. The key lies in finding a noncompeting market—either a publication that addresses an audience with different interests, or a publication that has a very different regional distribution.

Many authors do well selling reprints to noncompeting regional publications, such as magazines that serve a single city, county, region, or state. Even though the general "focus" or content of each magazine might be substantially similar, the audience is limited to a particular region, and therefore the publications are "noncompeting." By the same token, it is often possible to sell reprints of your work overseas. Print publications will sometimes accept material that has appeared electronically, and vice versa.

Q: How do I find markets for reprints?

A: The first step is to identify likely customers. It's actually a good idea to consider this step before you actually start writing your article; then, you can determine whether you need to gather additional information for revisions and retailored articles while researching the original. Brainstorm the potential markets for your topic, and jot down any ideas that come to mind. For example, if you're writing an article on natural healthcare for women for a major women's healthcare magazine, consider the potential for reselling the same article (or a retailored article) to other markets, such as:

• Women's healthcare magazines in other countries

• General women's magazines

• Magazines targeting specific age groups (e.g., teenagers, older women)

• General interest publications (especially if you can develop a newsworthy slant)

• Local and regional publications (especially if you can link the material to a local source or expert)

• Local, regional, and major metropolitan newspapers (target their "lifestyle" sections)

• Publications that address some subset of the topic, such as herb publications, natural health magazines, or New Age/spiritual magazines

• Online/electronic publications in any of the above categories

Once you've developed a list of potential markets, start hunting down information in the latest *Writer's Market* or online. Use an online newsstand or a guidelines database to gather more information about potential markets. If you can't find out from the listing whether a market accepts reprints, send a brief e-mail the editor and ask, or make a very brief, courteous phone call. Choose the markets that offer the highest pay potential first, and work your way down the list.

Q: What rights can I sell?

A: Whether you can sell a reprint at all depends first and foremost upon the rights you sell to the original article. If you sell "all rights" or produce an article as "work-for-hire," you cannot sell reprint rights, as you no longer own those rights. This doesn't mean that you should never sell all rights; however, if you do, be sure you're sufficiently compensated for the loss of potential future reprint income—or that no likely market for reprints exists.

If you sell "first" rights of any kind (e.g., First North American Serial Rights [FNASR], First Electronic Rights, etc.), you can then sell "second" rights to the same type of market (e.g., a North American publication), and in some cases you can sell "first" rights to a different market (e.g., a British publication). For example, if you've sold FNASR, you may be able to sell the article as a "first" to an overseas publication (although you'll find that many do prefer to handle such material as a reprint anyway). If you've sold first print rights, you can still sell first electronic rights, and vice versa. Regardless of the actual rights you've sold, however, many publications will still regard previously published work as a "reprint" (and treat it as such) even if some areas of "first" rights are still available.

When selling the reprint itself, you will generally offer nonexclusive "second" rights or "one-time" rights. "Second" serial rights can be sold over and over; the term simply indicates that the publication is no longer "first." (In other words, you don't have to worry about keeping track and offering "43rd serial rights.") Most reprints are sold "nonexclusively," which means that you can sell the same reprint to more than one publication, often at the same time. Sending out "simultaneous submissions" of reprints is also a little more acceptable than sending out simsubs of an original article; just be sure that the reprint isn't going out to competing markets.

When offering a reprint overseas, be sure to address issues of regional rights and language rights in your sale. For example, you might want to sell a reprint to a British publication, but hold onto the rights to sell the same material in English to another European country, as well as the rights to sell the material in other languages.

Q: If I rewrite an article, does it cease to be a reprint?
A: There is no hard-and-fast rule about how much editing or revision is required to change a reprint into a new, original piece. The keyword is usually "substantially"—i.e., the piece needs to be "substantially" different. If you just change a few words here and there, add a paragraph, or drop a sentence, this generally isn't enough to make a piece "new."

Rather than selling reprints per se, many writers prefer to tailor the same information to several different markets. For example, if you were writing a piece on relocating to a new city, you could slant one article to a business audience, another to a financial publication, another to a women's magazine, and yet another to a parenting publication. Each piece would have a focus specific to the market you're targeting, each would qualify as "original"—yet each is drawn from the same pool of research information. This is often the best approach, as many publications prefer that material be tailored directly toward their audience.

The best way to test whether something is rewritten sufficiently to be considered a new article is to put yourself in the reader's shoes. If you read the two articles in two different publications, would you think they were different articles? Or would you regard them as being the same? If you would regard them as the same (or regard one as being an excerpt of the other), then they are, essentially, the same. This means they are the "same article" with respect to the rights you're selling—you won't be able to satisfy one editor's request for, say, "first" rights or "exclusive" rights to a piece if you're selling a portion of that identical piece to someone else.

That being said, you can submit even the same article to two different publications *if* those publications are willing to accept non-exclusive one-time rights to the material. If, however, either publication (or both) wants first rights, or exclusive rights (e.g., exclusive electronic rights), then you can't. You have to honor whatever rights you're offering—and that usually means the rights that are requested by the publication (which you'll know by reading its guidelines).

Since most publications that deal with a specific topic are likely to be competing, this is even more reason *not* to try to pitch the same article (or very similar articles) to two at the same time. Most likely, each will get wind of the fact that you've sold something similar to a competitor, and that would be enough to make each editor decide never to work with you again.

Q: Do I need to query for reprints?

A: Generally, one doesn't bother to query on a reprint, as you have already written the article, so you're not really looking for an "assignment." Queries are more to save you time by preventing you from going to the trouble of writing a new article before you know that it will be accepted. Since a reprint has already been written, it's usually best to send it directly, with a cover letter. Just be sure that the publication accepts reprints, and that your material wasn't originally published in a competing magazine.

Q: Should I tell a publisher that a submission is a reprint?

A: It is considered proper to inform a publisher of any previous publications of a manuscript, regardless of the rights. A previously published piece is considered a reprint, whether you have the rights back or not. Otherwise, you would be (falsely) giving the publisher the impression that they are buying "first" rights. (By the way, if something has been previously published, you no longer have "all" rights to the work, as "first" publication rights, at least in a particular medium or area, have already been used and are gone forever.)

Q: Should I send the published article or the manuscript?

A: Since the publisher will have to format your article for publication if it is accepted, it's generally better to send the original (or edited) manuscript. Simply state where it appeared before. If the manuscript was heavily edited by the first publisher and you believe that this editing *improved* the piece, you might wish to retype the manuscript *as it was actually published* rather than as you originally submitted it. Keep in mind that the next publisher may also edit the manuscript.

If the original article included photos, then it's a good idea to send a copy of the clip so that the editor can see the images, without requiring you to actually submit the photos or photo files themselves until the editor accepts the piece.

Q: How much time should I spend marketing reprints?

A: That's up to you. As you build a collection of material, you'll probably find that some pieces are more appropriate for reprint sales than others. Don't waste a lot of time on those that aren't—and don't waste too much time on those that are! For example, you may not want to invest the same amount of time and money on sample copies for potential reprint markets as you would when researching markets for original articles, because there's less return on your investment.

Reprints can provide a viable source of income. However, to be able to market reprints successfully, you must first build a supply of "original" published articles. Never spend so much time trying to resell old work that you stop writing new material!

⌇31⌇

Writing for International Publications[1]

International publications can be an excellent way to expand your network of markets. If you live in the U.S., consider targeting the host of English-language publications that can be found in Canada, Great Britain and Ireland, Australia, New Zealand, India, South Africa, Singapore and other regions. If you live outside the U.S. and write in English, you have the option of expanding to *U.S.* markets. And if you speak and/or write fluently in another language, your market options expand even further, as there is a great demand for good translations of materials that have been previously published in English.

Unfortunately, it's not as easy to locate international markets on the Web as it is to find markets based in the U.S. While most U.S. publications have Web sites that make it easy to find an editor's e-mail, this is not always true abroad. In many countries, Internet use is not as well established as in the U.S., sometimes due to language issues, sometimes due to the fact that it's not always easy to obtain high-speed connections in rural areas. Hence, a great many non-U.S. publications have, at best, a "consumer" Web site aimed solely at potential subscribers (and often offering very little substantive information), or no Web site at all.

A variety of market guides exist to help you track down markets in English-speaking countries. For Great Britain and Ireland, you can choose from *Writer's Market UK and Ireland, The Writers' and Artists' Yearbook, The Writer's Handbook,* or the *Children's Writers' and Artists' Yearbook.* Australian markets can be found in the *Australian Writers' Marketplace;* Canadian markets are listed in the *Canadian Writers' Market.* For markets in other parts of the world, visit Worldwide Freelance Writer at *www.worldwidefreelance.com;* this site offers a weekly e-mail newsletter with market listings from around the world, and extensive compendiums of international markets.

Since so many international publications do *not* have a Web presence or, necessarily, an easily available contact e-mail for an editor, contacting such

---

[1]Excerpted from *The Writer's Guide to Queries, Pitches and Proposals* (Allworth Press, 2010)

publications must often be done the "old-fashioned" way, with a query sent by mail. When querying international editors, all the rules set forth in chapter 17 apply—and apply even more strictly than when dealing with U.S. editors. In the U.S., a certain degree of informality is often acceptable; however, what passes for "casual" in the States may be considered discourteous abroad. When in doubt, err on the side of formality, extra courtesy, and unwavering professionalism.

It's also important to know *what* to pitch overseas. Obviously, topics of limited local or regional appeal will rarely find a market elsewhere. (However, local "color" pieces can often be converted into useful international travel articles.) Even articles of a more general nature, such as pieces on health, or how-to articles, should be examined with care. An article on healthcare, for example, won't be useful overseas if the methods, treatments or medications are not available in the other country. Articles that rely on an understanding of American culture, society, idiom, humor or jargon are also rarely marketable outside the country. You may also need to make a convincing case for why an editor of a non-U.S. publication should buy from *you* rather than from a writer in his or her own country.

In both your query *and* your article, you should avoid American slang, idiomatic phrases, or humor that may not "translate" well, even if your article is going to another English-language publication. However, it's less important to worry about international spelling, punctuation, or usages such as the way of indicating dates, times, numbers, currencies and so forth; the editor of the publication will generally be able to resolve those minor issues. If you *do* know these international usages, so much the better—but if you don't, don't let that stop you from sending out a query.

Your query should be very clear and specific. Don't assume that an editor will "know what you're talking about." If you need to refer to recent events, news items, or articles, provide specific references (Web references are best). If you plan to interview an expert, spell out that expert's credentials. When it comes to your own credentials, determine if you can provide anything that indicates an understanding of your target publication's audience.

The good news is that once you've made contact with a formal query, you will probably be able to conduct the rest of your correspondence by e-mail. Most non-U.S. editors *do* have e-mail; they're just less likely to make it publicly available. This means that most likely, you won't need to include a self-addressed envelope with IRCs (international reply coupons); few editors actually want to have to make a trip to their local post office to redeem them. Even publications that insist on doing business by surface mail in their own country are generally willing to make an exception for international correspondence.

Another issue to be aware of when dealing with international publications is that many are far less concerned about lengthy, formal contracts than U.S. publications. Don't be surprised if all you ever receive is a letter (or e-mail) of acceptance. You may also find it difficult to convince an editor to "keep in touch" and let you know when your article is scheduled for publication, so follow up regularly (and politely). Be sure to request a contributor's copy when the article *is* published.

Payment issues can also be difficult; many international publishers will wish to simply issue a check in their own currency. Since this can cost you anywhere from $15 to $25 (or more) to deposit in a U.S. bank account, depending on your bank's charges for (a) international currency exchange and (b) a non-U.S. check, keep this in mind when doing your market research. If an international publication only pays the equivalent of $35 to $50 for an article, and you're likely to lose more than half of that in exchange and check-cashing fees, it may not be worth the effort. Fortunately, more and more international publications are turning to PayPal as a means of paying writers in other countries; while this, too, will involve some fees, they are typically much lower than what your bank will charge. Some larger international publications also maintain accounts with a U.S.-based bank, and can issue checks in U.S. currency.

While dealing with publications outside your own country can take some getting used to, the benefits can be extensive. International publications may be open to topics that you can't sell "at home," and they can also be excellent places to sell reprints of material you've already marketed in your own country. And, again, if you write fluently in a language other than English, your potential market area will be even greater. If you can write a great pitch, the world is your oyster!

❧32☙

Selling Photos

It has been said that a picture is worth a thousand words. In the world of publishing, this is not simply a parable, but the absolute truth. Magazines aren't simply a verbal medium; they are also a visual medium. That means that for every 1000 great words an editor receives, s/he will need at least one great picture.

If you have a knack with a camera, you may be able to make your editor's day—and increase your writing income—by offering packages of text and pictures. You don't have to be an experienced photographer to sell your photos. Granted, tourist snapshots of your trip to Rome won't make it into *National Geographic,* but they may be just what a smaller travel publication or your local newspaper travel section needs.

PHOTO "OPS"

Many editors make their purchasing decisions based on whether the author can provide photos. Keep this in mind, therefore, when you plan future articles. While some articles don't lend themselves to easy illustration, others are "naturals" for accompanying photographs, including:

• **Travel articles.** Whenever you travel, take your camera along, and use it. If you are using a film camera, don't worry about the cost of film; just snap every shot that looks remotely worthwhile. If you're using digital, then the issue of "cost" is irrelevant; snap *everything!* Failed shots won't cost you a penny, and the results may surprise you. While major travel publications accept only top-quality professional photos, many smaller publications welcome clear, focused shots that illustrate the sights described in your article.

• **Profiles.** Bring your camera when you go on an interview. Try to get a few "candid" shots of your subjects, in different types of light. If you're interviewing an artist or craftsperson, take photos of the person's work. If your interviewee has special interests, include those in the session. Also, ask your interviewee if he or she has publicity photos that you could include with your article. (Be sure that your subject is authorized to use this photo for publication; remember that the copyright of a professional or publicity photo is usually owned by the photographer, and the photographer's name should be listed in the credit line, if known.)

- **How-to articles.** Suppose you want to pitch an article on administering first aid to an injured pet. While your words may be vivid, nothing will get the idea across like a series of photos that demonstrate exactly how to apply a bandage, where to apply pressure, and so forth. The next time you prepare a how-to piece, consider setting up a "photo shoot" in which a friend or family member demonstrates the techniques you're describing, while you take pictures. (Or, if your friend is the better photographer, reverse the process!)

- **Craft projects.** Many magazines decide whether to buy instructions for a craft project based on a photograph of the finished result. They may not buy the photo itself; most will want to take their own photos of the finished piece. Your photo of how the finished piece will look, however, can be the key to selling your idea.

- **Events.** Photographic coverage of a newsworthy event can make the difference between a sale and a rejection. Try to avoid static "grip and grin" shots (where two people shake hands and smile at the camera), or dull head-shots. Instead, try to capture people in motion, with natural poses and expressions. Experiment with different angles and lenses (a telephoto lens, for example, can help you zoom in on individuals or zoom out for crowd shots).

BASIC EQUIPMENT

I won't try to tell you how to take great pictures. To learn more about photography, check with your local photo shop or adult education center; you may easily earn back the price of a class with your first photo sale. There are also now a host of excellent photography sites on the Web that offer free online "classes" and instruction in all types of photography (check out *www.apogee.com* as one example).

Today, the photography world is going digital. While there are still many publications that use film, these are more likely to be the magazines that also require professional, high-end photos. Even those often want images to be *submitted* digitally (more on that later), even if they weren't electronic to begin with. For the rest of us, converting to a good-quality digital camera is truly the best option.

The key here is "good quality." There are lots of inexpensive "point and shoot" digital cameras on the market that are great for capturing pictures of your toddler or friends at a wild party (if the ads are to be believed). But when it comes to taking photos that you can sell, aim for something a bit higher. Keep in mind that in the world of digital photography, size matters—specifically, the file size of your image. Now, it's possible to get a camera that provides 8-megapixel images for under $300. This gives you more than enough "file size" and image resolution to create photos that can be printed on a full magazine page or even as cover shots (something that was more difficult a few years ago).

Digital photography offers a host of advantages for those of us for whom photography is a secondary skill (secondary to writing, at least). Perhaps the greatest advantage is cost. You don't have to pay for film or to have that film developed—which means you can take as many images as you wish, without breaking your budget. When you're traveling, this is a wonderful advantage—because you can't just go back and try again if a shot doesn't come out right the first time. A digital camera gives you the freedom to experiment with different angles, exposures, and ideas that you might not want to "play around with" if every experiment were costing precious funds.

Digital cameras have another advantage in allowing you to preview and review shots. This, again, is helpful when you can't go back and take something over if it didn't come out right. You can tell at a glance if you lopped off the top of someone's head, or if someone walked in front of you just as you clicked the shutter, or if that castle is just a wee bit out of focus (or out of the frame). And finally, you don't have to worry about carrying film around with you or having enough on hand, or whether it will pass through the airport scanners without being damaged.

You *will* need to make sure that you always have enough batteries on hand, however. There's nothing worse than being at a once-in-a-lifetime destination only to find that your battery has run out and you don't have a replacement. I usually keep at least two fully charged batteries in my purse (and my husband keeps spares for his camera in the camera case that he attaches to his belt). Using your flash and reviewing your shots will both consume your battery faster than ordinary "shooting." Also make sure that you either have a large memory card in your camera (I use a 2GB card) or a spare—or both.

The downside of using a digital camera is that you will need to develop a certain amount of "tech savvy" with a photo-editing program. The industry standard for photographers is Photoshop. This program can be expensive (Photoshop Elements is cheaper and comes bundled with many digital cameras, but it doesn't do nearly as much). Photoshop can also be intimidating; it has loads of features and options that, quite honestly, you're never going to need. What you *will* need to be able to do is review your photos, rotate them (if you take a lot of vertical shots, like I do, you'll need to be able to turn them "right side up" on screen), and make some basic corrections to exposure and, in some cases, color balance.

All cameras come with a basic "program" for downloading photos to your computer and/or laptop, and a basic USB cable through which you can download images directly from the camera. It's simpler, however, to invest in an expensive "card reader" and just treat your memory card like any other storage device, transferring the photo files to a designated folder on your hard drive. (It's also faster; I've found that the camera-USB-computer transfer system tends to take at least three times as long as a card reader.) If you're traveling and take lots of photos, you'll probably want to take your laptop along so that you can download (and quickly review) each day's shots. (Another good reason to do this is to ensure that your photos are stored somewhere other than your camera at the end of the day. Digital cameras are tempting targets for thieves, and you wouldn't want to lose your entire photo collection if, perchance, you lose your camera.) There are also devices on the market that let you download and store your photos or even burn them to CD or DVD, but these generally cost several hundred dollars; a lightweight notepad computer is a less expensive and more versatile travel option.

But what about your old film camera—or more importantly, your old film photos? Does the age of digital mean that these photos are now worthless? Not at all! As I said above, many publications prefer film photos (particularly slides) that have been scanned to digital files. If you have an archive of, say, 35mm transparencies, it's a relatively simple matter to scan them and create digital files. While this can be done with a flatbed scanner that has a transparency converter (basically, a light in the lid), the easiest method is to invest in a standalone 35mm slide scanner, which will usually handle both transparencies and negatives.

If you have larger formats (2¼ transparencies, for example), things get a bit more complicated, as most basic scanners don't handle those. You can use a flat-bed scanner, invest in a more expensive standalone scanner, *or* pay to have your slides professionally scanned (this will cost around $2 per image). Prints, of course, are the easiest of all to convert; just scan them on a flatbed scanner at a minimum of 300 dpi. The good news is that once you've converted your film archives to digital files, you can tweak them in Photoshop just like original digital images.

If you're not ready to convert to a digital camera, and in particular if you take transparencies rather than prints, a couple of helpful tools are a lightbox and a "jeweler's loupe." The latter is a magnifying glass that you can use in conjunction with a lightbox to make sure that your images are clear and crisp before you send them in. (A photo can look very good at 35mm—but turn out to be amazingly blurry when it's enlarged several hundred times for a magazine.)

You'll also want to pick up some plastic photo-protector sheets corresponding to the size of slide or print you use. These sheets not only protect your photos during shipping, but also provide a safe way to store them; most are "archival quality," which means that they don't contain acids that can damage your film over time. Finally, you'll want to start saving 8x10 sheets of cardboard, such as the backs of notepads, so that you'll have something to further protect your photos during shipping.

SUBMITTING PHOTOS

The good news about digital photography is that it has made the process of submitting photos much less expensive. You no longer have to worry about losing your photos, or having them damaged in the mail (or by a careless editor's coffee cup), because you're only submitting a file.

That being said, there are some guidelines to be followed when submitting digital photos. Nothing is going to annoy an editor more than receiving an unsolicited article by e-mail—complete with a dozen 2-megabyte "sample" photo files. Conversely, another way to annoy an editor is to inform him (or her) that they will need to go to some obscure online photo-sharing Web site, create an account, and then individually download your photos. (That being said, a photo-sharing site *can* be a good way to enable an editor to *preview* the photos that you have to offer with an article. There are many such sites available, some of which are free. Such sites also enable you to specify who can view your photos.)

The first step in submitting digital photos is to contact an editor with your query or article submission, and inform the editor of the *availability* of photos. Let the editor know what type of photos are available. For example, if you're submitting an article on a craft project, do you have photos of the finished project only, or do you have step-by-step "how-to" photos illustrating how the project is made? If it's a travel article, let the editor know which primary locations or sites you have photos of, and any important information (e.g., "I have more than 50 excellent interior shots of Such-and-Such cathedral").

Then, ask the editor how he or she would like to review and/or receive photo files. Some editors may wish you to send reduced versions (i.e., smaller files) of a selection of sample photos. (This is why it's important to know how to reduce a photo's file size in Photoshop.) Others might prefer to preview your photos on a Web site or photo-sharing site. Others might prefer to have a selection sent on CD-ROM. The same applies when it comes time to actually submit your photos. Some editors will want to receive them as e-mail attachments; others will prefer to receive a CD-ROM. Most will *not* want to download them from a photo site or Web site, but this is an option in some cases.

If you are submitting physical photos, take the following steps to make sure they remain undamaged:

- **Put your name and address on each photo.** The easiest method is to attach a return address label to the back of each print, or to the cardboard mount of each slide.

- **Number each photo.** Do not write on the back of a print with a ballpoint pen or ordinary market, as the ink will smear (and if you stack prints, it will come off on the face of the photo beneath). Use a permanent marker to number prints (and write small), or print off labels that include the number of the print and the caption information.

- **Send slides and prints in plastic protective sheets.** These protect your photos from handling and postal damage. Editors can view slides through the sheets, and will only remove those they actually plan to use. (This also helps keep your photos together.)

- **Send proof sheets of black-and-white photos,** rather than making expensive enlargements.

- **Prepare a caption list that corresponds to the numbers of your photos.** Don't worry about inventing clever captions (the editor will do that). Just record essential information, such as the subject of the photo, and anything else the editor might need to know (such as the location, date, etc.).

- **Obtain model release forms for your photos, if necessary.** This is particularly important when photographing children; editors are very wary of publishing child photos without a parent's permission. You may need a model release when photographing individuals, or even when photographing private property. (For more information on the legal aspects of photography, see *Every Writer's Guide to Copyright Publishing Law*, by Ellen Kozak.)

- **Package your photos securely.** Put at least one sheet of cardboard into the envelope (usually your manuscript will be sufficient protection on the other side). Include a SASE with enough postage to cover the return of the photos, whether or not you want the manuscript returned.

OBTAINING PHOTOS FROM OTHER SOURCES

If you despair of taking good photos yourself, whom doesn't mean you have to despair of offering photos to editors. It simply means that you'll have to find another source.

One approach is to find a photographer whom you can work with, and sell a package deal to the editor. In this case, you'll have to work out an arrangement with the photographer with respect to who gets paid what—particularly if the publication offers a single rate for the entire text/photo package. It's a good idea to write up a brief contract up front, so that everyone knows what they can expect when the check arrives.

However, you may also find free sources of photos. When I write for pet magazines, for example, I'll often put out a call for photos on topical mailing lists (such as a cat-writing list). Generally, these photos won't be professional quality, and I usually don't offer the contributor any payment for them. Sometimes the magazine will use them, sometimes it won't. If payment *is* involved, I simply pass along the name of the photographer to the editor and let the editor handle payment for the photos separately.

When you're writing travel articles, check with tourist organizations for photos. Many tourist agencies offer free publicity photos, which will enhance your article without costing the editor another penny.

You may also be able to obtain free photos from online sources. For example, if you're writing an article about a travel destination in Great Britain, the site *www.britainonview.com* offers a wide range of photos that are available for free to the travel trade. While the publication to which you are submitting can access these photos, you can save editors time and trouble by creating an account and selecting appropriate images to accompany your article. Another source of photos is Wikipedia.org; most of the images on this site are available either via public domain or through the "Creative Commons" license, which allows them to be used in other publications. (To locate collections of photos on a particular subject, visit Wikimedia Commons.) Flickr (*www.flickr.com*) is also a good source for photos available for use under the Creative Commons license. (Never download a photo without being certain that it is available for use, and always provide an editor with full attribution as to the source of the photo, the licensing terms, and the name of the photographer to be credited.)

Finally, you may be able to locate photos from personal Web sites that can be used with permission. If you find "the perfect photo," don't hesitate to contact the owner of the site to find out whether the photo would be available for publication. Keep in mind, however, that photos posted online are often reduced in file size and not appropriate for publication in print; in addition to requesting permission to use the photo, you may also need to ask for a full-resolution copy of that image to submit to your editor.

SUBMITTING PHOTOS WITHOUT MANUSCRIPTS

If you can take high-quality photographs, you can also sell them independently, without an accompanying article. Many magazines buy shots of their basic subject matter year-round. For example, pet magazines always need generic photos of veterinarians examining animals, animals involved in various activities, animals interacting with different types of people (e.g., seniors, children), seasonal shots, and so forth.

You don't have to simply guess what editors are looking for. Many magazines offer photographers' guidelines that list upcoming articles and the types of photos that will be required. For example, a pet magazine may list the breeds it will cover over the next six months, plus special articles like "puppies" or "senior cats." These guidelines will tell you when photos must be submitted for each issue. By tailoring your photo shoots to these "need" lists, you'll have a better chance of breaking in.

You may even make more money by selling your photos separately than if you combine them with an article. While some editors pay the same amount for an article with or without photos (or add only a small bonus for the photos), they also have standard rates for photos alone. For example, a magazine might pay $50 per photo for inside use, and anywhere from $100 to $500 for a cover shot. Larger magazines pay more, of course, but also expect top quality. Smaller publications may pay $10 to $15 per shot. (To find out what magazines take independent submissions, and how much they pay, see *Writer's Market* or *Photographer's Market*.)

Finally, you may find that a photo submission can lead to an article assignment. If an editor falls in love with your photos, but has nothing on hand to use them with, she or he may ask you to write a piece to accompany them. Remember, editors think in two media—verbal and visual—so by sending a package that combines both, you stand a better chance of selling your work.

Oh, and if a magazine pays 5¢/word and $50 per photo, one picture really is worth a thousand words!

❧ 33 ☙

Selling (and Syndicating) a Column[1]

If you specialize in a particular subject area, or have an area of expertise that you'd like to write more about, you may start thinking about launching a column. A column is a great way to establish yourself as an "expert," and offers a steady income. Opportunities for columns can be found in magazines (usually monthly), newspapers (generally weekly but sometimes daily), and Web sites (most often weekly, monthly, or bimonthly).

While magazines generally offer the best pay rates for columns, this market also tends to be the most difficult to crack, as magazine space is the most limited. When a column opening comes up, most editors will turn to existing contributors—which means that the best way to get a shot at a magazine column is to become a regular contributor to a publication. Once you've sold several articles to a magazine, you might wish to pitch a column idea; even if it's not accepted, it will let the editor know that you're interested in a columnist position in case something opens up in the future. Magazines generally offer the highest pay rates for columns—anywhere from a few hundred dollars to $1,000—but also generally expect exclusive rights.

Newspapers represent the largest market for columns. Even the smallest regional papers generally run a few columns, often by local authors. Larger papers run a mix of local and national (syndicated) columns. Daily papers usually offer a mix of daily and weekly columns; weekly papers usually offer weekly columns. Weekend editions often have their own set of columns, often including review and "local event" and entertainment sections. Newspapers also offer the widest variety of content opportunities, as regular sections may cover health, cooking, lifestyles, women's issues, fashion, entertainment, sports, business, real estate, home décor, and more. Papers may also offer columns of specific regional interest. The downside is that the pay scale tends to be lower (anywhere from $10 to $50 in smaller papers); however, you can often "self-syndicate" your

---

[1]Excerpted from *The Writer's Guide to Queries, Pitches and Proposals* (Allworth Press, 2010).

column to more than one regional. (Most national papers buy exclusive rights, but also offer a much higher fee.)

Electronic publications offer excellent opportunities for columnists, as such publications have fewer space constraints. A Web-based publication could have any number of regular columns. An e-mail newsletter, on the other hand, will tend to have only one per issue, as most e-mail newsletters prefer to place limits on their length. (A newsletter might, however, feature links back to columns on a Web site.) Many commercial and "catalog" sites use columnists to offer material intended to attract visitors (and hence customers), and can often pay more than an independent "zine." Columns are usually archived, so that readers can access not only your current column but also all previous columns. Most electronic publications want exclusive rights, or at least exclusive *first electronic* rights, to a column, making it less likely that you'll be able to market the same column to more than one online publication (although you may be able to market the same column to an online publication *and* a print publication). The downside, again, is that most electronic markets pay less than print markets, except for those that are affiliated with commercial enterprises, print publications, or other media.

CHOOSING A COLUMN TOPIC

Magazine columns are generally governed by the same principles that apply to magazine articles, with "how-to" and informational columns being the most common. The easiest way to determine what type of column you might pitch to a magazine is to look at its regular content and choose a topic that could be covered on a monthly basis. Magazines may also feature editorial/opinion columns, news round-ups, review columns, and regional coverage (e.g., local restaurants, night spots, entertainment, events, personalities, etc.). Another popular type of column is the "advice" format, in which the columnist answers questions from the magazine's readership. (A pet magazine, for example, might have a medical or behavioral advice column, while a women's magazine might have an advice column on relationships or parenting.)

To write a magazine how-to column, you need to have some personal expertise in the field. Unlike a single feature article, where you can interview experts, a monthly column will be drawing on *your* knowledge of a subject, and a successful pitch will be based on your credentials. Don't try to pitch a gardening column, therefore, if you don't know a rake from a hoe! Similarly, if you want to pitch an advice column, you'll have to demonstrate that you have the credentials to *answer* those questions.

Newspapers may offer a similar array of columns, but will focus more on a general readership than on the "subject-specific" readership you'll find with most magazines. Since daily newspapers typically offer a different "special-interest" section each day, these offer a wide range of column possibilities. If your expertise is real estate, consider pitching a column about tips on buying and selling homes, or dealing with your local real estate market. If you have business expertise, consider pitching a column for the business section—and so on.

Newspapers also generally offer a variety of op-ed and "personal" columns. Op-ed columns typically focus on a perspective or viewpoint—e.g., liberal, conservative, feminine, minority, etc. To pitch an op-ed column, you'll need to persuade the editor that your opinion is worth hearing—and is likely to reflect the views of a substantial portion of the newspaper's audience. "Personal" columns tend to focus on a "slice of life" approach, again often focusing on local issues or on lifestyle topics that will be common to a large portion of the newspaper's readership. Some "slice of life" columns are humorous, but others are completely serious.

Newspapers also offer a range of review columns, covering movies, books, products (including high-tech products and computer games), entertainment, local events, restaurants, night life, and more. A newspaper's travel section might include reviews of travel destinations and accommodations. The best way to break in with this type of column is to pick a topic that isn't already being reviewed, and offer a convincing argument as to why the paper should cover this topic. This type of column often requires no special expertise or credentials (though if you're going to review something like computer equipment, you'll need to convince an editor that you understand technology). Such columns also tend to blur the line between information and entertainment; review columns are often chosen as much for the writer's style and voice (and wit) as for the reviews themselves. The bad news is that for this very reason, review columns are often the first thing amateur writers try to pitch, the most common being book reviews. To earn a space, therefore, you'll have to be able to ensure that your column rises above the competition.

It's also important to understand that a review column doesn't necessarily mean free tickets to movies, free dinners, free travel, or free books. I get lots of letters from writers who want to know how to get on a publisher's "list" for free books to review. Publishers, however, rarely send books directly to individual reviewers; instead, they tend to send them to *publications,* which then pass them along to established reviewers. The way to get "free books," therefore, is to become a regular book reviewer for a publication.

Newspapers also run humor columns—but as you have probably already noticed, these tend to be few and nationally syndicated (e.g., Dave Barry). This type of column is very difficult to sell (let alone syndicate), because the market for pure humor is limited—partly because a lot of people aren't nearly as funny as they think they are, and partly because newspapers will devote only a limited amount of space to this type of column.

PITCHING YOUR COLUMN

Once you've chosen a topic that you feel would make a good column, you need to develop a proposal that includes the following elements:

• **A catchy column title.** (Keep in mind that the editor may *change* that title once the column is accepted, but you still need to develop one that will get an editor's attention.)

• **An overview of the column's general subject area**—e.g., what the column will cover over time, why you feel that this coverage is important for the publication, and what the general "purpose" of the column will be.

• **A list of topics.** If you're pitching a monthly column, you'll need to provide at least six months of topics; if you're pitching a weekly column, try to develop topics for two to three months.

• **Three to six sample columns.**

• **A list of your credentials** (including an author bio and, optionally, photo). This may also include your publications list and, if appropriate, your resume, or curriculum vitae.

While it *is* possible to pitch a column by e-mail, you'll generally want to put together a physical package that can be sent by surface mail, particularly if you're pitching to a magazine. Most columnists recommend assembling these materials in a pocket folder, perhaps with a label bearing the name of the proposed column, and your name, on the cover.

Your package will include a basic query letter, which will be structured much like an article query. However, instead of proposing a single piece, you're proposing an ongoing series—so the goal of your query should be to present a rationale for why the target publication would want to cover your subject on a regular basis. Instead of going into detail about any single column, your query should present an overview of the nature and purpose of the entire column. Describe the subject, and explain why this subject is of sufficient importance (or interest) to merit ongoing coverage.

Any of the types of hooks mentioned in chapter 17 will also work for a column. For example, if you were proposing a column on natural health alternatives to a general-interest women's magazine, you might try any of the following hooks:

• **Problem/Solution:** "Many women today are becoming increasingly frustrated with the limitations of 'traditional medicine.' Often, traditional techniques—or harried HMO doctors with not enough time—just don't seem to answer women's questions or meet their needs. More and more women are seeking alternatives—and seeking accurate, helpful information to guide them toward those alternatives."

• **Informative:** "Natural remedies have become big business. No longer confined to strip-mall 'health stores,' they now line the pharmacy shelves of every supermarket. Now, more than ever, women are in need of accurate, reliable information on the products competing for their health dollars—and on how to safely incorporate natural health care into their lives."

• **Question:** "Are you bewildered by the array of natural products on your local supermarket shelves? Do you wonder whether these products are safe, whether they can actually meet their claims, or how to choose between them? If so, you're not alone; thousands of women face the same decisions every day."

• **Personal Experience/Anecdote:** "When I had my first baby, I wasn't prepared for the violent reaction I would have to XXX drug. Yet it was all my doctors could offer. The next time, I vowed to be prepared; I studied alternatives, and found natural solutions that eased my pain without ruining my health. Since then, I've talked to many women who wished they had the same options..."

• **Attention-grabber:** "Nature can be the death of you—even when it's attractively bottled in a supposedly 'safe' product on your supermarket shelf. While natural remedies offer a host of helpful alternatives to traditional healthcare, it's vital to know what you're doing—what's in that bottle, how much you can safely take, whether it actually works, and how it might react with other natural products."

Your hook should lead directly into your pitch, which will include not only the title of the column, but also its length and frequency (unless this is predefined by the frequency of the publication). If you're pitching to a newspaper, mention the section in which you believe your column should appear. For example:

A good pitch to follow the hooks above might read:

I'd like to offer you a [monthly, weekly] column covering the many facets of natural health care. Titled "Natural Health," this column would fit well within your "To Your Health" section. It would run between 750 and 1,000 words, and cover such topics as:

Follow this with the body of your query, in which you'll list a selection of topics that will be covered in the column. A bullet list often works well for this:

• Traditional home remedies: Which ones work, and why.

• How to read and understand the labels of "natural" products.

• Why "natural" doesn't necessarily mean "safe," and how to use such products safely.

• Understanding the health claims of natural products: What they're based on, whether they're true.

• Product interactions: Knowing which natural products can be taken together, and which can be harmful.

• Teas, tisanes, and distillations: How to best prepare a natural remedy.

• Natural remedies for pregnancy and childbirth problems.

• (etc.)

Finally, close with your credentials: the personal skills, expertise, education, job experience, or whatever that qualifies you to write this column—or to dispense advice to the publication's readers. Since an inaccurate column can damage the credibility of the entire publication, an editor will want to be sure that you're the right person for the job.

The final, closing paragraph of your query should offer a potential start date for your column, and may also be the place to specify your terms—the rights you're offering, and, if appropriate, the fee you would like to receive. Unless you're self-syndicating the column, however (see below), you'll generally leave these items for subsequent negotiation.

While you'll be sending sample columns with your proposal, you may also wish to include relevant clips that support your credentials and demonstrate your ability to write on the chosen topic. Be sure to reference any articles you've written for the publication you're pitching to! Clips from professional or academic journals can help establish your expertise and experience writing on your chosen topic, but they will generally *not* reflect the style you'd use for a consumer publication, so be sure to balance them with clips that show your ability to write for a more general audience. A published book also makes an excellent "clip," and is a great way to establish your expertise. If you can, send the publisher a copy of the entire book—or, photocopy one or two relevant chapters and copies of some favorable reviews.

Again, you'll generally submit this package by surface mail. If you're submitting a proposal to an electronic publication, however, you may need to put these materials into an e-mail. If so, find out from the editor whether you can send any of the materials (such as your resume and publications list, and sample columns) as attachments, or whether you need to place everything in the body of an e-mail. If you must put everything in a single e-mail, then you should limit that e-mail to a basic query, a list of topics, and *one* sample column; offer to send the editor additional materials (such as more columns, publications list, or clips) on request.

SELF-SYNDICATING YOUR COLUMN

Since newspaper readership is generally based on geography rather than on subject matter (as is the case with magazines and electronic publications), it is often possible to "self-syndicate" a newspaper column to more than one publication. You can sell the same column to newspapers in different states (provided that it applies to the area), or even to papers in different counties or cities in the same state, as long as those papers have little or no reader overlap.

Reader overlap is not necessarily determined by location. It is also determined by the size and distribution of a paper. While readers of a local paper in one town or county may not read a similar paper that is published in the next town or county, they *may* read a larger city paper that is distributed to *both* towns. For example, residents of Olympia, Washington may read the local *Olympian,* but may also read the larger *Tacoma News Tribune* and the national *Seattle Post*—but they may *not* read a local paper published in nearby Tumwater.

To self-syndicate your column, you must have a topic that "travels" well. You're not likely to be able to syndicate a local "review" column, for example, that focuses on purely regional subjects. Nor would you be able to syndicate a column that might have broader regional appeal—e.g., gardening in the Pacific Northwest—but that won't be useful to readers in a completely different climate. Columns on more universal topics, however, such as home décor, real estate, parenting, health, fitness, cooking, etc., can be distributed to a wide range of papers. Your column must also offer something unique; while you may be the only person writing about parenting for your home town paper, thousands of other writers cover this topic in other regions, so your column would have to offer something special to compete.

Finding Markets

You can locate newspapers through one of more than a dozen electronic "newsstands" on the Web. Many of these, however, simply provide a title and Web site URL for a paper; you'll have to dig deeper to locate the names of appropriate editors, and their address or e-mail. Nor do most of these sites offer information on a paper's distribution area or circulation; some won't even tell you if the paper is daily, weekly, or monthly. (Visit *www.writing-world.com/links/magazines.shtml* for a list of online newsstands.)

You can get more detailed information from the *Gale Directory of Publications and Broadcast Media,* which you'll find in the reference section of any library. The Gale Directory offers information about circulation, frequency, and staff. If, for example, you've decided you want to target daily newspapers with a circulation of over 20,000, you may wish to turn to the Gale Directory. You don't, for example, want to waste time submitting your column to weekly "shoppers," or to papers with no budget for freelance material.

Another resource is the annual *Editor and Publisher International Year Book,* also available in most libraries. This lists addresses and editors of U.S. and Canadian dailies, along with alternative and specialty papers. It also provides information on circulation figures, the paper's weekly sections and special editions, and whether it has a Sunday magazine.

If a region is served by several local papers and a larger state or big-city newspaper, you'll need to decide which to target first. This decision may not be as easy as it sounds. While a big-city paper may pay more (and will reach a larger audience), it is also likely to demand more rights (or even all rights). It is also more likely to want to post your material on its Web site, which can further limit your ability to distribute that column elsewhere. Smaller papers, though offering lower pay, may be less demanding of rights and less likely to have a Web site (or to put all their material on such a site).

Protecting Your Rights

Rights are a key issue in self-syndicating a column. Indeed, you should start thinking about "rights" long before you consider self-syndication; you should think about this issue when you sell your very first column to your very first paper. Don't assume that you'll never wish to expand. More and more publications (including small-town newspapers) want writers to sign over all rights to their columns, or even produce them as "work-for-hire" (which means that the newspaper owns the copyright to the material from the beginning). You may find that publications that pay as little as $10 to $50 per column still expect you to fork over all rights to that piece. I've also heard from a number of writers who have discovered that their local paper belonged to a larger syndicate that distributed their column to other papers in other regions without their knowledge or permission (let alone additional pay).

If you have any intention of selling your work elsewhere, you must ensure that you retain the rights to do so. Typically, you will want to offer a newspaper "one-time nonexclusive rights" to your column, perhaps with the guarantee that the column will not appear in a competing publication. An alternative is to offer "exclusive regional rights," and define "region" as narrowly as possible. The region should be limited to the area of the newspaper's general readership; if the paper is read only in Yakima, Washington, for example, don't let it restrict you from selling the same column to another paper in Seattle or Tacoma.

In some cases, a newspaper will want "first" rights. This may work if your first column sale is to your local paper—it gives you the ability to resell that column a week later to all your other markets. Since only one publication can ever be "first," however, think carefully before granting this option.

Don't be tempted to accept more money for "all rights." The goal of self-syndication is not to earn a huge amount from any single publication, but to gain the widest possible distribution for your piece. Payment for columns is always fairly limited—you're not likely to get an offer above $500 from even the largest paper. If you can sell the same piece to 20 newspapers that offer $50 apiece, you've already doubled that figure—and quite possibly doubled your readership as well. (If you have hopes of moving on to national syndication, readership figures will be vital to your success. It is better to be read not just by a large number of people, but by a large number of people distributed across a wide range of markets.)

Another thing to watch out for is papers that are owned by a larger conglomerate. I've heard from more than one columnist who has discovered that a column that was intended for one paper has been distributed by the paper's "parent company" to dozens of other newspapers—without permission or any extra pay to the writer.

Finally, you'll want to determine a minimum rate you're willing to accept. Some small newspapers still offer as little as $10 per column—but that amount can add up quickly if you can sell your column to several papers. Some columnists set a fee based on circulation—e.g., 50¢ per 1,000 subscribers.

Preparing Your Package

Self-syndication has one downside: Expense. Most newspapers still prefer to receive column proposals by surface mail than by e-mail. This means that to pitch your idea to a wide range of markets, you'll have to invest in postage, printing, and envelopes.

Your submission package will be much the same as that described in the previous chapter, including a cover/query letter, three to six sample columns, a list of topics, your credentials, clips, and a SASE or a self-addressed, stamped postcard with "check boxes" for an editor's response. Newspaper editors often prefer a postcard to a SASE, as it enables them to check the appropriate response rather than having to write an acceptance letter. Your postcard might read something like this:

Date: _____

Dear (Your Name):

Thank you for submitting your proposal for a column titled "Natural Health Tips for Seniors."

_____ We would like to use this column on a weekly basis. We will pay you a fee of $_____ for one-time, nonexclusive rights (per your guarantee that the column will not appear in a directly competing publication).

_____ We regret that we cannot use your column.

(Signed) _____

Editor's Name: _____

If you plan to submit your column to a large number of newspapers, you'll probably want to have all your materials printed in bulk. Have your cover letter printed on a good-quality paper stock; your clips and column samples can be printed on plain 20-lb. bond. Most print shops will also be able to print your return postcard. To save costs (and weight), print your clips double-sided.

It *is* possible to pitch a newspaper column by e-mail, though it is more difficult. First, you'll have to build a list of e-mail contacts. As with pitching a regular column, you won't be able to send as many materials as you would by surface mail; usually, you'll be limited to a *short* query letter, a brief list of topics, a description of your credentials, and one sample column. Offer the editor the opportunity to receive more materials either by mail or e-mail if interested.

Don't be surprised if you never hear anything from the majority of the editors you query. Most newspaper editors don't bother with rejections; they respond only if they are interested in a submission. While you can certainly follow up on non-responders, your follow-ups may not produce a response either. If you don't hear from a market, just drop it from your list and move on.

When an editor *does* respond, don't be surprised if he or she wants to modify your terms, perhaps by suggesting a different word count or a lower price. It's up to you to decide whether to accept editorial changes. If you're distributing your column to a large number of publications, it's usually easier to send the same column to everyone (and let individual editors make their own changes or cuts) than to try to tailor several versions for different markets. On the other hand, if you're working with only a few editors, this can be a good way to build a better relationship with them—and possibly gain other assignments in the future.

Self-syndication is a wonderful way to build your portfolio. Be sure to ask for copies of the issues in which your column appears, or at least for a tearsheet of your column. Once you have a regular column with a local paper (even if it's not local to *you*), you can list yourself as a "contributor" or "stringer" to that publication. This may be just the stepping-stone you need to propel your column into the big leagues—such as national syndication.

~34~

Writing (and Selling) a Nonfiction Book

A t some point in your writing career, you're probably going to say, "Wow, I could write a book about that!" Unfortunately, many writers stop at that point, intimidated by the prospect of writing something as large as a book—or by the horror stories they've heard about the difficulties of getting published.

Writing a nonfiction book doesn't have to be an intimidating process, however. Often, it's the logical "next step" in your career, and can provide a number of benefits. While articles are often forgotten once a magazine or newspaper hits the recycle bin, people keep books on their shelves for years. A book is considered a more significant "expert" credential than an article. And if a book stays in print, you could receive royalty checks for years to come.

The market for nonfiction books is huge. Walk into any bookstore and you'll see that the nonfiction titles vastly outnumber the fiction titles—and that's not counting the "specialty" bookstores that focus on a particular topic, such as travel, self-help, military history, crafts, and so forth. There are also more nonfiction publishers than fiction publishers, ranging from huge commercial concerns to smaller "niche" publishers that focus on a particular topic or region. Nor is it that difficult to get a nonfiction book published. (Most of the horror stories you've heard relate to fiction.) It rarely requires an agent, and you can often sell your book before you write it.

Writing a book involves most of the same basic skills required to write and market nonfiction articles: The ability to develop and refine a topic, organize your subject matter, conduct research and interviews, and write and polish your material. It also requires much the same credentials. Plus, any articles that you've already sold on a topic will help you "prove" your ability to write a book about that topic.

These are all reasons why I've referred to writing a book as a "next step." I don't recommend attempting to *start* your writing career with a book. Even if you've got the "perfect book idea," keep it "on hold" until you've mastered the process of writing (and selling) articles. Don't tackle something as significant as a book project until you're thoroughly comfortable with the writing process, and feel sure that you won't mind spending several months writing and researching a single topic. A book project is a great way to apply and expand the skills you've developed as a freelance writer—but isn't the best place to try to *learn* those skills.

WHY WRITE A BOOK?

Writers choose to branch out to book-length manuscripts for a variety of reasons, including the following:

1) **To share your knowledge or expertise.** If you're an expert in a particular subject, chances are that you're already writing about it. You may have found, however, that there are only so many articles you can sell on the topic—and so much more that you want to say. A book may be the ideal way to get this information across.

2) **To fill a niche.** Frequently, as you conduct research on a topic, you find a gap that is just begging to be filled. For example, at the time of this writing, I've noticed a sudden influx of books covering *women* in the Civil War—an area that has been neglected amid the flood of books addressing battles, leaders, and so forth. Your inability to find information can be an incentive to provide that information yourself.

3) **To help people.** Many books are written out of a desire to help people with a particular problem. For example, I wrote my first book, *Coping with Sorrow on the Loss of Your Pet*, after discovering through a magazine survey that hundreds of pet owners felt they were "alone" in their grief. The desire to reach out to others can be a powerful motivation to write a book.

4) **To bring your written work together in one place.** Many writers compile collections of columns or articles into a book. Mary Emma Allen, for example, turned her series of columns on Alzheimer's into *When We Become the Parent to Our Parents*. The book you're reading is based on the columns and articles I've written for various writing publications.

5) **To ensure that an important event or person is not forgotten.** Autobiography, biography, and genealogy are all potential sources of material. I know of one writer, for example, who is working on the history of an ancestor who was a Buffalo Soldier. Many writers want to ensure that future readers will be able to know "what happened" or "what life was like when."

Note that one motivation I *didn't* list is "to make lots of money." While some nonfiction books earn a great deal of money, others earn only a few thousand dollars in royalties. Most writers find other incentives more powerful than the lure of cash.

GETTING STARTED

It may seem like a big jump to go from writing 2,000-word features to writing a manuscript of anywhere from 60,000 to 100,000 words. The first step, therefore, is to stop thinking about your project as a "book" and start thinking about it as a series of "chapters." Then, think of each chapter as being equivalent to a 2,000- to 5,000-word article. If you already know that you can write an article a week, then you know that you can write a book chapter a week. If you have twenty chapters, your book will take about twenty weeks, not counting research time. While a book may actually take anywhere from six months to three years to write, most contracts anticipate a delivery time of one year.

Choosing a Topic

Choosing a book topic is similar to choosing a topic for an article. Once again, you may start with a general subject (e.g., dogs) and move to a more specific topic (e.g., health). Then, begin brainstorming subtopics. The difference is, when you're writing a book, each subtopic may become its own chapter.

When you choose a topic, you may find you either have too much information or too little. For example, a subject like "dogs" is too broad for an article *or* a book. A topic like "canine health," however, is too broad for an article, but *could* be turned into a book. Narrowing that topic still further—e.g., "natural health care for dogs"—will make your book even more focused, and thus more marketable.

A book that targets a more specific market niche is often more marketable than a more "general" book. For example, a book focusing on "how to have a healthy dog" might have a broader market appeal ("all dog owners") than a book on "how to care for the older dog." However, it will also have more competition. Your book on older dogs may have a smaller audience, but it may also stand out as the only book of its kind on the shelf.

Focusing on too narrow a topic, however, can leave you with insufficient information to write an entire book—and too small an audience. For example, it might be difficult to write a book about "chiropractic care for dogs." However, you could expand that topic to "holistic health care for dogs," covering not only chiropractic but acupuncture, Reiki, massage, herbal therapies, and so forth. This will expand your book *and* your market.

Organizing Your Book

When you start writing a book, you face that same question you faced when writing articles: "Do I need an outline?" The answer is "yes"—if only because you'll need a chapter-by-chapter outline when preparing your proposal.

Fortunately, the techniques I recommended in chapter 9 apply just as well to books. The difference is that each subtopic is likely to be an entire chapter. For example, if you're using the "logical sequence of events" approach (this happened first, this happened next...), each major event may be a chapter. Your introduction and conclusion, instead of being limited to a few paragraphs, will be chapters in their own right.

Once you've developed a basic chapter structure, use each chapter "heading" to organize your research. Many writers set up a file folder for each chapter, and use it to store research information. If you find that a chapter has too much information, you can always split it; if a chapter is too short, you can often combine it with another chapter.

Another common question is whether to write your book from beginning to end, or whether you can write a chapter here and a chapter there. The answer, of course, is: Use whatever method works best for you! Some people like to write the easiest chapters first, then progress to the more difficult ones, and finally tie it all together. Others prefer to write chapters sequentially, particularly when it's important to know what you've "already covered" in earlier parts of the book. If you find that one approach isn't working for you, try the other.

Write, then Revise

Your writing can bog down if you attempt to edit your book as you go. It's usually better to simply try to "get it all down" first—even if the end result is considerably longer than your allotted word count. Once you've written a first draft, it's easier to determine where to make cuts or add information. It's also easier to polish a manuscript all at once rather than a piece at a time.

Most writers recommend giving yourself a "cooling off" period of at least a week before attempting to edit or polish your manuscript. Then, you'll find it easier to approach your words from the perspective of the reader, rather than as a parent trying to edit a beloved "baby."

This can be essential when you discover, for example, that your book is 20,000 words longer than the limit. At first glance, you may not be able to imagine how to cut 20,000 words. After a break, however, you may find that you can manage to part with a paragraph here and a minor concept there, or even a chapter that seemed interesting but isn't vital to the whole. You may also find that you can cut words by creating contractions (e.g., changing words like "you are" to "you're" and "you will" to "you'll"). You'll also be amazed to find how easy it is to tighten up phrases and paragraphs—for example, if your book is 2,000 paragraphs long, you only need to cut an average of ten words per paragraph!

FINDING A PUBLISHER

As I said earlier, it's often possible to sell your book before you write it. To accomplish this, you'll need to submit a proposal to an appropriate publisher.

Before I continue with this section, let me make it clear that I am referring to a *commercial, royalty-paying publisher*. Today, writers are bombarded with information from a host of subsidy print-on-demand publishers who want to convince you that they are "real" publishers. Professional writers know that a "real" publisher is one who pays *you*, not one that you pay. If you want to see your book in bookstores and libraries, and (possibly) reviewed in the press, you need a commercial publisher. There is no cost associated with submitting your book to a commercial publisher; if it is accepted, you will receive an advance and (eventually, if you're lucky) regular royalties.

That doesn't mean that there is no place for print-on-demand and other forms of subsidy and self-publishing. Sometimes these may, indeed, be the right option—and these options are discussed in more detail in the next chapter.

The first step in submitting your book to an appropriate commercial publisher, of course, is *finding* an appropriate publisher. Don't just grab a directory of markets and look in the topic index for, say, publishers who handle books on "dogs." Instead, try these steps:

• **Check your bookshelf.** Who publishes the books *you* refer to on this subject? Would your book fit into their line? Take note of any publisher who appears more than once on your shelf.

• **Check a bookstore.** What publishers are offering similar, or complementary, titles? Do you find that you're picking up books by one publisher more often than others? This could mean that your interests mesh with those of that publisher. While you're browsing, ask yourself these questions:

  ♦ **Do you like the look and feel of the publisher's products?** Is the paper high quality? Do you like the cover? Is the type easy to read? Would you like your book to look like this?

  ♦ **Does the publisher offer the type of book you're planning?** Does it have the same depth of content? If the publisher uses lots of color photos, can you provide them? Conversely, if you're planning to use lots of artwork, does the publisher support it?

  ♦ **Do the books match your style?** If you write in a "conversational" style, don't pitch to a publisher who offers highly technical or academic books.

  ♦ **Are your credentials comparable to the publisher's other authors?** Do you need a special degree or professional experience?

  ♦ **What is the price range?** Does it match the likely budget of your audience? You may like the idea of having your book published in glossy coffee-table format, but will your audience shell out $30 or more for it?

• **Review the guidelines.** You may find these on the publisher's Web site, or in a guideline directory. (You'll find lists of book publisher sites at *www. writing-world.com/links/bookpubs.shtml*.) Also, try to find the publisher's current catalog; this will tell you what books have recently been published. If a publisher has recently published a book similar to the one you're proposing, it isn't likely to want another—but a competing publisher might! Make sure your book matches the publisher's requirements, including length, illustrations, etc. Finally, make sure you know what terms the publisher offers—including royalties, rights, etc.

Chances are, your research is going to turn up more than one "appropriate" publisher for your book, and that's good. You'll want a backup plan if your first choice doesn't come through. The question is, can you submit your proposal to more than one publisher at a time?

There is no clear answer. Some publishers still resist "simultaneous submissions," but others acknowledge that when it can take six months or longer to review a proposal, it's asking a lot to expect authors to submit proposals "sequentially." One approach is to submit simultaneous *query* letters, asking whether you may follow up with a proposal and sample chapters. If a publisher says "yes," you can then ask whether the proposal must be "exclusive" (sent only to that publisher) or whether you can send it to other interested publishers. A book query is functionally the same as a magazine query (see chapter 17), and you can often send it by e-mail.

PREPARING A PROPOSAL[1]

Once you've found a publisher, you need to develop a professional proposal that includes the following elements:

The Overview

The overview of your proposal is presented in narrative format, and may have several sections, including:

Title. A title helps establish the concept of your book in the editor's mind. Amy Shojai, author of *New Choices in Natural Healing for Dogs and Cats,* points out that a title "must not only describe the book and/or concept, but be that illusive thing that editors/agents describe as 'sexy.' The title must strike an instant chord of recognition with the editor." At the same time, she notes, "don't get too attached to titles. Editors change them all the time, often for something that's boring."

Content. Your overview should offer a general summary of the content. Don't go into excessive detail; instead, try to convey the general focus and purpose of your book, including the benefits it will offer to readers. (The concept of "benefits" is key: Your overview should clearly indicate what readers have to gain from your book.)

Rationale. Your overview should also explain who will buy your book (and why that audience will want to buy the book *now*). "Back up the need for the book with stats," says Shojai. "Editors want numbers; don't just say 'everybody who loves pets will buy my book.' Tell them how many owners there are who have dogs who chew used bubblegum and would benefit from *12 Steps to De-Gumming Da Dog.*"

When pitching her book on natural healing, Shojai began with broad statistics to define the potential market: the fact that, at that time, Americans owned 66.2 million cats and 58 million dogs. She then narrowed that audience to those who "welcome pets into their hearts and homes as full members of the family. This pet-generation is eager to provide quality care for their furry families." She explained the timeliness of her proposal by noting the "national obsession with health and fitness."

---

[1] A more detailed explanation of how to write a nonfiction book proposal, along with several samples of successful proposals, can be found in *The Writer's Guide to Queries, Pitches and Proposals* (Allworth Press, 2010). This book also discusses how to research one's book competition on Amazon.com, and how to submit a book to an international publisher.

Competition. What books will you be competing against, and *how* will you compete? To answer this question, of course, you must first *research* the competition—something that, hopefully, you did before you started writing. Says Shojai, "The competition section is probably the most important part of any proposal. I try to *never* slam the competition, but to put my proposal in a favorable light compared to whatever might be out there. In this case, I felt that some of the competition was quite good—just way, way out of date, which meant my proposal was timely. Of course, I added lots of new elements the competition didn't have, too."

Your discussion of the competition should list specific titles (including author, publisher, and publication date). It should then explain how your book differs from those titles: How it improves, differs from, or goes beyond what has been written before. For example, Shojai listed several representative titles in her proposal, then noted that while most of her competitors focused on single therapies, her book would present a range of approaches.

What if you can't identify any competition for your book? This is not necessarily a good thing! Shojai notes, "If there is no competition, find some. Put something in, even if it's a stretch, because if nobody has done the topic before, the publisher/editor will figure... it's not a saleable idea. You want books on your topic to be out there and successful; that means you have a ready-made market. Then it's a matter of making your book different enough... to make the idea viable."

Format. This section should list the book's title and subtitle, the number of words you anticipate, and any other information relevant to the production of the book. Mention whether your book will include any graphics (tables, charts, figures, diagrams) or illustrations (photos, line drawings, etc.), sidebars, appendices, and so forth. Indicate whether the publisher will need to assist with artwork or whether you will be providing it yourself. If color artwork is included, make sure you provide a rationale for the cost.

Market. Explain how your publisher can reach the book's target audience. List magazines in which the book should be reviewed, organizations and groups that might be interested in the book, specialized bookstores or other market outlets, etc. Note whether the book could be used as a classroom text. (You'll be asked for this information anyway once your proposal is accepted, so start gathering it now.)

Chapter-by-Chapter Summary

Most publishers expect to receive a list of proposed chapters, with a brief (one- to two-paragraph) summary of each. If you haven't written your book, you may not know exactly how many chapters it will contain—but you should be able to flesh out a summary from your basic outline. This information isn't "set in stone"—you can always change the number of chapters, or their organization, later. There's no "right" number of chapters; however, a book with too few chapters (e.g., less than five) may seem too "light," while one with too many (e.g., more than 30) may seem unwieldy.

Some publishers will also ask for sample chapters. If so, find out whether they need to be sequential (e.g., the first three) or whether you can send the most *representative* chapters.

Author Bio

What are your qualifications for writing this book? Your bio should answer this question in the space of (about) a single page. It should be written in narrative format, and in third person—e.g., "John Smith is an award-winning decoy carver who has practiced and taught the craft for more than twenty years." As with magazine publishers, a book publisher is likely to expect credentials in one or more of the following areas:

- Educational background
- Professional background
- Personal experience/expertise
- Previous writing credits

Be sure you know what credentials are expected of you by the publisher and by the market you are attempting to target. If your book focuses on scholarly information, chances are good that you'll be expected to have academic credentials. If your book focuses on business or technical information, you may be expected to provide relevant professional experience. If your book addresses more popular how-to or self-help topics, you may be able to market your proposal on the basis of professional *or* personal expertise.

Personal experience can be tricky. It is, of course, essential for a book that is an *account* of your personal experiences, but is usually less helpful in marketing how-to or self-help titles. The more impact your book might have on a reader's well being, the more credentials you will be expected to have. While you might sell a book on fly-fishing on the basis of a weekend hobby, you may have trouble selling a book on child-care if your only "credential" is being a parent.

Writing credits are useful if they are relevant. If you have published other nonfiction books, for example, this demonstrates that you can finish *and* sell a book-length manuscript, even if it's on a completely different topic. Articles will also help demonstrate your skill and marketability—but publishers often aren't impressed by articles on an unrelated topic. Fiction credits may not impress an editor at all. Keep in mind that you're not just trying to prove that you can write; you're also trying to demonstrate that readers should believe what you say!

Supporting Materials

You may also wish to include the following materials:

- **Resume or curriculum vitae,** if it supports the credentials listed in your bio.

- **Publications list** that cites *relevant* publications (and any books that you've already published).

- **Writing samples.** Some publishers like to see writing samples, others don't. Check the guidelines first, and send no more than three (relevant) samples.

- **Business card,** so that a publisher can easily contact you.

- **SASE.** Unless you have an overwhelming reason to want the publisher to *return* your proposal, simply send a #10 SASE.

- **Reply postcard.** If you want to be informed that your proposal was received, include a self-addressed, stamped postcard that the recipient can toss in the mail. The postmark itself will give you the delivery date.

Don't send your photo (you'll only need to provide this *if* the proposal is accepted), testimonials or reviews (especially from friends and family), irrelevant writing samples, copies of other books you've written, or "imprinted" business products (such as personalized pens, card-magnets, calendars, etc.). Most of all, never send anything that would appear unprofessional!

THE PUBLISHING PROCESS

Selling your proposal is just the beginning. Here's what happens next:

1) **The contract.** The first step in the publication process is the contract. Read it carefully; if there is anything you don't understand, ask for clarification. Be sure you know what rights you are giving up (don't sign a "work-for-hire" contract by mistake!), what royalties you'll receive, and the basis for those royalties. Some publishers pay royalties on cover price, others on "net" price (after bookstore or distributor discounts, which can be as high as 60%). This can make a significant difference in what you're paid; for example, while 10% royalties on the *cover price* of a book priced at $15 would be $1.50 per book, 10% of *net* on that same book might be as low as 60¢. Find out what you'll be paid for "subsidiary" sales, such as electronic or audio editions, translations, or movie rights (the standard rate is 50%).

2) **The advance.** Once you've signed and returned the contract, you should receive a portion of your advance. Most publishers pay 50% on signing the contract and 50% on delivery of an "acceptable" manuscript; some, however, pay the advance in thirds. If you fail to deliver the book, or if it is not considered "acceptable," you may have to return the advance.

3) **The author questionnaire.** At about the same time as you receive your advance, you'll receive a (long) questionnaire asking you to describe possible marketing outlets for the book. The publisher will use this questionnaire to guide the book's promotional campaign, so be as thorough as possible!

4) **The manuscript.** Your contract will specify a delivery date for the manuscript, and the form in which it is to be delivered (e.g., hard copy, disk, etc.) Your publisher will announce a publication date and begin promoting the book long before you deliver it, so meeting that deadline is important. (If you can't, contact your publisher as soon as possible.)

5) **First review.** Once you've delivered the manuscript, it must be reviewed by the publisher before you receive the second half of your advance. Often, this takes one to three months, so don't expect a check immediately. I recommend following up after six weeks of delivery.

6) **Editing.** First, your book will be reviewed for content issues, and you'll be asked to clarify anything that seems unclear, or perhaps to add (or cut) information. (This is a great time to reread the manuscript yourself and make any necessary editing changes.) Next, your book will be copy-edited and proofread, and you'll be asked to review and approve suggested changes. You may be given only a few days for each review.

7) **Galley proofs.** Once the book is typeset, you'll be sent "galley proofs" for a final review. Today, these are often sent electronically as PDF files. Your job now is simply to make sure that no typos or errors have been introduced in the typesetting process; the publisher will *not* appreciate editorial corrections unless you spot a major error. Again, you may have less than a week to review galleys.

8) **Indexing.** At the galley stage, you may be asked to create an index for the book. (I have found that the easiest method is to sit down with a notepad and go through the book page by page, jotting down terms that should be indexed with the corresponding page numbers.) If you don't want to index the book yourself, the publisher will arrange for indexing, but will usually charge the cost (which can be several hundred dollars) against your first royalty check.

9) **Printing.** Your book may go to press anywhere from six months to two years after you deliver the manuscript. When it does, you'll receive the number of author copies specified in your contract (usually ten). You'll also have the option of buying more copies at a discount (usually 40%); you will *not* receive royalties on copies you buy. You may also have the option of preordering a quantity of books at a higher discount (e.g., 60%); this is useful if you expect to sell books at talks, classes, or other personal appearances.

10) **Royalties.** Most publishers pay royalties twice a year, based on royalty periods beginning in January and June. If your book is published in June, your first royalty period would end in December, and you'll see your first statement around February or March. You won't actually receive royalties, however, until your book has sold enough copies to "earn out" the advance you've already been paid. For example, if your book is priced at $15, your royalty is 10%, and your advance was $3,000, you'll have to sell 2,000 copies of the book ($3,000 ÷ $1.50) before you receive additional royalties.

❧ 35 ❧

Do-It-Yourself Publishing

Many authors, frustrated by the time-consuming process of submitting a proposal and waiting a year or more to see their book in print, are tempted to "do it themselves." Today, there are a variety of options for the DIY publisher, including self-publishing, electronic publishing, subsidy print publishing, and subsidy print-on-demand publishing. And many authors have been successful with these approaches. One of my own books, *Coping with Sorrow on the Loss of Your Pet,* started out as a self-published title, was sold to a commercial publisher, and then reverted to me after languishing for several years. It is now published in a combination of print-on-demand and self-published formats, and earns me several thousand dollars each year.

First, let's look at the options. There are four basic ways to do it yourself:

- Self-Publishing
- Subsidy Print Publishing
- Subsidy Print-on-Demand Publishing
- Electronic Publishing

SELF-PUBLISHING

It's important to understand the difference between "self-publishing" and "subsidy" publishing, particularly as there are a host of subsidy publishers in the marketplace who seek to blur the distinction between these two approaches by referring to all forms of "DIY" publishing as "self"-publishing.

The simplest way to understand the difference is to realize that when you self-publish, you literally become a publisher. Everything begins and ends with you. If your book has an ISBN, that ISBN points directly to you—either to your own name or to the name you've established for your publishing company. (And yes, you "own" a publishing company, even if you've only published one book.) You pay all the expenses, wear all the hats—and reap all the revenue.

It also generally means that you will have to set yourself up, officially and legally, as a retail business, which can mean obtaining a business license in your state, county or city, and quite probably obtaining a sales tax license. You may also need to set up a "doing business as" statement to enable you to use the name of your publishing house as your business name. This will enable you to accept checks in the name of your publishing house (which, typically, also means that you'll have to open a separate business bank account).

Traditionally, a self-publisher invests in having a limited number of copies of his or her book printed by a book *printer*. (Note the distinction: The company that produces your books is a printer, *not* a publisher.) If you use a traditional printer, you'll probably end up printing anywhere from 200 to 1,000 copies of your book, which you will then (most likely) store somewhere in your home or garage while you work on getting them into the marketplace. You will pay the entire cost of having your book printed (typically, the more copies you print, the lower the per-book cost will be). When you sell your books, the full revenue comes straight to you; you do not receive royalties, as when you publish through a commercial or subsidy publisher.

A self-publisher is responsible for every aspect of book production. If you choose this route, your job is just getting *started* when you write the last page of the book. You are your own editor and proofreader; it's up to you to make sure that your book is free of grammatical errors and typos, and that it says what you want it to say. You are your own book designer; you're responsible for designing both the interior of the book (including the layout of any artwork) and its cover. You handle the typesetting (these days, that's a piece of cake on the computer), choosing a printer, and getting the book produced. Then, you are responsible for marketing: getting people interested in *buying* your book. If you want to send your book to reviewers, it's up to you to build a list and send out review copies, along with an appropriate information kit. And when people order your book, it's up to you to (a) find a way to receive payment and (b) get that book into your customers' hands as quickly as possible.

Of course, the good news is that you can "farm out" as many of these tasks as you wish. Unless you're a superb graphic artist, for example, it's usually a good idea to hire a professional to design your cover. Fulfillment houses can store your book and ship copies to customers as orders are placed; some can even accept credit cards on your behalf, and some also offer an 800-number ordering service. Obviously, however, the more services you pay for, the lower your profit will be.

The best part of being a self-publisher is that you're in complete control of every step of the process, because you're the owner. If you decide you want to *give* your book away, you can. The book is 100% yours.

SUBSIDY PUBLISHING

In the old days, if you wanted to produce a printed book but didn't want to become a self-publisher, the only option was to go to a traditional subsidy publisher. For a whopping fee (often thousands of dollars), a traditional subsidy publisher will print several hundred copies of your book, store them, and pay you a small royalty (often no more than that paid by a commercial publisher) if and when your book sells.

The differences between self-publishing and subsidy publishing are legion, beginning with the key difference that you do not *own* the finished product. Despite the huge sum of money that you pay to have your book printed, it belongs to the publisher, not to you. If you wanted additional copies of your book, you'd have to buy them from the publisher, despite the fact that you've *already* paid to have them printed in the first place. You often have little or no control over the design of the book or its cover. Quite often, as well, you may find yourself locked into a book contract that is every bit as restrictive as a commercial book contract—and that you can't get out of if, for example, you suddenly find a "real" publisher for your book.

Traditional subsidy firms still exist; they usually advertise with phrases like "new authors wanted!" I have yet to hear from a writer who has been delighted with the results of this form of publishing; fortunately, the growth of print-on-demand publishing now gives authors another option.

SUBSIDY PRINT-ON-DEMAND PUBLISHING

Print-on-demand (POD) publishing is an alternate way to develop a printed book without having to take on quite as many tasks as a self-publisher. While there are a handful of *commercial* print-on-demand publishers (with the same submission requirements as any other commercial publisher), the majority of print-on-demand agencies are subsidy publishers. This means that you pay them to produce your book, and you receive a royalty. You do not *own* the finished book, and if an ISBN is issued, it will generally be issued in the name of the subsidy publisher (although some publishers, like Lulu.com and Amazon.com's CreateSpace, make it possible for you to use your own ISBNs).

The POD process literally enables books to be printed when they are ordered. This means that you can offer readers a high-quality print book, without having to have hundreds of copies printed in advance. In many cases (though not all), the quality of the printing is indistinguishable from a commercially published book.

The cost of POD publishing varies widely, depending on how much time and effort you're willing to invest in the process. Companies like Xlibris and iUniverse have publishing packages ranging from several hundred dollars to thousands of dollars. Sites like Lulu.com, CreateSpace, and Blurb.com have no upfront "package" costs, but generally offer a range of production services such as editing, cover design, and interior design that you can purchase separately if desired. Thus, the more you're willing (and able) to invest into the process of developing your own book (e.g., editing, proofreading, interior design, and cover design), the less you'll need to spend.

The advantage of POD publishing, particularly through the free sites, is that you can get your book into the marketplace with a minimum of cost and fuss.

You don't have to worry about orders or shipping; orders are generally placed directly through the company. Some POD publishers will place your books on Amazon.com and other online bookstores as part of their basic package (and in the case of CreateSpace, which is run by Amazon.com, this is standard and comes at no extra cost); in most cases, however, if you want your book to have an ISBN so that it can be sold beyond the publisher's own Web store, you'll have to pay extra.

The downside of POD publishing is that it is an expensive process, and books produced this way invariably cost more than their mass-produced counterparts. It can cost from $5 on up to produce a basic paperback, which means that you have much less leeway in offering quantity discounts. Also, since you don't own the book, you'll have to buy your own copies at (usually) the production cost, which can make it expensive to send out copies to reviewers. The high cost and non-returnability of POD titles also means that these books are rarely accepted by bookstores. And once again, the burden of marketing your book rests entirely upon you.

ELECTRONIC PUBLISHING

A host of electronic publishing options exists today, ranging from the complete "do-it-yourself" approach to the option of submitting your book to a "commercial" royalty-paying e-publisher. Other options include subsidy e-publishing, e-publishing through sites that offer print-on-demand publishing, and publishing through venues like Amazon.com's Kindle.

Ten years ago, electronic publishers were cropping up across the Web like mushrooms after rain, hoping to capitalize on the notion that (a) there were thousands of writers whose books had been rejected by commercial publishers and (b) there were thousands of readers who'd want to buy those books. While the first half of this equation proved true (there were, and are, thousands of writers desperate to get their book published by any means available), the second half did not. Readers quickly discovered that a great many books had been rejected by commercial publishers for very good reasons. Readers were also not thrilled when commercial publishers also jumped on the bandwagon, offering bestsellers electronically at only a slightly lower price than what one had to pay for the print edition.

Now, the e-publishing industry seems to be maturing. The number of readers interested in e-books is growing—but those readers have made it clear that they are interested in getting the same level of quality that they expect from commercial print books. A handful of e-publishers have not only survived but thrived by following the time-honored practice of publishing only high-quality work, rather than throwing up any e-book that came their way. In addition, readers have more options on which to read their e-books, including Kindle and other hand-held devices, and apps for iPhones and BlackBerries.

While e-publishing originally included such options as physically mailing a computer disk or CD-ROM to the buyer, now it generally involves downloading or transmitting a file. For the self-publisher, this will generally be a PDF file, though other formats can be used. (Kindle, for example, does accept PDF, but this is not always the best format for that particular device.) The major advantage of electronic publishing remains the low cost: One doesn't have to pay for paper, printing, or mailing or storage. Issues of interior design and even cover design are also less important (though an attention-getting cover is still a good idea).

If you wish to self-publish an e-book, it's as simple as putting up a Web site and setting up a shopping cart through a service like PayPal or ClickBank. You can even set up affiliate programs that encourage *other* Web site owners to market your book. If you offer more than one e-book, you may need a more complex shopping cart system (I use Softseller.com, which charges 25 cents per transaction and enables buyers to purchase through PayPal; it also offers a means to set up your own PayPal-based affiliate program).

If you'd rather not worry about selling books directly, it's relatively simple to upload an e-book to a site like Lulu.com, where you pay nothing to "publish" and receive the majority of the revenue when your e-book sells. Many other subsidy print-on-demand sites offer the option of issuing his or her book in both print and electronic formats. Anyone who owns the rights to their material can also publish through Kindle (which is also a good place to publish public domain materials). Finally, you can submit your book to a commercial e-publisher, who, like a print publisher, will pay you royalties (but rarely an advance).

The downside of e-publishing is that, like any other DIY venue, the burden of marketing your book lands entirely upon you. No one else will get it to reviewers or to the attention of readers. Though Kindle titles appear on Amazon.com, most other e-books do not, and of course they aren't available in brick-and-mortar bookstores. This can be an effective option for a well targeted nonfiction book; it's often less successful for fiction (unless you are dealing with a well established e-publisher in a niche market, like Ellora's Cave [*www.jasminejade.com*], which deals in erotica romance—and which, ironically, is now expanding into print publishing).

However, the business side of e-publishing is definitely less demanding than for print self-publishing. You don't have to worry about the physical side of publishing: No print runs, boxes of books in the garage, or shipping books to customers. Nearly all your transactions will be handled electronically. And since you are only marketing "information" or "data," rather than a physical product, you generally don't need to register as a "retail business." If you opt for commercial e-publishing or subsidy e-publishing through a site like Lulu.com, life is even simpler, as you are now no longer an "independent" publisher at all; like any author, you're simply receiving royalties.

Before you venture down the "do it yourself" road, be sure you understand what is involved. Becoming your own publisher (whether you self-publish or choose a subsidy option) means becoming more than just a writer. In fact, it means that your job is only starting when you finish *writing* your book. Now, you are taking on all the chores that you would normally expect to hand over to a publisher. You will become your own editor, proofreader, bookkeeper, marketer, designer, distributor, shipper, and more—or, you'll pay someone else to handle these tasks, which will cut into your profits. Keep in mind that the more time you must invest as a "publisher," the less time you'll have for actual writing—so if you'd rather spend your time writing, this may not be the best option for you.

In addition, it is almost impossible to get "DIY" books of any type (self- or subsidy-published) into brick-and-mortar bookstores. If you'd like to see your books on the shelves of real-world bookstores across the country, this probably isn't the best choice. (On the other hand, many self-publishers are successful in placing their books in non-traditional outlets that regular publishers might not exploit.) It's also very, very difficult to get a DIY book reviewed by the mainstream press (though if you have a particular subject niche, you may be able to get reviews in publications that specifically address that niche).

Most importantly, the job of finding readers and buyers for your book rests entirely upon your shoulders. Though commercially published authors point out that their publishers often do very little to promote their books, the very ability of a commercial publisher to get a book onto bookstore shelves puts them far ahead of you in the promotion game. *You* have to be able to find a way to reach readers *without* being able to catch their eye in a bookstore. The more avenues you can find to market your book, the more successful it will be—and many authors have, indeed, done exceedingly well with DIY publishing. It's vital, however, to know what you're getting into *before* you make that decision.

PART VIII:

Commercial Freelancing

❦ 36 ❦

Writing for Businesses

by Dawn Copeman

Writing for businesses probably isn't the first thing you considered doing as a freelance writer. It certainly wasn't high on my list of priorities when I started out. I wanted to write articles. Yet within months I learned that one way to make steady money as a writer was to start writing for businesses.

Writing for businesses, also known as commercial writing or copywriting, may not seem as exciting as writing articles, stories, or a novel. But it is an exciting, growing field—and more importantly, a lucrative field that you ignore at your own cost. There will always be a need for copywriters. Commercial writing pays well and is a varied and interesting line of work, particularly if you enjoy learning about new things and working with language, as most writers do.

For example, I've been paid to find out about conservatories, orangeries, sardines, cake sprinkles, tequila, the health benefits of red grapes and cocoa, and the top-selling Christmas toys—and then to write about these things in press releases, brochures, recipes, company newsletters, and sales letters. And once the commercial job is over, I can then put this newfound knowledge to use in articles. The fact that I can get paid to explore topics that I can then apply to magazine articles is just one of the perks of the business. Another is the sheer variety of work available.

WHAT DOES A COPYWRITER DO?

A copywriter, or freelance commercial writer, writes "copy" or text to help businesses communicate with their customers—and more importantly, potential customers. Every advertisement, brochure, catalog, and sales letter you've ever read was written by a copywriter—as were the words to all the radio and TV ads you hear, and those fundraising letters you get from charities.

A copywriter is employed by a client, who may be the business itself or a public relations agency hired to create material for the business. The type of material you can be called upon to write falls into three main areas:

- **Business-to-Business Communications:** Sales letters, reports, or articles for trade magazines designed to promote the client's products or services to other businesses.

- **Business-to-Consumer Communications:** Any materials designed to draw the consumer's attention to what the business has to offer.

- **In-House Communications:** Material such as reports and newsletters designed to bring staff up-to-date regarding the company's news, aims, and intentions.

Within the first two areas, a copywriter may be called upon to write some or all of the following materials:

- Press releases
- Advertisement copy for flyers, leaflets, postcards, and press advertisements
- Brochures
- Sales letters
- Catalog descriptions
- Company newsletters
- Web site content
- Web site advertisements
- Scripts for television/radio advertisements
- Scripts for promotional films
- Scripts for training films
- Direct mail campaigns
- Articles for publication in trade/specialist magazines
- Advertorial articles—advertisements "disguised" as articles
- Speeches

A copywriter working on in-house materials may also be called upon to write:

- Internal corporate newsletters
- Training manuals
- Office procedures
- Job advertisements

- Corporate vision statements

- Company reports

A copywriter working on in-house materials may also be called upon to provide "knowledge capture." This involves going into a company and learning about the company's procedures in order to prepare such materials as operating manuals.

There is always a demand for copywriters, even during a recession. During a recession, companies still need to advertise their products and services, and using a freelance writer is often the most economical way to do so. When the economy is good, companies still often prefer to use freelancers rather than employ someone in-house because freelance writers are only paid when working on a specific job, and do not cost the company "overhead" fees (such as health benefits and vacation time). It's also easier for the company to change writers if they're not satisfied with the service they've received. This can work in your favor if you're called in to replace another writer—but it also means that you could be the one fired if you don't provide the best service you can.

WHAT DO YOU NEED TO BE A COPYWRITER?

To become a copywriter, you don't need to invest in any extra materials. You need the same supplies as for any other form of freelance writing: A computer, an Internet connection, a printer, a workspace, and a telephone. You will, however, find it easier to start work in this field if you invest in the following resources:

A Swipe File

Most copywriters advise you to build up a "swipe" file. This is a file of all the direct mail that you and your friends and family receive, including sales letters, brochures, postcards, and flyers. Some copywriters even advise signing up to receive different catalogs just to receive more (and more varied) types of direct mail.

You will never look at "junk mail" the same way again. Soon, you will get into the habit of analyzing each piece you receive to see if it works or if it doesn't. Does it catch your attention? Does it make you consider using the firm that produced it? If so, it works; if not, it doesn't.

Go over each piece of copy you have in your swipe file and look at how it has been put together and if it's good, note down why it works. If it's bad, try and write it so that it works. This is a great way to learn how to write postcards, flyers, and brochures, and especially sales letters.

A Web Site

Most copywriters have a Web site of some sort to advertise their services and showcase their writing skills. This can cost you as little as $20 for Web hosting and $25 (less if you sign up for more than one year) for a domain name. If you have little or no experience with Web design or HTML, look for a host that offers templates, or for an easy-to-use Web creation program (you can find a number of these at no cost on shareware sites).

Your Web site should include:

- **A brief description of your experience and the services you offer.** Ensure that this is grammatically accurate and has no spelling mistakes. Simply state who you are and what you offer, and your experience if relevant. Do not, however, list your rates. This marks you as an amateur, as seasoned copywriters know that there's no such thing as a typical project with a typical fee. (See chapter 38, "Commercial Freelancing: Where's the Money," below.)

- **Samples of your work.** These can be real samples or ones you've made up to showcase your skills. Many beginning copywriters start by making sample brochures, press releases, and flyers for imaginary companies. This demonstrates to prospective clients that you can actually do the job. On my first site, I used samples of work I'd done in previous jobs: course content, training handbooks, and political campaign material (which was written by me, for me, and won me a seat on the local council). You could also volunteer to do some copywriting for a local church, charity, or nonprofit and use this as a sample. This is a good idea for two reasons: It gives you practice in listening to and meeting a client's needs, and it shows a prospective client that you have done work for others.

Here is the text from my very first Web site. It isn't perfect, but it did the trick:

WriteAway is your first choice for affordable, creative writing solutions.

I know that you know your business best and you do what you do best in running your company. I also know that if you want your firm to succeed where others fail, you need a professional writer. I take time to understand your business so that I can give you a writing product that fully meets if not exceeds your demands.

I am Dawn Copeman, an approved member of Freelancers in the UK, who has had articles published on travel, food, cookery, history, health, writing and British traditions. I am a columnist and contributing editor at *www.timetravel-britain.com* and contributing editor at *www.foodanddrinktowers.co.uk.* I am also the newsletter editor at *www.writing-world.com,* a site with over 725 pages of writing information, and also editor at *www.newbiewriters.com.* I hold a BA (hons) degree in business administration, as well as a Post-Graduate Teaching Certificate. I am a qualified writer and also a part-qualified accountant. Fluent in French and German, I have many years' experience in business and education and can bring my knowledge to bear in writing about and for your business.

In the field of commercial writing I have written:

- Web pages
- Successful political campaign material
- Sales letters
- Brochures
- Company newsletters
- Press releases
- Advertisement brochures for small businesses
- Course content for French, German and ICT courses
- Training manuals for chartered surveyors, secretaries and trainee teachers
- Procedure manuals for after-sales departments, office staff and health & safety.
- Curriculum vitae

Click here to see samples.

In short, if you need fast, compelling, accurate writing, then WriteAway is the site for you. Take a look around the site and contact me to discuss how I can meet your writing needs.

As you can see, I presented myself as a professional writer with experience in certain industries. As my experience widened, I removed some of the earlier samples from my pre-copywriter days and replaced them with more up-to-date samples.

Business Cards

It is also a good idea to have some business cards printed with your name and the title "Freelance Copywriter" or "Freelance Commercial Writer." You can obtain business cards very reasonably online (or even, occasionally, free at such sites as VistaPrint, (*www.vistaprint.com*) where all you pay for 250 cards is postage). Most online sites have templates that enable you to design your own card quickly and easily. Or, you can design a card on your computer and print it out on perforated card stock (be sure to get the kind that leaves no perforation marks on the edges).

Don't fall into the trap of putting too much information on your card. Some people get double-sided cards that include their name and contact details on one side and all the services they offer on the other. This can make you appear to be a jack-of-all-trades (and master of none). I prefer single-sided cards that refer companies to my Web site for further information.

Useful Books

At the very least, you'll need a good thesaurus and dictionary to help you find powerful, selling words. If you're serious about becoming a copywriter, you should also check out *The Well-Fed Writer* by Peter Bowerman. This is the industry standard on how to become a successful commercial freelancer.

GETTING THE WORK

This is the part that often fills writers with fear. You know how to write a query letter, but how do you find commercial assignments? In fact, getting copywriting work can be much easier than finding a home for an article. Here are some of the best methods:

- **Word of Mouth.** Simply tell people that you are a copywriter. Tell your friends, bank manager, family, people you meet socially, people you meet in elevators and in restaurants, people you meet on vacation. You never know when someone *you* meet will meet someone else who is looking for a copywriter. Hand out your business cards whenever you can. I've picked up many jobs through this method; try it and work is bound to come your way.

- **Web site.** Your Web site's job is to sell your services 24 hours a day, seven days a week. Ensure that you have the words "copywriting, copywriter, commercial writer, business writer" and your hometown entered as tag words. This will help search engines locate you when someone searches for a copywriter in your area.

- **Memberships.** Join local or national freelance groups. One of the first inquiries I received came about because I was listed on the Freelancers in the UK site as a copywriter and editor. Most of these organizations are free or have a nominal fee. Also consider joining organizations that relate to types of subject matter in which you have expertise. If, for example, you love to write about gardening, join a regional gardening society—and you may start picking up jobs from local nurseries and other businesses related to gardening.

- **Cold Calling.** This involves telephoning local businesses to ask if they need a copywriter. I have never done this, but many freelancers believe it is a good way to contact clients. To cold-call, you need to work out your script: What, exactly, you are going to say when someone answers the phone. Then you need to work out who to call. You could look through your local phone book, or get a list of local companies from your chamber of commerce. Don't overlook any potential client. Don't always think big; many smaller companies also need copywriting. Don't forget to contact local marketing companies and PR firms. Finally, keep

---

The Cold Call, by Peter Bowerman

Peter Bowerman is a firm believer in contacting clients through the cold call. "If people aren't expecting your correspondence, chances are excellent it'll go into the trash unopened. You really need to establish that connection with someone so that they know what your package is when it shows up on their desk," he notes. Here's his approach to the cold call:

Your Script. Know exactly what you're going to say when your prospect answers a record of whom you have called and when, and whether you have been asked to call back. Be sure that your Web site is set up so that you can refer potential clients to it. You must also be prepared to mail out a portfolio—a physical copy of your samples, along with a brief introductory letter and two business cards, within a pocket folder. To succeed in cold calling, you must be persistent and prepared for rejection—but hey, you're a writer, you're used to that!

• **Social Networking.** Many freelancers now get work via social-networking sites such as LinkedIn, Plaxo, MySpace, and Facebook. Some freelancers who responded to a recent survey in the Writing World newsletter reported getting two or three assignments a week from such sites. Just like your Web site, your profile on a social networking site can be working for you 24/7. Just make sure you update it regularly and check your profile daily to ensure you're not missing out on any work. (See chapter 28 for more information on now to network effectively.)

• **Freelance Work Sites.** Many sites and newsletters that list freelance writing jobs also list calls for copywriters. You can also pay to join job-bidding sites such as Elance.com, where you can maintain a profile that potential clients can view, and bid for a variety of copywriting jobs. The pay for these jobs, however, can be significantly lower than those found through other means.

the phone. Write it out word-for-word on a 3x5 card and keep it in front of you. Always say it, and never say anything but. In my opinion, this is a critical secret to staying focused during prospecting, while removing one potential source of anxiety from the process. Keep it brief (15 seconds or less), simple and to the point.

My basic version goes like this: "Good morning, my name is Peter Bowerman, and I'm a freelance writer, making contact with local banks [for instance], to determine whether you have any ongoing or occasional needs for a good freelance writer to help create marketing collateral material: brochures, newsletters, ads, etc. Who might be the best person to talk with?" The word "collateral" is industry standard. Use it and you'll fit in.

Ideally, you'll have a name, but if not, this'll do and it's always enough to get some reaction, which then drives the rest of the call. Hopefully, you know what to say if they respond, "Great! Your timing couldn't be better." It happens.

How to Talk. Slowly, clearly, and evenly. When you get someone on the phone, don't just chat away like you normally would. Adjust to accommodate people who don't know you and weren't expecting your call. Make it easy for them to switch gears.

What Not to Say. Refrain from cuteness like an ultra-cheerful, "How are you today!?" unless they ask you first. Coming from you, it fairly screams "Salesman Butter-Up Line!!" If they ask, it can be like a cool drink of water. Simply reply politely, "Very well, thank you. Yourself?" Resist the urge to jump all over them with dirty paws like a golden retriever greeting its master after a two-week absence.

❧ *37* ❧

Becoming a Successful Copywriter

by Dawn Copeman

Copywriting, like many other areas of writing, has some ground rules that you must learn to improve your chances of successfully landing a job. You need to know how to get the client to tell you exactly what he or she wants, which isn't as easy as it sounds. Then you need to know how to transform those wants into a clear, easy-to-read format that will generate interest and sales. To accomplish these tasks, it's helpful to keep these three things in mind:

- The target consumer—who is going to buy the product
- The golden nugget—the fact that will help you to create your sales material
- The USP—the unique selling point of the product or service you are writing about

Finding the answers to these questions can be the trickiest part of the job—but there are steps you can take to make it happen.

LISTEN TO THE CLIENT

This may sound easy, but many clients are quite vague about what they want you to do. They have a rough idea of what they want to achieve, but you will need to work hard to get them to communicate their ideas to you. Or, they may be so focused on their new product or service that they assume you know all about it!

Take your time. Ask clients to explain what they want you to do. Take notes and ask more questions. Ask them in detail about the new product or service. Don't be afraid of looking stupid; if you don't understand the product, how can you explain it to others? Explain that you need to know everything about the product that the target consumer needs to know.

Don't rush this phase. When I was contacted to write Web content and brochures for a conservatory company, I followed the managing director as he took me for a walk around the showroom. I asked about the different styles, how long it takes to build a conservatory, methods of construction, planning permission, security, uses of conservatories, heating, guarantees, and even how to clean them. By the end of the visit, I knew what I needed to explain the world of conservatories to the general public.

Here are some questions you should put to a potential client:

- What is so special about this new product/service?
- What is its Unique Selling Point (USP)?
- Who is the target consumer for this product?
- What type of marketing approach are you considering?
- Will there be any samples or photos available for journalists to use?
- Are you willing to offer a discount to generate interest?

Finally, ask if the client has any previous sales letters, brochures, flyers, or press releases—and ask to take a copy of each with you so that you can see what approaches have been tried before. Ask which ones had the best and worst results, so that you don't inadvertently go down the same path as a previous copywriter.

RESEARCH

This is the most crucial part of your job. If you're going to write about a product, you need to know it inside out. You need to learn everything there is to know about this particular product and the company producing it, as you never know what will prove to be the precious nugget you can use to help sell the product. Don't rush this step. Copywriters must be inquisitive and thorough. They must go beyond the information provided by the client to ensure their work is the best it can be. Here are some ways to approach your research:

- **Review Company Materials.** Look at any and all material the company can give you. By spending a few hours reading the brochures and leaflets of the conservatory company, for example, I found that it had won several design competitions and were one of the first companies in the area to win a prestigious award—all useful information for sales literature that the company hadn't thought of mentioning!

- **Look at the Web Site.** When I was asked to create a press release for a new brand of cocoa, I discovered from the company Web site that some of their profits went to community projects in a Third World country—something no one had thought to mention. One phone call later, I learned that in the past year they'd built a school. This was a golden nugget that would help sell the product.

- **Look at Competitors' Web Sites.** By reviewing the competition, you can get an idea of what is and isn't working in this particular trade, and you may also discover USPs for your client. By looking at the Web sites of other conservatory companies, for example, I found that my client offered a much longer guarantee than any of its competitors—a definite USP!

- **Find Out About the Target Consumer.** Ask clients who the product is aimed at. If they are breaking into a new market, who are they hoping to attract? Many businesses will have a "Media Card," a card that contains information about the typical age, sex, and income of their target consumer. If they don't, ask what type of magazines they think their target consumer will read, and visit those magazines' Web sites and check their media cards. This will help you write copy in a tone that will appeal to the target consumer.

- **Use the Internet.** This is most useful when you are looking for extra facts to help spice up your copy, especially if you are writing a press release and need something newsworthy to grab the attention of journalists. While writing a press release for the cocoa company, I came across a new piece of scientific research that suggested that drinking cocoa could help prevent Alzheimer's disease. This, combined with the information on the company's Third World projects, provided me with all the information I needed to create a successful press release.

WRITING COPY

Once you've gathered your facts, it's time to sit down and write. Just as in article writing, there are specific rules to follow. These include:

- Put Yourself in the Target Consumer's Shoes
- Write as You Speak
- Remember the Power of You
- Discuss Benefits, not Features

Put Yourself in the Target Consumer's Shoes

Your copy must be written in a way that will appeal to the consumer. Is the product aimed at the elderly or the young? At working moms, family men, singles, office administrators, doctors? For each type of market, you need to find a tone that will appeal to the target audience. To find that tone, you must put yourself in the shoes of the target consumer. If you're trying to sell a new type of life insurance for blue-collar family men, think like one. What would push your buttons? What would make you read further? And what would make you throw the letter in the trash?

Write As You Speak

When you're talking to different people, you use different words. You don't talk to your boss the way you talk to your friends. When you've worked out what tone would be best for your target consumers, imagine that you are sitting next to them and having a conversation with them. What words would you use to describe the product? How would you get them interested? If you write as you would speak in this situation, your copy will be more natural and appealing.

Remember the Power of You

Successful sales literature may be written in a multitude of styles, but it has one thing in common: it appeals directly to the reader. As I wrote in my press release on cocoa, "You won't only be helping your brain; you will be helping others too." Ensure that your copy is liberally sprinkled with the word "you." Bad copy goes on and on about the company or product; good copy re-phrases this information to focus the emphasis on the benefits for the consumer.

Consider these two statements.

We have 20 years' experience in the field of building conservatories. We only employ the best skilled craftsmen and we guarantee our conservatories for ten years."

Okay, but what's in it for me? Let's rewrite it with "the power of you."

With over twenty years' of experience our expert team will design and install the perfect orangery or conservatory to meet your needs, your lifestyle, your budget and your home. You can rest assured of a quality service from start to finish, because unlike many of our competitors, we employ all our own craftsmen from builders, to plasterers, electricians to installers, carpenters to heating engineers."

By using "you," you are instantly creating rapport with readers, and getting them interested in what the client can do for them.

Discuss Benefits, Not Features

A common mistake made by first-time copywriters is to simply take the information the client provides and reproduce it. When clients create a new product or service, they get very excited about the features. Consumers, however, don't care about features. They care about benefits: What it will do for them, how it will make their lives easier, how it will make them feel better, etc.

For example, here are some features of a hypothetical writing software called WriteWorld:

- *British-English, American-English, and Australian-English Spell Checkers.*
- *British-English, American-English, and Australian-English Thesaurus.*
- *Chicago and AP Style Guides built in.*

Now, let's write these as benefits:

- *You'll never have to worry about misspelling words again. Simply select the destination language and WriteWorld will automatically change all your spellings. Color will become colour and vice versa at the click of a mouse, making it easier for you to sell your work to international markets.*

- *Avoid confusing readers! With our built-in thesaurus, WriteWorld will scan your text for words that have different meanings in the destination country, and offer you a choice of more appropriate words, so that your text retains its original meaning and your article is more likely to find a home in an overseas publication.*

- *Do you need to write in AP style but don't know how? Simply choose AP from the menu and at the click of a button it will advise you where to make changes so that your text is AP style. It does the same for Chicago style too, meaning you need never miss out on a freelance opportunity again.*

Note that writing about benefits takes more words than writing about features. That's OK; your job is to communicate those benefits to the reader.

While these tasks apply to most forms of copywriting, some tasks require a different approach.

DIRECT SALES LETTERS

Direct mail, also known as junk mail, is a surprisingly effective means of generating sales, especially in the charity sector. You'll need to do all the research steps above, but also ask to see any previous sales letters and find out what response they generated. This can save you from wasting hours on a format that has already been tried.

When it comes time to write your letter, keep all the rules above in mind, but also add the following to the mix: Picture, Promise, Price, and Action. You paint a *picture* of the consumer's life with the new product; you make a *promise* (your life will be easier with this, you will be helping orphans to a better life); you close with the *price* and the call to *action* (buy the item, take a test drive, sign up to support the charity).

Imagine, for example, that you are writing a sales letter to generate more sponsors for a charity that educates children in Bangladesh. Here's how to put picture, promise, price, and action into the letter:

- *Picture: Paint a picture in words about the life of young seven-year-old Patha—how she has to work twelve hours a day to help support the family, and cannot go to school. Many copywriters use a story as an easy way to get ideas across. Good story pictures appeal to the emotions of the target consumer.*

- *Promise: Now, paint a picture of how Patha's life would be different if only "you," the target consumer, would sponsor her. Show the reader how every cent of their donation goes to help Patha and her family.*

- *Price: Now and only now, state the price for giving someone the chance of a new life.*

- *Call to Action: Reply today! Every day we wait for your reply means another day without schooling for Patha.*

PRESS RELEASES

Press releases are one of the most effective means of business advertising. They are basically a one- or two-page announcement of a new product, trend, business premise, or anything that can be described as newsworthy. Well written press releases are loved by journalists and editors, as they provide much needed content, either as short news items or items that can be developed into longer articles. This is why press releases are so effective: They don't look like advertising, but if done well, can generate lots of publicity for the client.

It is estimated that between 3,000 and 10,000 press releases are written every day. Only the best will be published. If your press release is going to make the news, you need to know how to write it effectively.

The first step is to understand the layout:

Company Name or Logo

Press Release (in 10 or 12 pt. font)

Date it can be used (this is either "For Immediate Use" or "Not To Be Used Before a Specific Date.")

Title of Press Release (keep to 1 line)

Body of Press Release. Interesting Hook. Opening paragraph.

Paragraph

Paragraph

If the press release runs longer than one page, type "1 of 2" and "conts" at the bottom of the first page. At the end of the press release, type the word "ENDS" at the bottom of the page.

Notes to Editors

This section contains fact-checking material to support any claims made in the text, such as details of surveys, opinion polls or references to scientific studies. It normally appears on a separate page if the release is one page long, or directly underneath the content if the release is two pages. This section should list whether any photos or samples are available. All notes should be numbered. This section should also contain the e-mail address, URL, telephone numbers, and contact details for the person within the company whom journalists can contact for more information.

Is that all there is to it? Well, no. This is how to format a press release, but not how to get one published. Following the format won't help you one bit if your press release is dull. The key is content.

How do you write a release that is newsworthy and grabs the attention of journalists and editors? The first thing to do is learn as much about the product or item. Think creatively, and take all the steps described earlier: Ask the client questions, get them to send you details or samples of the product, check their Web site, and then hit the Internet for further research.

For example, one of the first press releases I wrote was about cocoa. It didn't seem the most thrilling of topics, but my job as a copywriter was to make it so. As I mentioned above, I found out that profits from the sale of the product were being used to fund community projects, and I also found a health study on the benefits of cocoa—giving me not just one but two newsworthy items for my release.

Press releases are short, but must be well written. Just like an article, they require an attractive hook, followed by paragraphs that flow and are written in an engaging, easy-to-read style with facts sprinkled lightly through the text. Finally, they must finish with a good ending. Often, you don't have much time to accomplish all this. When I worked for a food public relations agency, I often received the details around 8:30 a.m. and was expected to submit my press release by mid-day or 4 p.m. at the latest.

For the cocoa press release, I combined the health benefits of cocoa with an appeal to its traditional drinkers, the elderly, to create the headline: "A Cup of Cocoa a Day Keeps Alzheimer's at Bay." This was followed by a hook: "Our grandparents know more than they are letting on when they tuck into their nightly cocoa; not only does it give them a good night's sleep, it is helping them to keep their brains healthy too." The rest of the article flowed with scientific facts about the known and newly proven health benefits of cocoa, plus information on why the reader should buy this particular brand: "It has a higher proportion of flavonoids—the health-giving aspect of cocoa—than most other brands." Finally, I stated in the ending, "...X not only keeps your brain healthy, it helps others, too."

This particular press release ran, in many cases exactly as I wrote it, in several UK daily papers and many local newspapers—a great result for the client and a great sense of satisfaction for me! As a copywriter, of course, I get no byline and am only paid once, no matter how often the release is used. It does niggle slightly, seeing your words with someone else's name attached, but that's copywriting!

Once you've completed your press release, submit it first to the client for approval, then submit it to press release sites or by e-mail or fax to local newspapers. Some press release sites will distribute your press release for free; others have a sliding scale of charges. While a paid service will get your release into more inboxes, it still won't guarantee that journalists will read or act on the release; only you can do that by making it interesting to read. Following are some press release distribution sites:

- Daryl Wilcox Publishing – *www.dwpub.com* (sign up to the Response Source service to receive press releases in your chosen areas—great for research!)

- PR.com – *www.pr.com/rss-feeds*

- PR Log – *www.prlog.org*

- 24/7 Press Release – *www.24-7pressrelease.com*

- PR Fire – *www.prfire.co.uk*

WRITING WEB CONTENT

One of the cardinal rules of writing copy that goes onto your client's Web site is to keep it short and sweet. Web pages are not read in the same manner as printed text. People skim Web pages for the content they are looking for. If they don't find what they want within 30 seconds, they will click elsewhere. If you can't grab their attention or tell them what they want to know within that time, they will move on. This is why writing Web content is a specialized area of copywriting and one that takes time to master.

There isn't enough space here to go into details on how to write effective Web copy, beyond the rules I've already provided for copywriting in general. Text should be written in smaller, easily scannable chunks. Keep in mind that you probably won't be responsible for formatting the Web content, which is a completely different task.

Here are some sites that can be helpful in learning how to write Web copy:

- Writing for the Web – *www.useit.com/papers/webwriting*

- Gerry McGovern – *www.gerrymcgovern.com*

- High Rankings – SEO/SEM Resources - *www.highrankings.com/seo-resources*

❧38❧

Commercial Freelancing: Where's the Money?

Commercial freelancing differs from writing for magazines and other periodicals in one more, profound respect: It is the one form of freelancing where you get to set your own rates. Of course, the rate you set must be a rate a client will be willing to pay—but here, at last, you are not held hostage to a magazine's standard "per word" rate.

Setting your commercial rates typically begins by preparing a "bid" for your client. A bid should present your client with the following information:

- What you will do

- How long it will take

- What you will charge

On the surface, that all sounds simple enough! In practice, however, developing an effective bid can be quite a challenge—especially if you're not accustomed to setting your own rates or estimating how long a project will take. The most common "beginner" mistakes are failing to clearly define the project, underestimating the time factor, and setting rates too low. Here are some ways to avoid those mistakes.

DEFINING THE PROJECT

The first step in submitting a bid (or in determining whether to bid in the first place) is to determine exactly what the project involves. If, for example, the client wants a brochure, find out how much information will be provided, how much you'll have to dig up on your own, how it should be presented, and whether you are expected to provide a finished product or just written copy. Determine the goal of the brochure, including its audience and the "image" the company wishes to project.

Similarly, if you're asked to edit a document, review the material first. Find out what level of editing is desired: Proofreading for typos, copy-editing for grammar and style, or content editing for readability and accuracy? Does the copy need a lot of work, or is it fairly clean?

Once you've determined what is expected of you, spell that out in your bid, in writing. In other words, tell the client what the client has told you. This is your only protection against unexpected demands, changes, or requests for endless revisions.

DETERMINING A TIMELINE

Once you have defined what a project entails, you'll need to determine when it can be delivered. In many cases, the client will set the deadline, whereupon you'll have to determine whether you can meet it. In other cases, however, the client will ask you how long the project will take. You may be required to offer a completion date, an estimated number of hours, or both, depending on how you will be billing the client.

Think carefully before you answer this question! It is easy, especially in the beginning, to underestimate how many hours a project will require. Be sure to leave room for unexpected delays, difficulties, changes in direction, and people who don't deliver their part of the work on schedule. If you have to submit the project for corporate approval at various stages before completion, remember that this can add significant delays.

Also consider any other projects you have. Can you fit this project into your existing schedule? Will you have to drop or postpone other projects or clients? Will you be able to take on new projects? Again, budget extra time for the unexpected: If problems arise in another project, will they delay this project?

Resist the temptation to underestimate the amount of time required in an effort to "impress" the client with your speed and efficiency. Often, this can backfire: Too short an estimate can convey the impression that your work is hasty and slipshod. Though clients value speed, they also want to know that you are giving their work your full attention.

As a writer, you may be accustomed to thinking only about "writing" time. As a business writer, however, you'll be billing for all the time you spend on that project—including telephone time, meetings, research, errands, revisions, more revisions, etc. Be sure to include all those hours in your estimate.

SETTING FEES

Writer's Market lists fees for a wide range of writing services such as copy-editing, copy writing, speech writing, brochures, and so forth. In some cases, these fees are listed by hour; in others, they're listed by project.

Most of these listings offer a range of fees—usually somewhere between $20 and $100 per hour. Where you should place yourself on that range depends on a variety of factors, including your experience *and* your geographic location. Freelancers based in New York City, Los Angeles, or Silicon Valley will be able to charge higher rates than freelancers doing the exact same work in Kansas or Nebraska.

Don't assume that you have to start at the bottom of the rate scale. Instead, call around and try to determine the "going rate" in your area. Look for editors online and contact them to determine their rates.

Just as you shouldn't underbid on hours, you should also avoid underbidding on price. It's tempting to bid low, on the assumption that a client will prefer to hire the cheapest contractor available. In reality, clients tend to avoid contractors who price themselves too cheaply; just as you might wonder why something is "marked down" to a bargain price, your client may also wonder why you charge so much less than your competitors. Also, avoid the temptation to "underbid" the competition. It's wiser to build good relationships with other business freelancers, who may then refer clients to you when they're overloaded.

Once you've determined your hourly rate, you can calculate how much a project is worth. Your final decision is whether to price the project on an hourly basis, a flat rate, or some other rate scale. Each has advantages and disadvantages.

If you are concerned that a client will think your hourly rate is too high, a flat rate may work best. The advantage of a flat rate (i.e., "$300 per brochure") is that you get the same fee even if you put in fewer hours than you originally estimated—more profit to you! The disadvantage, obviously, is that if the project runs longer than you anticipated, you won't get more money. Some clients like flat rates; others don't. Often, this is something you'll need to determine by working with the client.

An hourly rate has the advantage of being more open-ended. If the client wants revisions, makes changes, or adds extra tasks, you just add extra billing hours. The disadvantage of billing by the hour is that some clients have no understanding of how long things really take and may assume that you're "padding" your bill. Again, it may not be possible to determine the best approach until you've actually discussed the project with the client.

A third approach is to bill by some other measure, such as "per page" (which is a good way to charge for editorial services). The way to determine this type of rate is to simply estimate how many pages you can edit in an hour, and then divide your hourly rate by that number! The advantage of this approach is that it is easy to calculate: The client only has to count the number of pages in the project to determine the final cost. Another advantage is that, like the flat rate, you'll get paid the same amount even if the work goes more quickly than expected. The disadvantage, of course, is also the same: If the work goes more slowly than you expected, you get paid less.

The final element you'll need to calculate into the billing portion of your bid is expenses, if any. If you will need to purchase special software to handle the job, or subcontract portions of the job to others (such as artists or designers), be sure to include an estimate of those amounts in your bid. Make sure that these are listed separately from your own billing hours. Try to determine exactly what those costs will be, so that you don't surprise the client at the end of the job with an unexpected list of outside expenses.

GET IT IN WRITING

When you bid on a project, submit your bid in writing. E-mail is often acceptable. Don't be surprised if you have to negotiate before your final bid is accepted. Don't start the project until the client has accepted your bid in writing.

Here's a sample bid letter from Dawn Copeman, offering a variety of copywriting services to a single client. Note that each section of the bid includes detailed specifications of the services that will be covered for that portion of the project, including planning meetings, revisions, and sample designs.

Dear [Client]:

Thank you for inviting me to your offices yesterday to discuss your copywriting needs.

As per our discussions yesterday I understand that you would like me to come up with a new look for your Web site for your Web site builder to install. You would also like me to write new copy for your Web site, including any additional pages that we decide you need following our meeting to discuss and approve a Web design. Finally, you need content for a new, 16-page A4-sized glossy brochure.

Here is my bid for providing these copywriting services.

Web Site Design Advice

I will provide you with five different suggestions and mock layouts of your Web site within two weeks of your go-ahead. My fee for this service will be $400 to include all conceptualization, research and one planning meeting.

Web Content Writing

My fee for writing the content of the Web site will be $1400. This will include two revisions and two planning meetings. The copy will be delivered to you within one week of approval of final Web design and agreement of page content. Following our first planning meeting, I shall return any redrafts to you within 48 hours, and following our second meeting, the final copy shall be with you within 24 hours.

Brochure Content

To write copy for a new 16-page, A4-sized brochure, my fee will be $500. This is to cover an initial planning meeting with you at which we shall discuss photos to be used and the focus of the brochure, all conceptualization, research and two sets of revisions. As I understand it, you wish to have the new Web site up and running before commencing work on the brochure.

Before commencing on the Web design conceptualizing and the Web content writing, I would require half my fee to be paid in advance, with the remainder to be paid within 30 days of delivery of final approved copy and design. Before commencing work on the brochure I would likewise require half my fee to be paid in advance with the remainder within 30 days of delivery of final approved copy.

If these terms are acceptable to you, please sign and date the agreement below and keep a copy for yourself, returning a copy to me via post or e-mail.

I look forward to working with you,

Sincerely,

Dawn Copeman

I have read and agree to the above terms and payment conditions.

Name:_____

Print Name:_____

Date:_____

And here's a sample "letter of agreement" to provide a newsletter for a business Web site, also from Dawn Copeman:

Letter of Agreement

Dear

Following our recent e-mail conversations, I have agreed to write and edit the newsletter for your site. I will produce one 400-500-word article per month on the topic you provide to me. In addition to this I will format and edit the newsletter, inserting links and advertiser promotions and ensuring that all content is grammatically correct and reads well.

My fee for this service is $XX per newsletter, with half the amount to be paid in advance and the remaining half within 15 days of completion of the project. This fee includes one rewrite per newsletter. Payment is to be made via PayPal to my e-mail address.

I hereby confirm that you will own all rights to the articles and the newsletters as this is a work-for-hire agreement.

We have both agreed that this agreement is a temporary one valid only for the next three issues of the newsletter. We will both review the situation after delivery of January's newsletter.

I will provide you with the first article by Friday November 10th 201X, with the second article by December 5th and the third article by January 5th.

If this agreement is acceptable to you, please sign below, keep a copy for yourself and return this copy to me. (I will accept confirmation via e-mail stating you understand and agree to these terms.)

I look forward to working with you,

Sincerely,

Dawn Copeman

Understood and Agreed _____

Date: _____

You also need to determine when and how you will get paid. If you're undertaking a large job (e.g., worth more than $500 or $1,000), you may wish to ask for payment in installments. Some writers ask for payment in thirds: One third when the bid is accepted or the contract is signed, one third halfway through the project, and one third on completion. Others ask for half down and half at the end. If you have to buy materials or software to complete the project, ask for payment for those items in advance. If you need to subcontract part of the work, you'll usually ask for reimbursement of those expenses after the work has been completed.

Business clients expect to be invoiced. Accounting departments are more likely to respect a professional-looking invoice; it's worth going to the office supply store and buying a pack of preprinted forms. Find out whether you need to provide a purchase order number to get paid.

FOLLOW UP!

Once you've completed a job, follow up! Find out whether the work was considered satisfactory, and remind the client that you would welcome other projects. Ask the client to refer you to other companies, and ask whether the client is willing to be used as a referral when you contact other prospects.

A word of warning, however: Not every corporate client is easy to work with. A bad customer can waste your time—and in the business of corporate freelancing, time is money. Don't spend time dealing with clients who don't know what they want and are never satisfied with what you give them. Don't let such clients deter you; just finish the job and move on. There are lots of other prospects available; use your newly gained clips and go after them!

PART IX

Conclusion: Taking the Plunge

⚜ 39 ⚜

Full-Time Freelancing: Taking the Plunge

Wouldn't it be great to quit the rat race? To leave bosses and time-clocks behind, skip the commute, ditch the heels or tie, and work in the same clothes you wear to weed the garden?

It's called "taking the plunge," and if you're at all serious about writing, you've probably dreamed about it. But you may also have regarded that dream as, at best, nothing more than an improbable fantasy. Writing may be the career you love, but chances are it's not the career that's keeping food on the table and a roof over your head.

I can't tell you whether you can make that dream a reality. But I can offer a few tips on making the decision: To plunge or not to plunge!

WHEN TO PLUNGE—AND WHEN NOT TO

The first question to ask when considering "the plunge" is: Where is your writing career today?

If the answer is "just getting started," stop right there. If you have only a few clips to your resume, or no clips at all, you're unlikely to be able to support yourself at your craft.

I hear from many writers who say they would like to quit their jobs and "start writing." To such writers, I say: "Start writing now. Quit later." If you haven't started yet—or if you're just starting—you simply won't know enough about this complex business to earn a living. So start writing. Get your feet wet. Find out what you can and can't do, what you enjoy, what you don't enjoy. Discover your strengths, and the areas that could use improvement. Find out whether you really wish to pursue writing as a business, or whether you'd rather pursue it as an avocation.

Writing can be a career or hobby or anything you care to make it. *Writing for a living* is a business, pure and simple. If you wouldn't dream of quitting your day job to run, say, an auto repair shop without any training as a mechanic, then don't dream of quitting your day job to become a writer without a comparable level of experience.

But how much experience *is* enough? Should one have been writing for a year, or three, or five? Can writing experience even be measured in terms of "years"?

I suspect it can't. The real question is "where you are," not how long it has taken you to get there. The following checklist may help you determine whether you may be ready to consider "plunging."

A WRITER'S CHECKLIST

1. **I write more than 5 hours per week, every week.**
   You have discipline. It's tough to find five hours a week for writing when working a day job. You've already passed one of the biggest hurdles writers face.

2. **I submit at least one new query or article per week.**
   You have a high output. Clearly you don't spend those five hours a week (or whatever) repolishing old material, or stuffing your work in a drawer. You're already "in the marketplace."

3. **More than 50 percent of my queries and/or articles are accepted.**
   You know how to target markets effectively, and you obviously write well enough to impress the majority of the editors to whom you submit. (With that kind of acceptance rate, there's a good chance that your rejections aren't due to poor quality.)

4. **More than 50 percent of my markets pay more than $100 per article.**
   You've found the guts to break out of the low-paying "ghetto." You have confidence that your work is worth more. You won't be held back by self-esteem issues.

5. **I have at least one "regular" market that has accepted several of my articles.**
   You have a steady source of income.

6. **I have at least one "regular" market that contacts me with assignments (i.e., ideas generated by the editor rather than in response to a query from me).**
   You are reliable and dependable. You meet deadlines and produce quality work. Otherwise, editors wouldn't come to *you* with ideas.

7. **I am familiar with the practices and terminology of the publishing marketplace (e.g., I know what "FNASR" and "SASE" mean and I know how to format a manuscript).**
   You know the basics, and won't waste precious time "gearing up."

8. **I own at least one current market guide.**
   You know the importance of obtaining the tools of the trade.

9. **I subscribe to two or more writing publications.**
   You keep current with your field.

10. **I know how to cope with rejection.**
    You won't be daunted by the inevitable disappointments of this type of career.

11. **I earned more than $5,000 from writing activities last year.**
    It won't keep a roof over your head, but it's more than many freelancers ever make in a year. It's one of those invisible lines: If you know how to earn this much, you know how to earn more. Probably the only thing holding you back is lack of time.

12. **I currently report writing income for tax purposes, and know how to maintain proper business/tax records of income and expenses.**
    You know that "writing" isn't just putting words on a page. It's also a matter of records, accounting, and good business practices.

13. **I keep a household budget.**
    You already have an idea of what it will take to support your household—which means you know how close you are to being able to go full-time.

While scoring 100 percent on this checklist is no guarantee that you're ready to quit your day job, a low score is a pretty good indication that you need to build up more of a foundation for your writing career before attempting to rely on it for a paycheck.

MAKING A PLAN

So you've scored a perfect 13, you're totally fed up with your day job, and you're sure this is what you want to do. What next?

For most writers, the answer is *not* "quit your day job today." The answer is "make a plan." Typically, if you hope to become a full-time writer, you'll need to plan at least six months to a year ahead before actually "taking the plunge." What will you do during that year? Lots! Here are some of the steps you'll need to take before saying farewell to a regular paycheck and "hello" to the joys and uncertainties of the freelance life.

1) **Discuss your desire to become a fulltime freelancer with everyone in your personal life who will be affected by that decision** (e.g., spouse, significant other, children). Presumably, your desire to write won't be a total surprise. However, family members who supported your "hobby" may not be as enthusiastic about losing a significant chunk of family income. They may not be happy about making adjustments, such as providing extra

income themselves or accepting cutbacks and lifestyle changes. Don't be surprised if you encounter resistance or even sabotage. (I've heard of some wacky "conditions" imposed by spouses.) Don't dismiss those concerns as unfeeling; if your decision will affect others, the needs of those others should be a part of the decision-making process.

2) **Evaluate your household income requirements.** If you don't track your monthly expenses, this is a good time to start. Before you can make an effective plan, you need to know exactly where every penny of your income goes. Try tracking expenses on a simple spreadsheet, with categories such as:

- Rent/mortgage
- Groceries
- Utilities
- Insurance
- Auto (gas and repairs)
- Medical
- Household expenses (e.g., maintenance)
- Clothes
- Children's expenses
- Meals and Entertainment (e.g., restaurants and movies)
- Miscellaneous

It's also wise to break "miscellaneous" into more detailed categories, such as "books, CDs, videos, pets, crafts, subscriptions," etc. A good rule of thumb is to establish a separate listing for every category that exceeds $50 (or even $20) per month.

If you're never tracked your expenses in such detail before, you could be in for a shock. You didn't know you spent $100 a month on books? Or that those twelve magazine subscriptions (that you never have time to read) cost more than $500 per year? Your budget may be a rude awakening, but it can also be a welcome one, as certain categories emerge as ripe for cost cutting.

3) **Create a projected budget.** It's "trim the fat" time. Go over your current expense list, and determine what you can cut and what you can't. Be realistic: Don't imagine that you can go a year without buying a new CD or book, or without eating out even once. (By resolving to buy those CDs or books used instead of new, however, you may cut those categories in half!) Be sure to budget for unexpected expenses; you can bet that sometime in the next year, the car will need repairs, the dog will get sick, or the roof will leak.

4) **Determine the difference between your projected budget and your current take-home income.** If, for example, you can trim $10,000 in expenses, and you currently take home $30,000, you'll need to earn $20,000 as a writer to pay the same costs—one way or another.

5) *Save.* Most writers suggest having a full year of income saved (or at least enough to cover a full year of expenses). You need a cushion to pay those regular bills while waiting for irregular checks. Savings will be easier once you trim the budget, however. For example, if you've determined that you can cut $10,000 in expenses, you can save that over the next year. You can also ramp up your writing (by producing more articles or seeking higher-paying markets), and bank every penny of that income as well. If your shortfall is $20,000, and you save $10,000 in expenses and earn another $10,000 in writing over the next year, you'll have covered the difference.

6) **Create a business plan.** Determine your existing income sources, and explore ways to increase that income. Should you pitch more articles to your regular customers? Should you seek new, higher-paying markets? Should you focus on a specialty or expand your range?

7) **Be realistic.** Nothing will sabotage your dream faster than setting impossible or unsatisfying goals. One writer I know attempted to increase her regular workload in order to build up her savings, *and* triple her writing output to gain more clients at the same time. Needless to say, this didn't work, and her "plunge" has been postponed indefinitely. Another common cause of failure is "plunging without a net"—with no savings backup. It only takes one missed rent check to get you back behind that hated office desk.

Your goal is to improve your life, not ruin it. Many writers take the plunge so that they can spend more time with loved ones—so don't create a schedule that shuts those loved ones out of your life! Many also want to find more time to do what they love—so don't create a plan that forces you to give up the types of writing you love in favor of higher-paying projects that bore you to tears. In short, don't sabotage your plan—or your life—in your attempt to make that life more rewarding. Writing is a rewarding activity in itself; being able to write for a living can be the icing on the cake.

About the Author

Moira Allen has been writing professionally for more than 30 years, and has published several hundred articles and columns in a variety of magazines and newspapers. She is the author of several books on writing, including *The Writer's Guide to Queries, Pitches and Proposals* (Allworth Press, 2nd Edition, 2010) and *Writing to Win: The Colossal Guide to Writing Contests* (CreateSpace, 2010). For the past ten years, Allen has hosted Writing-World.com (*www.writing-world.com*), one of the world's largest and most popular Web sites for writers. She has served as a magazine editor, business and commercial writer/editor, columnist, and desktop publisher; she is now hard at work on a novel. Allen lives in Maryland with her husband and the obligatory writer's cat.

About the Contributors

Peter Bowerman (Chapter 36: sidebar) is a veteran commercial freelancer and business coach, and the author of the award-winning self-published Well-Fed Writer titles, the how-to "standards" on lucrative commercial freelancing writing for businesses (*www.wellfedwriter.com*). He chronicled his self-publishing success (52,000 copies of his first two books in print and a full-time living for seven-plus years) in the award-winning 2007 release, *The Well-Fed Self-Publisher: How to Turn One Book into a Full-Time Living* (*www.wellfedsp.com*).

Dawn Copeman (Chapter 36: Writing for Businesses; Chapter 37: Becoming a Successful Copywriter) is a freelance and commercial writer who has published more than 100 articles on travel, history, cookery, health, and writing. As a copy writer Dawn has written press releases, Web content, brochures, newsletters, company reports, articles for trade journals and newspapers, and has devised recipes for clients to use in press releases. She is the editor of the Writing World newsletter (*www.writing-world.com/newsletter/index.shtml*)

Penny J. Leisch (Chapter 28: How Social Networking Helps Writers) is a writer, author, and book reviewer. Her work appears in newspapers, magazines, online, and in anthologies. She also wrote *Writing & Photography: A $Winning$ Combination*. Penny is available as a speaker and as a facilitator of writing workshops in Austin, Texas. Learn more about Penny: at *www.pennyleisch.com*. She also has profiles on MySpace, LinkedIn, and Facebook.

Sue Fagalde Lick (Chapter 15: Writing for Newspapers) is the author of *Freelancing for Newspapers,* published by Quill Driver Books. In addition to many years as a staff reporter and editor, she has published countless freelance articles and three books on Portuguese Americans, including *Stories Grandma Never Told*. Her articles, short stories, and poetry have appeared in many magazines and newspapers, as well as two Cup of Comfort anthologies. She lives with her dog, Annie, on the Oregon Coast. Visit her Web site at *www.suelick.com*.

Index

Books from Allworth Press

Allworth Press is an imprint of Allworth Communications, Inc. Selected titles are listed below.

The Writer's Guide to Queries, Pitches and Proposals, Second Edition
by *Moira Anderson Allen* (6 × 9, 288 pages, paperback, $19.95)

The Author's Toolkit: A Step-by-Step Guide to Writing and Publishing Your Own Book, Third Edition
by *Mary Embree* (5 ½ × 8 ½, 224 pages, paperback, $19.95)

The Writer's Legal Guide: An Authors Guild Desk Reference
by *Tad Crawford and Kay Murray* (6 × 9, 320 pages, paperback, $19.95)

Business and Legal Forms for Authors and Self-Publishers, Third Edition
by *Tad Crawford* (8 3/8 × 10 7/8, 304 pages, paperback, $29.95)

The Complete Guide to Book Marketing, Revised Edition
by *David Cole* (6 × 9, 256 pages, paperback, $19.95)

The Complete Guide to Book Publicity, Second Edition
by *Jodee Blanco* (6 × 9, 304 pages, paperback, $19.95)

Marketing Strategies for Writers
by *Michael Sedge* (6 × 9, 224 pages, paperback, $24.95)

Successful Syndication: A Guide for Writers and Cartoonists
by *Michael Sedge* (6 × 9, 176 pages, paperback, $16.95)

Writing the Great American Romance Novel
by *Catherine Lanigan* (6 × 9, 224 pages, paperback, $19.95)

Making Crime Pay: An Author's Guide to Criminal Law, Evidence, and Procedure
by *Andrea Campbell* (6 × 9, 320 pages, paperback, $27.50)

The Birds and the Bees of Words: A Guide to the Most Common Errors in Usage, Spelling, and Grammar
by *Mary Embree* (5 ½ × 8 ½, 208 pages, paperback, $14.95)

The Elements of Internet Style: New Rules of Creating Valuable Content for Today's Readers
by *Tad Crawford* (6 × 9, 192 pages, paperback, $24.95)

The Perfect Screenplay: Writing It and Selling It
by *Katherine Atwell Herbert* (6 × 9, 224 pages, paperback, $16.95)

The Journalist's Craft: A Guide to Writing Better Stories
by *Dennis Jackson and John Sweeney* (6 × 9, 256 pages, paperback, $19.95)

To request a free catalog or order books by credit card, call 1-800-491-2808. To see our complete catalog on the World Wide Web, or to order online, please visit **www.allworth.com**.